Advance Praise for GenX Religion

"So much attention has focused on baby boomer spirituality that GenX religion has been almost completely ignored. The essays in this book offer a rich inside look at the pastiche of worship styles and spiritual practices that America's young people have come to embrace—and a poignant portrait of a generation desperately seeking to be loved."

—Robert Wuthnow, Princeton University, author of
After Heaven: Spirituality in America Since the 1950s

"This volume represents the opening gambit in a larger discussion of the eclectic, innovative, and unconventional spirituality of Generation X. If this collection of compelling essays is any indication, it promises to be a lively conversation indeed."

—Randall Balmer, author of *Blessed Assurance:*
A History of Evangelicalism in America

"*GenX Religion* looks deep into the gap between traditional by-the-book churches and solitary postmodern spirituality to find a thriving world of youthful religious gatherings—a Christian tattoo parlor, a Baptist nightspot, a Latino drama troupe, a Korean students' Bible study, Sunday services for hip African Americans, shabbat and schmoozing for Jewish singles, committed fellowships and casual associations— with hardly anyone over thirty! This is a fascinating book."

—R. Stephen Warner,
University of Illinois at Chicago

Gen X Religion

Edited by

Richard W. Flory
Donald E. Miller

Routledge
New York   London

Published in 2000 by
Routledge
29 West 35th Street
New York, NY 10001

Published in Great Britain by
Routledge
11 New Fetter Lane
London EC4P 4EE

Routledge is an imprint of the Taylor & Francis Group.

10 9 8 7 6 5 4 3 2 1

Library of Congress Cataloging-in-Publication Data

GenX religion / edited by Richard W. Flory and Donald E. Miller.
    p. cm.
    Includes bibliographical references.
    ISBN 0-415-92570-3. ISBN 0-415-92571-1 [pbk.]
    1. Generation X—Religious life.   I. Title: GenX religion.
  II. Flory, Richard W.   III. Miller, Donald E. (Donald Earl), 1946–

BV4529.2 .G46   2000
261.8'34242'0973—dc21   00-036594
                                                           CIP

Contents

Preface

Both of us were feeling a little guilty. Research should not be this much fun. But here we were in an upscale Mexican takeout restaurant talking to Lori, who was about to get a tattoo. She was nervous, because it is a painful process. That was news to us. None of Dick's surfing cronies had tattoos. And the closest that the graying/balding member of this trio had come to the subject was when he told his daughter, when she was sixteen, that she could not get a tattoo on her ankle because it was illegal!

Lori had been Dick's star undergraduate student at Biola University. Don was one of her mentors at USC, where she was completing a Ph.D. in sociology. In a crazy revelatory moment, we had collectively seized on the idea of writing a paper for an upcoming meeting of the Society for the Scientific Study of Religion, on Christian tattoo parlors. Lori already had a respectable collection of Jesus tattoos, but said that she had been thinking of getting one more. Actually, it was two more—a matching set of doves, one on each shoulder, with each of these symbols of peace carrying a banner in its beak: one reading "grace" and the other "compassion."

The balding researcher had his camera in tow. It was a defense to make certain that no one thought he was a candidate for graphic artwork. Dick pulled out a notebook as we entered Sid's Tattoo Parlor, and for the next three hours we talked with members of the staff and patrons, as Lori's shoulders were decorated.

A few months later we presented our paper at the conference, complete with photographs. Religion reporter David Briggs was in the audience, and it ended up being a race between him and *Los Angeles Times* writer Elaine Gale as to whose article would first make it into print. Within the next few weeks, Christian tattooing articles appeared in over two hundred newspapers, including the *New York Times*. Almost overnight, we became experts on GenX religion as reporters barraged us with questions.

It was in the heat of the media battle that we realized that many clergy and churchgoing parents and youth leaders are worried about the religious heritage of their children. We also became aware of the paucity of good descriptions of churches and synagogues that have been connecting with Generation X, which sent us on a search. The first place we turned was to graduate students finishing dissertations on GenX topics, and we started visiting congregations in the southern California area that were connecting with this age cohort.

The product is this book of case studies, sandwiched on one end by an introductory chapter on social and cultural influences on Generation X and a conclusion that develops a theory out of the case studies. While this is obviously not a representative sample of GenX congregations, we have attempted to include a broad spectrum of different racial and ethnic groups, as well as religious traditions.

We have not written the last word on GenX religion. However, we have a strong desire to contribute to a conversation about the relationship of this generation to religion in the new millennium.

Donald E. Miller,
University of Southern California

Richard W. Flory,
Biola University

Introduction: Understanding Generation X

Values, Politics, and Religious Commitments

Donald E. Miller and Arpi Misha Miller

He dashes out the door to his Ford Explorer with a mug full of cold, home-made latte and a briefcase. "Thank God for the Starbucks travel mug," he thinks, flying through yellow lights in an attempt to save time en route to the inevitable—gridlock traffic. Fortunately, the cell phone has transformed his urban assault vehicle into a mobile office cubicle, making time for additional meetings during the once-dreaded hour-long commute.

Is this your job?

No, it's your *dad's*.

Now grab a soy milk, hop on board a San Francisco trolley car, and check out where the GenXers have been hiding.

Their hair might be Apple green to match their computer, they have been known to wear pajama pants to work, and they might be pierced in places you do not want to go, but one thing is for sure; they are redefining the work-place, and with no sacrifice of their personal salary. This is Internet start-up land, home of the multimillion-dollar business that pays its employees well, grants them explosive stock options, and has created a livable, if not flat-out enjoyable, workspace. There are no separate offices, no time cards, no visible hierarchies, and only two expectations: that you output creativity and you get the job done. Sitting behind their personal $2,500 laptops at desks littered with stuffed animals and freakish icons, this is GenX. They may not be burn-ing their bras or rallying in the streets, but they are leading a global informa-tion revolution, and they are doing it with style.

The workplace is not the only arena in which creative thinking and com-munity are being spawned. On a microscale, small gatherings like Thursday Night Group are cropping up among the members of Generation X. From the outside, this might look like an AA meeting or even Bible study, and perhaps, in some ways, it is. It is a place where people from different walks of life—a botanist, several teachers, a surfboard designer, dancers, a musician, a traveling academic, an Internet guru—can gather and find both support and inspiration. "Group" could be called a social cooperative; there is no one leader, no constant agenda, and no set location. Like any good underground party, the plans evolve spontaneously and find a home wherever there is room. The only certainty is that, come Thursday, people will gather. Sometimes there is food, often wine, occasionally charades or art projects, movies and discussions. But the basis is that these young people need each other. And rather than remaining isolated, they are filling in where family, community, and religion have let them down.

It is no mystery that the mainline denominational church has done a terrible job of holding on to these GenX youth in the 1990s. There is an obvious clash of culture here—one more rigid and traditional, the other marked by innovation and progression. The result of this clash has often been the misinformed notion that GenX is both apathetic and irreligious. However, as the chapters that follow will attest, religion is still alive and well in this country. Many young adults are finding their way into churches, temples, and synagogues, but the *medium* that communicates the message of these traditions has changed radically. In fact, to parents and grandparents, some forms of youth culture religion are nearly unrecognizable, if not shocking. The music in GenX churches is contemporary (gone are the eighteenth-century hymns). The worship space is utilitarian (stained glass and icons are out, being identified with hierarchical and authoritarian religion). Worship involves the body in ways that Enlightenment rationalism would never have predicted (feelings, including physical touch, are at the forefront). But it is also true that many young adults, perhaps the majority, are pursuing a form of spirituality that is subtle, individual, and hence unrecognizable to the older generations. This form of spirituality is expressed in attitudes toward nature, a strong attraction to community, voluntary acts of service, a more permissive view of "natural" drug use, and a rather strong belief in mysticism and dimensions of reality beyond the purely physical.

The reflections that follow have emerged out of ongoing conversations between a twenty-three-year-old daughter and her fifty-three-year-old father. This thirty-year generation gap has been wonderfully generative, and has provided the basis for many hours of debate and discussion—in the hot tub, over dinner (she keeps coming back to live with her parents), and during those fabled "final" family vacations. The intention of this book and this chapter is to invite you, the reader, into the discussion. There are no formulas for how religious leaders should respond to the GenX mentality. But there are

2

some social and cultural factors common to this generation that need to be understood if continuity is to exist between the historical religious traditions and GenX young adults.

The Problem of Definition

GenXers are the 80 million Americans who were born between 1961 and 1981. This is the "buster" generation, the children of the so-called baby boomers. While they are a diverse lot, they also share many common cultural experiences related to advances in technology, the failed marriages of their parents, changes in the structure of the economy, and the liberation politics that transpired during their childhood and youth. Initially, the media labeled GenXers as slackers, cynics, apathetics, drifters, and malcontents. More recently, these stereotypes are being challenged, in part because of a recent outpouring of entrepreneurial activity. For example, 70 percent of currently operating start-up businesses were founded by people between twenty-five and thirty-four years old. Hence, commentators are increasingly proposing that we look beyond dress styles and work habits in order to recognize the ambitious quality of this independent, pragmatic, and often self-sufficient generation.[1]

Throughout this book's case studies, it will be apparent that generalizing about Xers, both socially and religiously, is not easy. Traditional variables related to social class, education, race, and ethnicity play an important role in the decisions that they make. In fact, unlike the countercultural conformity of the 1960s and '70s, recognition of difference is something GenX prides itself on. One generalization that seems to be true, however, is that young adults are simply not attending traditional mainline churches in great numbers. This observation sometimes diminishes the fact that Xers are a deeply spiritual generation, seeking meaning and purpose while simultaneously avoiding what they perceive to be inauthentic attempts to mediate the sacred. Indeed, a new worldview is emerging, and it stands in stark contrast to the text-based, linear, rationalist empiricism of the Enlightenment. Traditional definitions of reality are fuzzy for this generation. Their failure to commit to traditional religious and denominational structures does not signal their lack of interest in questions of meaning and values. Instead, it signals that new institutions are being birthed, and that current ones must be reinvented if they are to survive within this environment.

Benchmark Experiences for GenXers

GenXers have sometimes been referred to as the lonely generation, and for many young adults this label fits because of the rootlessness they have

experienced. The divorce rate doubled between 1965 and 1977. By age sixteen, 40 percent of this generation had spent time in a single-parent house-
hold. Furthermore, this is a generation of children who had mothers working
outside the home, prompting the labeling of Xers as the latchkey generation.
Not only was no one home after school, but the extended family network had
all but vanished, along with neighborhood networks that minded children in
their parents' absence. When parents *were* home, they were often exhausted,
sometimes abusive, and frequently drained of emotional energy, although
they were continually touting the virtues of "quality time." The television set
became the dominant presence in many children's lives.

Not every child was left to raise herself. But there was a curious philosophy that permeated the households of even two-parent families. Parents hes-
itated to stuff religion down their kids' throats. They wanted their children to
choose for themselves, which meant that active churchgoing was not on the
Sunday agenda for many families, as it had been in the past. Consequently,
many children had nothing to rebel against as they moved into their teenage
years, and simultaneously no set path to follow. The television set became the
moral mentor of this generation, with role models being drawn from a cast of
sitcom characters, rock stars, athletes, and moviemakers.

The tremendous freedom experienced by this generation can be viewed
both positively and negatively. On the one hand, they inherited the liberties
established during the civil rights and women's movements led by their parents. While these freedoms have often been taken for granted, they have also
become the basis for a critically thinking and openly progressive generation.
But as beneficiaries of these freedoms, GenXers became the experimental project of a society testing the effects of changes in family structure and dynamics.
As a result, many Xers experienced loneliness in their childhood and entered
adulthood confused by the meaning of love and relationships. "Hanging out"
became the watchword for community. And these group relationships were
taken very seriously—more seriously oftentimes than individual commitments. If they couldn't be loved unconditionally by one person—a parent, a
classmate, a boyfriend—then the group would be there for them as "family."

If GenXers have been disappointed by their parents, changes in our economy have also had a powerful shaping effect on this generation. This is the
first cohort of young adults who may have lower lifetime earnings than their
parents. Corporate downsizing became the mantra during their childhood
and young adult years, with 43,000 jobs being lost between 1979 and 1995.
While unemployment has remained low, well-paying factory jobs have been
replaced by low-paying service sector jobs that lack health care and retire-
ment benefits. The expectation of lifetime employment has disappeared as
managers look to the bottom line on hiring decisions. The middle class has

shrunk, and while some GenXers have made fortunes in high-tech jobs, many young adults are feeling the impact of the fact that real median wages have been falling since 1973. Thus, although no previous generation has attended college at a higher level (over a quarter are graduates), many GenXers feel stalemated and bitter, weighing the enormous costs of their higher education against its value within the job market, all the while surrounded by the media's depiction of athletes and movie stars, their get-rich-quick mentalities and lavish lifestyles.

The bright side of this generation's experience is the amazing revolution that has occurred in digital technology. If there is a culture gap between the generations, it definitely has been influenced by computer literacy. GenXers relate to this new technology with the same comfort level at which their parents drive cars, drawing comparison to their grandparents' struggle to move from the horse-and-buggy era into the age of the automobile. For one thing, GenXers are no longer bound in their self-expression by the print media and linear thinking. Digital imaging allows for visual self-expression that only the privileged classes could afford a half century ago, and the Internet continues to democratize access to information in ways never before possible. But equally as important, definitions of reality undergo transformation in the hands of Xers, as is revealed in movies such as *The Matrix*, where the distinction between reality and imagination is not all that apparent. Furthermore, electronic games and more sophisticated digital computers have blurred the boundaries between everyday experience and fantasy. Critical challenges to reality are no longer locked away in academic theory but manifested readily in pop culture through media expression.

The Values and Politics of GenXers

In some ways, it is perfectly understandable why Xers might be slackers, cynics, and malcontents. Their economic situation is dismal. Even if they work, they have a hard time getting ahead. Furthermore, they may have a right to feel cheated by parents who cheated on each other, and then on their kids by abandoning them to pursue their own personal goals. In addition, they have gone through a political period in which government has been knocked rather than championed by politicians, and with much thanks to a cynical and drama-hungry media corps.

Voting rates among Xers are substantially lower than among their parents, sometimes a result of apathy or lack of information but often because of a pessimism regarding the worth of their individual vote. In 1972, half of those aged eighteen to twenty-four voted in national elections. In contrast, by 1996 only a third of that age group voted. Furthermore, Xers are cynical about the differences between Republicans and Democrats; both parties are viewed as corrupt, with politicians putting self-interest over the good of the people. Consequently, Xers tend to vote Independent at much higher rates than the general population—when they choose to vote. Furthermore, Xers have grown cynical about the taxes that they pay. Over the past twenty-five years, government spending on infrastructure, such as education and research, has declined from 24 to 14 percent of the federal budget. Xers believe that they are going to be stuck paying for the social security of their parents, with nothing left for them. But most important, the ebullient economy of the late twentieth century does not seem to be paying benefits to Xers—excluding those working in the high-tech industry and a few other well-paying jobs—as they struggle to move out of their parents' houses and become self-supporting.[2]

In many ways GenX is not more cynical than previous generations, but simply more realistic, living within the bleak reality of a society no longer whitewashed with a *Leave It to Beaver* front. What they seem to want more than anything else—from their politicians, as well as from parents, bosses, friends, and religious leaders—is honesty, realism, and authenticity. Having witnessed the failure of relationships and education, as well as surviving a time unparalleled in terms of violence, Xers are not afraid of the truth, nor are they fooled into thinking they can change the world. They have by and large given up on large-scale utopian schemes and are working for practical change in their own lives, those of a few close friends, and, when feeling expansive, that of their neighborhood. Thus there exists a duality within their mentality: the coexistence of harsh reality and a desire and hope for better days. They respect people who live below the hype of expectations. Indeed, this is a cynical generation, but it is this way because it wants something more from relationships and people in authority.

This generation is also very materialistic, which should come as no surprise when considering the amount of time it has spent in front of the television. The billion-dollar advertising campaigns designed by GenXers' parents have proved to be very successful. GenX has been raised to think they are entitled to the same things that their parents have, and perhaps a bit more. Hence, they keep taking advantage of the credit card offers that arrive in their mailboxes. Designer labels seem to have great meaning at the very same time as political labels have lost all meaning. And they hedonistically adorn themselves with multiple earrings, nose rings, lip rings, and tongue studs and tattoos, expressing their desire to separate themselves from their parents' generation and redefine traditional definitions of beauty, creating "la vie Bohème" of their era.

This generation is not used to denying its impulses, even when it comes to sex. Indeed, premarital sex, for many, is inevitable, with the major question being whether it can be done safely. At the same time, the threat of AIDS has cheated Xers of the "free love" practiced by their parents' generation. More important, there is great confusion about the meaning of love and sex and how the two interact. While this generation is having sex earlier than previous generations this century, there is no indication that they are enjoying it more. Nevertheless, they have developed routines for avoiding the consequences of sex and are subsequently delaying marrying to historically late ages. Living together prior to marriage is the norm, not the exception.

Xers are a very tolerant group. They enjoy differences. Multiculturalism—unless it affects one's admission to college or graduate school—is in, while assimilation is out. A favorite expression "Isn't she such a freak!" is a term of endearment. It identifies the individual's uniqueness, her creativity. In addition, it is chic to be an ethnic of one stripe or another, and interracial dating is common. To be gay or lesbian is just a part of life, and bisexuality is in vogue. While racism and homophobia still abound in some sectors of society, the ethic of tolerance and acceptance is normative for many Xers. Much of this tolerance also applies to drugs, even if one has chosen, personally, to be drug free. While hard-core drug use is viewed as a problem, eating "shrooms" or relaxing with a little weed is viewed as a personal choice that by and large does not deserve judgment. It is okay for people to be into their own thing as long as it is not hurting anyone else.

Being mellow is a great virtue for many Xers. Perhaps in response to the workaholism of their parents, Xers take a different view of time. Frequent appeals are made to having a Zen attitude, which seems to mean that one should not let personal ambition grow too rampant. Goals are okay, but everything will happen in its own time and in its own way. One should "go with the flow" and, meanwhile, take in as much goodness and positive energy as one can find. Xers are the generation of the "hurried child" who was rushed by socially aggressive and upwardly mobile parents from one activity to another. Hence, it is now time to relax, to take it easy, to seek out a higher good and a more authentic way of being. When bad things happen, it is simply karma; things happen for a reason and usually work out in the end. If they do not, friends will be there for support. Xers do carry with them residual anger toward government, and consequently seldom engage in the political protests and rallies of times past. Rather, conspiracy theories and views of the evils of society are spread through music, rap, graffiti art, and other forms of artistic expression. Simultaneously, anger is directed inward, resulting in depression. And when alienation and anger do make their way out, they are sometimes inappropriate—resulting, for example, in acts of random violence.

Donald E. Miller and Arpi Misha Miller

The Philosophy and Epistemology of GenXers

Many analysts of Generation X see parallels between postmodernism in its many manifestations and the spiritual commitments of young adults.[3] One of the hallmarks of postmodern philosophy is rejection of metanarratives that relate a unified story of reality. For GenXers, reality is simply not that neat and simple. The possibility of universal principles is rejected, abandoned because they too often reflect someone's narrow self-interest. Xers tend to believe that values and metaphysical affirmations are conditioned by people in positions of power, with a desire to control others. Hence, the task of the critical thinker is to deconstruct all claims to supposed absolute truth.

In its cynical form, postmodern thought is destructive—it constantly debunks all attempts to define reality. On the other hand, a postmodern attitude can be viewed as enormously liberating if one is being oppressed by a hegemonic theory. Thus, many liberation movements have embraced this turn in philosophy and social analysis. But when embodied by GenXers, postmodernism typically takes two forms. On the one hand, it supports their cynicism toward anyone claiming to hold the universal key to knowledge and insight. Conversely, postmodern approaches to knowing open up the quest for truth in new and fresh ways that break out of all the standard boxes of perception.

Enlightenment-inspired epistemology from the "modernist" period—as opposed to the postmodern era—stressed abstract rationality, linear thought, and intellectual propositions. Divine revelation and supernatural activity related to miracles, prophecy, and mystical encounters came under heavy fire by philosophers and scientists who favored naturalistic explanations, insisted on replicable experiments, and were optimistic about conquering evil through enlightened reflection. In contrast, Xers are creating a new epistemology that has profound implications for their religious appropriations. Rationalist apologetics are rejected in favor of experiential knowing. Abstract doctrines, propositional creeds, and dogmatic affirmations are viewed with suspicion. Instead, experience replaces reason, feeling is more important than form, and the heart triumphs over the head. If traditional religions are going to have any meaning, it will be in the quality of their communal practice and experience of the faith, not because of pronouncements by external authorities.

The hegemony of one religion over all others is challenged in our postmodern world. GenXers embrace pluralism. In their view, that there are many religions makes the world a more interesting place. Buddhism, Hinduism, Judaism, Christianity, Islam, and a few thousand other religions, ancient and modern, have a right to exist, each in their own distinctiveness, say Xers. In contrast, modernists tend to demythologize these religions as vestiges of a more primitive time and impulse, or alternatively to homogenize them, searching out universal commonalities. Implicit in the modernist agenda is a rationalism that separates truth from fiction, as well as holding on to the idea of universal truth.

What is distinctive about Xers is that subjective knowing is valued above propositional truth. The quest for higher forms of knowing is not abandoned entirely, but such truths are better embodied in stories and myth than in dogma and doctrine. Filmmakers are viewed as the prophets of our age, and the messages they communicate are to be caught more than taught. GenXers favor implicit over explicit messages, which is why they are sometimes rather inarticulate about the spirituality that they embrace. Religion is a feeling, or sometimes it is expressed as a relationship. Intuition is important, as is metaphor, in expressing realities that guide one's life. GenXers are typically willing to give others their space, rather than building community that is based on right thinking.

GenX Religion

In spite of many common cultural experiences, there is no singular expression of GenX religion. In broad stroke, there are individuals with a generic interest in spirituality, but who find it a bit confining to attend a church, temple, or synagogue. Then there are the religious dabblers, who appropriate various elements from this religion and that one, and may even get serious for short periods of time as they do yoga, practice meditation, or revert, like good romantics, for a short dip back into the religion of their heritage. From the dabblers, we get many interesting hybrids of new religious combinations, but authority is vested in the individual, not in any particular tradition. There are also those who prefer the darker side—Gothic clubs, gangs, and other quasireligions that, of course, are not religions in the narrow sense but have their own rituals, rites of passage, and communal structure.

The chapters that follow, however, primarily focus on institutional expressions of GenX religion. There are Korean, Latino, African-American, and Anglo examples—each trying to solve a different problem for its members. There are also Jewish and Christian case studies, as well as Pentecostal and fundamentalist. In addition, there are those who spend hundreds of dollars getting Jesus tattoos, and there are modern-day GenX saints who have given up the luxury of the suburbs to be subtle witnesses for Jesus in their inner-city neighborhoods. It's a pretty wild assortment that, if nothing else, makes the point that GenXers resist formulas.

Nevertheless, there are some common themes. For one thing, each of these case studies offers a portrait of people gathering together to offer each other some support, some nurturing, and some love. One wise commentator on GenX religion has said, "Today's generation is not asking what must I do to be saved, but what must I do to be loved." This is in stark contrast to Philip Rieff's statement about the therapeutic impulse of the boomer generation, which is that these folks were substituting hedonism and material wealth for salvation. Xers are a generation of young adults who have been bruised by their parents and disappointed by their society. When they turn to organized religion, it is often to get a little structure in their lives, as well as find a source of authority. Therefore, we should not be surprised that one of the groups described in the case studies is called Committed, even though it outgrew a surf shop and now owns its own building.

In all of these groups there is a warmth and feeling of community that exceeds almost anything one might find in secular society. For example, the International Church of Christ is an amazing blend of racial and ethnic backgrounds. Many of the members are from blue-collar families, but they dress up in suits and ties and their Sunday best when they come to worship. More striking, however, is the fact that this rainbow coalition of believers embrace and hug each other when they meet, and then link brown, black, and white arms as they sit together to worship and pray. Newcomers are attracted to these groups because of their quality of community. People genuinely care for one another. They are rebuilding the bonds that existed in yesteryear but have been fragmented in our complex urban society.

Given the need for group cohesion and belonging, it is not surprising that multiple resources, ranging from music to religious pop art, are unifying mediums for GenX religions. Each group tends to have songwriters who compose lyrics and music, thus creating a signature sound; likewise, artists within the community create logos and other material expressions that uniquely symbolize the group. Even more innovative, however, is the way in which these groups use media. In addition to expensive sound systems, many are introducing videos and other multimedia elements into their worship settings. These are home-grown products that our digital age makes affordable, and some churches, such as Mosaic, have extraordinary individuals scripting computer-generated art with music videos, interviews, and original sound tracks—all for the glory of God! Worship is anything but sterile.

In addition to being multimedia, worship is multisensory. In fact, some GenX churches are now sneaking candles and incense back into their worship spaces. This is not an attempt to re-create medieval Christianity. Rather, these ancient tools of the sacred are mood setters. While GenX religion is often iconoclastic in breaking down traditional dichotomies between the sacred and profane, in another sense GenXers seek encounters with mystical, transcendent realities. Hence, the GenX church of the future may not be the made-over warehouse or supermarket, devoid of all religious symbolism. Rather, some of the dark and dusty spaces of bankrupt mainline churches may be just the setting in which to invoke the spirits of old. On the other hand, don't expect Xers to put the old-time religion back into these stone fortresses. Postmodern religion is going to rock and roll, dazzle with contemporary jazz, and quiet the soul with Gregorian chant. Indeed, it is precisely this juxtaposition of elements that will mark the maturing forms of GenX religion.

Movies such as *Dogma* demonstrate that, while there is a cynical streak in Generation Xers, they are also quite willing to open the door to angels and even demons. The old worldview of Enlightenment rationalism has a crack in it. So do psychoanalysis and all the pop "isms." There is nothing wrong in being playful with the sacred traditions and appropriating from them what is personally transformative. Consequently, even ancient practices such as fasting are coming back into vogue—not as cheap diets, but to purge the impediments to hearing one's call. After all, the Hebrew scriptures are filled with stories of God revealing himself in dreams and burning bushes. And did not Jesus spend forty days in the wilderness in prayer and fasting? While baby-boomer parents are reading books about monasteries and cloisters, their sons and daughters are tempted to actually try out some of these practices.

At the core of this paradigm shift is the realization that the old dichotomy between mind and body has to be discarded. Worship is that moment when we are one: in Christ, in nothingness, in nirvana. At Harvest Rock Church, young adults are calling out to God for revelations; they are publicly confessing their sins; they are speaking in the tongues of men and angels. From an outsider's view, these various forms of spiritual warfare and spirit invocation may seem primitive. But to practitioners, they are the instruments of healing and wholeness.

Obviously the range of integration between mind and body is going to differ from group to group. After all, GenXers have not abolished the traditional variables on which social scientists have established their profession: namely, race, class, and, increasingly, immigrant status. There will be "different strokes for different folks," with the upper-middle-class crowd represented in the opening vignettes of this chapter pursuing, in all probability, a different course toward religious commitment than those who are struggling to survive financially. Stated more specifically, the role of authority and the desire for discipline may be direct results of the problems that religion is addressing. On the other hand, cultural trends, including globalization, are affecting us all, and therefore it is meaningful to identify what is common to this generation of young adults as well as what separates them.

Will GenXers reinvent mainline churches and synagogues in the new millennium? Will they create altogether new houses of worship and religious practice? Or will they opt for a privatized spirituality? The chapters that follow offer some alternative models in response to these questions.

Notes

1. An excellent source of commentary and information about GenX religion is to be found on the "Generation X Internet Onramp" (http://home.pix.za/gc/gc12/genx/links/index.htm). Topics include postmodernism; generation X and the other generations; generation X and the church; generation X and evangelism; genX worship; generation X defined; generation X and music; generation X and the media; and many others. Also see "Smashing the Gen-X Stereotype," *Los Angeles Times,* September 3, 1999, 1.

2. The statistics in this section are drawn from Ted Halstead's highly informative article "A Politics for Generation X," *Atlantic Monthly,* August 1999, 33–40.

3. Our understanding of Generation X religion has been greatly enhanced by discussions with Todd Hunter, national director of the Association of Vineyard Churches. See the Vineyard's Internet site for updated articles on GenX religion (http://www.vineyard.org/). In addition, the Leadership Network has a very progressive Internet site that deals with GenX religion (http://leadnetinfo.org/leadnetinfo/).

Part 1

Spirituality Embodied

1

Marked for Jesus

Sacred Tattooing among Evangelical GenXers

Lori Jensen, Richard W. Flory,
and Donald E. Miller

Do not cut your bodies for the dead or put tattoo marks on yourselves. I am the Lord.

—Leviticus 19:28

One will say, "I belong to the Lord"; another will call himself by the name of Jacob; still another will write on his hand, "The Lord's," and will take the name Israel.

—Isaiah 44:5

Do you not know that your body is a temple of the Holy Spirit, who is in you, whom you have received from God? You are not your own, you were bought with a price. Therefore honor God with your body.

—I Corinthians 6:19–20

Let no one cause me trouble, because I bear on my body the marks of Jesus.

—Galatians 6:17

On His robe and on His thigh He has this name written: KING OF KINGS AND LORD OF LORDS.

—Revelation 19:16

Sid's Tattoo Parlor

Housed in an L-shaped, 1950s-era strip mall, Sid's Tattoo Parlor is located on the border of the cities of Santa Ana and Tustin, in Orange County, California. It resides next to a vintage clothing store, a bar, a beauty salon, and a lawyer's office in the run-down strip. Classic cars dot the parking lot, and on occasion vintage motorcycles are parked on the sidewalk in front of the shop. A large, retro 1950s-style sign proclaims "Sid's Tattoo Parlor" and gives an immediate feel that one is stepping into the past on entering the shop. The glass front of the shop invites walk-ins and the curious to take a peek at the fascinating happenings inside, and in general, the place is more bright and open than most tattoo shops. Although Sid's is not explicitly known or advertised as a Christian tattoo shop, all four of its tattooists are evangelical Christians, as are the majority of its clientele.

When you walk into the tattoo parlor, two things immediately confront your senses. First, the buzzing cry of the electric tattoo guns grates upon the ears, and second, the crisp smell of astringent rubbing alcohol tickles the nose. Loud music is played as well, a random combination of punk rock, rockabilly, and big band. Looking around, you see a vintage couch backed up against the front window, flanked by side tables that hold tattoo magazines, a Christian devotional book, and a faux leopard-skin Kleenex box cover. In the front corner is an antique Pepsi machine, and off to the right is a pool table. About halfway in is a waist-high wall separating the three workstations from the waiting area. Up front is Sid's station, behind him is Rob's, and off to the right is Eric's. The fourth tattooist, Jen, shares Sid's station.

The walls are covered with "flash," or drawings of tattoo designs. Some of these designs are by the tattooists who work there, some are by other prominent tattooists from around the country, and a sizable number are reproductions of midcentury traditional designs by "Sailor Jerry." A handwritten sign in traditional-style writing proclaims, "In God we trust, all others pay cash," another reads, "Warning: Tattooing May Be Addicting," while still another prohibits alcohol, smoking, and drugs on the premises. Various pictures of schooners, black-and-white portraits of heavily tattooed men and women from early in the century, and a Norman Rockwell reproduction of a tattooist and an old sailor add to the nostalgic feel of the shop.

Sid's, however, is not just a tattoo parlor, conducting only tattoo business. It also is a site of community, as well as spiritual fellowship. On our visits, there were people from out of state who came specifically to Sid's because they knew about it through other people, as well as a number of people just hanging out, socializing at the premises with no intention of getting tattooed at that time. Thus, Sid's is a station of the larger tattoo network, which is an interconnected, tightly knit word-of-mouth system. In the words of one of the tattooists, "I hate to say this, but I could pass gas right now and someone in New York would find out about it next week, and that's the way the tattoo industry is."[1] Moreover, Sid's also functions as its own localized site of community, serving much the same purpose as barbershops and the local diner did in small-town America. It is a central meeting place for a symbolic neighborhood that is separate from work, church, and school, where like-minded people hang out together to find community and solidarity.[2] Part of this hanging out involves spiritual community, as Bible studies are regularly conducted in a room next to the shop, Christian radio is often played over the speaker system, and conversations often revolve around sacred topics.

More than just a business and a site for localized community and fellowship, Sid's Tattoo Parlor can also be viewed as a cultural reference point. The rockabilly scene has the tattoo parlor—especially those shops that specialize in traditional-style work—as a central cultural location. This mostly GenX subculture revolves around rockabilly music (think early Elvis or Johnny Cash, or contemporary bands like Social Distortion, Reverend Horton Heat, or the Stray Cats), classic cars ('49 Merc, '56 Ford T-Bird, '57 Chevy Bel Air, and the like), vintage clothing (rolled up Levis and white T-shirts and pompadours for the guys; dresses, sweaters, and saddle shoes for the gals) and midcentury popular culture, which often runs on the seedy side (Betty Page, Vargas pinup girls, Viva Las Vegas). And of course, the Sailor Jerry–inspired traditional-style tattoos are essential—pledge tattoos, pinups, and panthers, as well as flames and dice. Thus, many scenesters frequent tattoo parlors as the "cool" or "hip" place to hang out (regardless of whether they are being tattooed at the time), and many tattooists themselves partake in the rockabilly subculture. Sid's Tattoo Parlor is no exception, as the tattooists there are part of this scene, as are many of their clientele.

And so we began our journey into the mysterious, often paradoxical world of sacred tattooing. Although an ancient practice, such tattooing has been much neglected not only by sociologists but by mainstream culture as well. Despite being tied to religious practice across cultures and across time, the notion of evangelical Christians permanently decorating their bodies with sacred (and sometimes not-so-sacred) symbols seems contradictory. Yet for a small but growing subculture within evangelical Christianity, religious tattooing is becoming an increasingly legitimate expression of individuality, identity, and faith. By taking a closer look at one example of this phenomenon—Sid's Tattoo Parlor—we will explore the subject of evangelical Christians who are getting tattooed, and offer some initial analysis as to how and why the phenomenon is occurring. We will meet the people at the shop, examine the history of tattooing, and explore how this generation of evangelical Christians views tattooing. Finally, we will seek to explain how and why tattooing among evangelical GenXers is growing in popularity.

We visited Sid's Tattoo Parlor twice during September 1998 to explore this topic. During our first visit, one of us was tattooed, while the other two took photographs and interviewed the tattooists, their clients, and others just hanging out in the shop. We returned about a week later to do a more intensive follow-up interview with Rob, who also gave us a condensed version of a Bible study class he had once given about Christians and tattooing. In order to supplement this fieldwork, we also distributed questionnaires regarding Generation X evangelical Christians' attitudes toward tattooing in several classes at Biola University, an evangelical institution, collecting 130 in all. Let us now continue, meeting some of the colorful (in both personality and skin) people at Sid's Tattoo Parlor.

The Tattooists and the Tattooed

The owner of the shop, Sid Stankovits, got his first tattoo at the age of eighteen from a high school friend. He has been tattooing for eight years now, and opened his own shop two years ago. He attends church at a local Calvary Chapel, and is married to the granddaughter of Chuck Smith Sr., the founder of the Calvary Chapel movement and head pastor of the mother church, Calvary Chapel, Costa Mesa. On one of our visits, Sid was wearing a Calvary Chapel T-shirt. He estimates that 50 to 60 percent of the tattoos produced at his shop are of a religious nature, while the rest are secular. He says that his work in the shop is "definitely a ministry," but he also takes his trade seriously and challenges himself with different tattoo styles and techniques. His favorite style of tattooing is traditional, as well as Japanese and "psychobilly," which is "traditional with a shot of punk rock thrown into the mix." He recently has been experimenting more with thin-line, realistic work such as portraits (Delio 1998).

Rob Silva became interested in tattooing at the age of eight, upon seeing an ice cream truck driver who was heavily tattooed (Delio 1998). He was in the tattoo world long before becoming a Christian and experienced much persecution because of his conversion. He was fired from three tattoo shops for being a Christian, because "every time they said the G-Dammit word, I used to tell them, you know, 'God's last name is not Dammit, it's Wonderful, it's Awesome.'" For a while, then, he was "mobile," working on his own in people's homes. Rob had previously met Sid at another shop, and when Sid opened his own, he sought Rob out to work with him. Rob also views his tattooing as a ministry, and believes he may one day go into full-time ministry, perhaps as a pastor. Regarding Christian ministry opportunities, he says that "we led, like in two years, three or four people to the Lord, that we know of for sure, here in the shop, and many other people have rededicated their lives, man. I would say, countless times—I can't even count the times—how many people we've ministered to. That's what it's all about."

Eric Jones is the newest addition to the shop. He met Sid through friends, and soon began apprenticing with him and Rob. Sid saw some tattoo designs Eric had drawn up, thought he would make a good tattooist, and invited him to learn the business. Because of that invitation, Eric has been tattooing for about a year now. While still relatively new to the trade, Eric shows a lot of promise. He does primarily traditional-style designs, and has a large amount of traditional flash hanging on the walls in the shop (Delio 1998).

Jen Smith married Sid in October 1996. She began getting tattooed by him, and started apprenticing soon after as well. She has become a regular fixture at the shop, doing her own tattoos. She remarks, "It turned out really well having a female tattoo artist at Sid's because everyone in the shop is Christian and the guys won't tattoo girls on their private parts. With me around, we never lose the business!" She says that her favorite type of tattoo to do is the traditional-style head of Christ (Delio 1998, 50, 53).

Jason is another regular fixture at the shop. Although he does have a lot of tattoo work done by Sid, he regularly drops by just to hang out. He and Sid are childhood friends and are still very close. Jason sometimes visits the Monday-night services at Calvary Chapel in Costa Mesa, and goes occasionally to his Assemblies of God "home church," as well as visiting other churches in the area. Jason provides an interesting case of mixing the sacred and profane with his tattoos. On his chest, he has a makeshift World War II "cross": a B-52 bomber crossed by a pinup girl. He has a three-quarter backpiece of Moses parting the Red Sea, and below that, a picture of the *Star Wars* character Yoda holding an upright bass. When asked about why he chose such a unique tattoo as Yoda, he said it was because he has always been "into *Star Wars*" and that "Yoda's my man." And since he is also "into" rockabilly and psychobilly music, Yoda is playing the stand-up bass.

Another (semi) regular in the shop, Dave, is someone who takes both his tattoos and his Christianity very seriously. Although he lives in Portland, Oregon, Dave was passing through southern California on his truck route on the way to Arizona. He decided to make a stop at Sid's along the way to add to his already impressive collection of religious skin art. That particular night he was getting two large skulls on his kneecaps, which were eventually going to be part of a larger design with a Christian theme. Through the course of the evening it was discovered by one of the authors that she and Dave shared mutual friends in Portland—tattooist Mav Mess and his wife Nichole, both Christians who used to live in southern California before moving to the Northwest a couple years ago. This revelation reinforced the small-world feel of the tattoo culture in general, as well as strengthening the barbershop aspect of Sid's, where not only is business conducted but relationships and community maintained as well.

Dave's arms and torso are practically covered with religious art. His chest reads, "My Heart Belongs to Jesus," a Sacred Heart is placed over his heart, a rope is around his neck and attached to an anchor that stretches from his collarbone to just above his navel. Across his stomach is printed, "JUST-IF-IED Never Sinned," a play on words that refers to the Christian doctrine of justification commonly talked about in Calvary Chapel circles, and in laymen's terms means "just as if I'd never sinned." Dave has an elaborate backpiece depicting the risen Christ wearing a robe made up of various national flags, and flanked by warrior angels. He is fully "sleeved" with tattoos on both arms, with a miscellaneous mixture of both sacred and profane symbols. He also has more typical religious designs, such as a Praying Hands, a Christhead, and a small Sacred Heart; these are combined with "Twice Born" written across the inside of his wrist.

Dave is very knowledgeable and articulate about tattooing, and clearly has an apologetics in place for why it is acceptable for Christians to be tattooed: there was Christian tattooing as far back as the turn of the century, and more Christians are becoming "educated" about it now.

Indeed, Christian tattooing is not strictly a southern California phenomenon. Rob Silva has recently been in contact with other Christian tattooists from across the United States, as facilitated through a fledgling national organization, the Christian Tattoo Association (CTA). The CTA is managed by Christian tattooists from the Cherry Creek Tattoo Studio in Willmar, Minnesota. In its early stages of development, the CTA has this twofold statement of purpose:

- To spread the gospel to tattoo artists and enthusiasts through the printed page, personal witness, workshops and small group meetings at local events and national conventions.

- To promote health and safety issues in the field of tattooing and encourage moral and professional standards in the tattoo industry. (Christian Tattoo Association 1988a)

The main goal is to "share the gospel" with those in the tattoo world, primarily through personal evangelism. To further aid the fulfillment of this goal, the CTA has designed an evangelistic tract, *Eternal Ink,* using tattooing lingo to communicate the message of Christianity (Christian Tattoo Association 1988b). Here the permanence of marking one's flesh is compared with marking one's spirit, but in this case with God's ink: "Now God doesn't do coverups. He only inks a clean canvas. . . . God's forgiveness will wash away all your sin, all the bad ink of your life. . . . If you haven't met the Master Tattooist, you can. God does have an appointed time for you, but He doesn't take appointments. God takes walk-ins. *All* walk-ins." The tract then has a prayer for the person to pray for salvation. It concludes with this message: "Your canvas has been washed clean. . . . He has some awesome art planned for you! His hand is gentle. His lines are true. His colors are brilliant. And His work is indeed *most excellent!* Get hold of a Bible and read the Master's after-care instructions." Thus even the very tenets of the Gospel are compatible with the tattooing world, according to the Christian Tattoo Association.

In addition to the CTA, newspaper reports on evangelical tattooing in different parts of the United States and Canada have been reported to us, which provide some perspective on how extensive this activity actually is. Reports from such disparate locations as Vancouver, British Columbia; South Bend, Indiana; Nashville, Tennessee; and Kalamazoo, Michigan, suggest that evangelical tattooing is not just a California, or even urban, phenomenon.[3] Rather, GenX evangelicals in a wide variety of locations are participating in this religious expression.

Tattooing History and Interpretations

To gain some perspective on tattooing, religious or otherwise, a brief outline of tattooing history, as well as some initial scholarly analysis, is in order.

Tattooing History. During biblical times tattooing was a common practice, not only for pagan cultures in the Middle East but arguably for Jews and Christians as well. It was usual for the Arabs of the nations surrounding Israel to tattoo their foreheads and hands with magical symbols, and the Baal worship so often decried in the Bible involved the tattooing of worshipers' hands. Some scholars have theorized that Moses instituted sacred tattooing among the Israelites (see Exodus 13:9, 6), and thus the Levitical prohibition against tattooing would only be against heathen forms or symbols (Gilbert 1996a, 1).

Western forms of tattooing have also been practiced for centuries, since the time of the Roman Empire and before. The ancient Britons are believed to have established tattooing in Europe, and the Roman military during their conquest of the British Isles picked up the craft. Emperor Constantine subsequently banned tattooing in the empire in the third century, as he deemed it "violated God's handiwork" (Sanders 1989, 13). However, Procopius of Gaza, in writing a commentary on the Old Testament Book of Isaiah in A.D. 528, reported that many Christians were still being tattooed on their arms with a cross or with the name of Christ (Gilbert 1996a, 1).[4] Furthermore, a 787 edict by the Council of Northumberland (Gilbert 1996a) distinguishes between religious and secular tattoos: "When an individual undergoes the ordeal of tattooing for the sake of God, he is to be greatly praised. But one who submits himself to be tattooed for superstitious reasons in the manner of the heathens will derive no benefit therefrom" (2). Soon after this, though, the Catholic Church banned tattooing until the tenth century as a "form of deviltry" that disfigured the body created in God's image. However, medieval crusaders traveling to Palestine picked it up again. They were often tattooed with a cross on their arms, as either souvenir or a sign for Christian burial should they die upon their journey (Sanders 1989, 13–14; Gilbert 1996a, 2).

Religious tattooing for pilgrims continued in Jerusalem, where travelers marked themselves with Christian symbols to commemorate their journey and represent their faithful devotion. In fact, such tattooing (still practiced today) remained the only significant form of tattooing in the West until the 1700s, when explorers such as Captain Cook encountered tribal tattooing and brought it back to Europe (Sanders 1989, 14).

As a result of European contact with Polynesian culture, a "tattoo rage" broke out across Europe among both the nobility and the lower classes. Sailors, soldiers, artisans, and the aristocracy (including nobility from Russia, Germany, and England) were the primary tattoo consumers during the 1800s. The most popular designs during this time were South Sea and nautical images, religious tattoos, love vows, and military or craft insignia (Sanders 1989, 15). Tattooing soon crossed the Atlantic to America, where it flourished, especially due to the invention of the electric tattoo gun. Lew "the Jew" Alberts was one of the first professional tattooists, working in the first part of the 1900s. His designs—"sentimental, patriotic, and religious"—are the roots of what is now called traditional-style tattooing, which still involves an unusual mix of religious and secular images (Gilbert 1996b, 3; Sanders 1989, 17).

Interpretations of Tattooing. In Emile Durkheim's classic study *The Elementary Forms of the Religious Life*, he offers perhaps the first sociological treatment of tattooing and its religious associations. Here, Durkheim (1915) makes reference to the aboriginal practice of tattooing, wherein clan members put the image of their totem "upon their persons; they imprint it upon their flesh, it becomes a part of them" (136–37). He claims that this is done to "bear witness to their common existence"; it is "the most direct and expressive means by which the communion of minds can be affirmed" (265). As such, it is a mark of identity and belonging to the group, a symbol of common belief and practice.

Georg Simmel (1950) also dealt with tattooing from a sociological perspective, although only briefly, in his writings on adornment. He claimed that tattooing is the "closest" type of adornment, and that it is unique in that it is "so inexchangeable and personal" (340). For him, adornment served as a tool of individualization, of extending the personality. Moreover, this enhancing of the individual "is an inextricable mixture of physiological and psychic elements: the sensuously observable influence which issue from an individual in

22

the direction of his environment also are, in some fashion, the vehicles of a spiritual fulguration" (339).[5] Thus adornment (and among its various forms, tattooing), although markedly physical, also has a spiritual element to it, as it reveals and reflects a person's inner self.

More contemporary treatments of nonreligious tattooing include Samuel Steward's *Bad Boys and Tough Tattoos: A Social History of the Tattoo with Gangs, Sailors, and Street-Corner Punks, 1950–1965* (1990). Steward, a former English professor who left the academy to become a tattooist, examines firsthand the more seedy side of tattooing, including its associations with sexuality and deviance. Clinton R. Sanders examines the "art and culture of tattooing" in *Customizing the Body* (1989). This is perhaps the most extensive sociological treatment of the subject, with much insight on the process of "becoming and being a tattooed person," the tattoo relationship of risk and social control between artist and recipient, and social definitions of art and artistic production. Although both of these works are extremely helpful in understanding the general context of tattooing, virtually no mention is made of the contemporary relationship between religion and tattoos. To further explore this connection, we now examine evangelical GenX Christians' approach to, and understanding of, the practice of tattooing.

Evangelical Attitudes toward Tattooing

To gauge the general view of the current generation of young evangelicals toward tattooing, we distributed a brief attitudinal survey to various classes at Biola University, an interdenominational evangelical Christian university located in La Mirada, California. Although not a random sample, the 130 respondents were representative of the university population in that 85 percent were between the ages of eighteen and twenty-two years old; 74 percent were white; two-thirds were female; and 85 percent claimed some sort of conservative, evangelical religious affiliation.

Of the 130 respondents, 11 said they had a tattoo, but only 2 had a tattoo with any religious significance. However, of the 119 who did not have a tattoo, 75, or 63 percent, had thought of getting one at one time or another. When asked to rate the strength of their consideration of getting tattooed, 22 percent of the 119 tattoo-free respondents said it was definitely more than "just a passing thought," with about half of those claiming they were "ready to get one tomorrow." About 30 percent said getting a tattoo was "just a passing thought," and about 13 percent considered it even slightly less than that. However, about 33 percent claimed that "never in a million years" would they consider getting a tattoo.

Respondents were then asked what has kept them from getting a tattoo. Of the 135 total reasons given (some multiple responses), only 19, or 14 percent, of the reasons presented were of a religious nature, and these were quite varied. Some thought getting a tattoo would "cause their brother to stumble," others looked to specific biblical passages, still others simply responded "God." One young man, who had considered getting tattooed, gave his religious justification for deciding against a tattoo by writing, "I know that everything is permissible and not beneficial, and that if I love God first, it [tattooing] would be OK. What I was considering were verses and a crown of thorns. Then I realized how silly it would be to have a verse on my arm and not in my heart. If I had that verse in my heart, where else would I need one? Is it not better to proclaim God's glory, kindness, love, patience through actions and not the surface of one's body?"

Other significant deterrents to being tattooed were one's parents/family (8 percent), pain (11 percent), permanency (14 percent), cost (10 percent), regretting it later (10 percent), and how it would look when one is older (5 percent). Miscellaneous responses included health risks, not being eighteen yet, viewing tattooing as being "juvenile" or seeing it as a fad, and not knowing what design to get, where to place it, or where to get it done.

When asked if it is acceptable for Christians to be tattooed, the majority—70 percent—said yes. Fourteen percent were not sure, and only 13 percent said no. Another 3 percent thought the question was irrelevant. Of those who thought it was acceptable, many clarified that the acceptability of Christians being tattooed was dependent on the design and motivations behind it. It was often seen as a permanent symbol of their religious commitment, and could be used as a "witnessing" tool. Some responded that it was acceptable because Christians are no longer under the Old Testament law (which prohibited some forms of tattooing) but rather under grace. Others compared tattooing to getting one's ears pierced or cutting one's hair; as one individual stated, "It doesn't do any permanent damage to a person's soul."

Of those who were not sure if it was acceptable for Christians to be tattooed, some thought it was too worldly, but said that it did not necessarily have eternal significance. It could bring others down, and was also seen as unwise stewardship of one's body. Others had just not thought about it enough to come to a clear decision.

For those who opposed Christians being tattooed, the most common argument against it—offered ten out of eighteen times—was that it "defaced" the body, which is the "temple of God." Others thought tattooing was "messing with God's design"; "if God had wanted us to have permanent marks on our bodies, we would have been born with them." One person claimed that "you are blatantly sinning" if you are tattooed. Nevertheless, despite some sharp disagreements, the overwhelming majority was not against Christians permanently marking their bodies with tattoos.

Tattooing in Innovative Cultural and Institutional Spaces

So what then are we to make of this phenomenon of evangelical tattooing? First, we see that there is a newly created cultural space within the larger evangelical culture that gives a general context for tattooing to emerge. Historically, evangelical Christians have sought to control the presentation and expression of the human body, framed by a biblical rationale for their guidelines. By implementing various strategies such as implicit/explicit dress codes, the (un)acceptability of wearing jewelry or makeup, and enforcing gender-appropriate hair styles, evangelicals in various settings have traditionally controlled bodily expression as they have deemed biblically appropriate. Moreover, expression through use of the body—such as dancing, charismatic worship, and the like—has also historically been prohibited (see Flory 1996).

However, our findings, as preliminary as they may be, indicate that among this younger generation of evangelicals, there is a cultural space that for the most part accepts tattooing. That only 13 percent of the college students surveyed believe it is unacceptable for Christians to be tattooed is indicative that the historical evangelical emphasis on the control of the body is waning. Indeed, others such as James Hunter (1987) decry the loss among the "coming generation" of evangelicals of symbolic boundaries of control such as prohibitions against playing cards, dancing, and attending R-rated movies, which marked evangelical orthopraxy during the first half the century. Thus a general acceptance of traditionally banned cultural expressions and forms is becoming more prevalent among young evangelicals. As such, tattooing, and specifically the sacred tattooing we have been describing, subverts this historical evangelical emphasis on a controlled, conservative presentation of body and self by permanently marking the body as a symbol of Christian experience. Certainly, religious tattooing presents a "counter (evangelical) cultural" expression of the body; it is an "un-orthopraxy" that, although rejecting traditional evangelical cultural forms, nevertheless expresses a new form of a "total commitment" to evangelical Christian orthodoxy.

Second, we see that beyond the general cultural space that allows bodily expression such as tattooing, there is a specific institutional space within contemporary evangelicalism that allows (even encourages) such cultural expressions to flourish. From our observations, it seems that "New Paradigm" churches,[6] such as Calvary Chapel, give the specific, necessary context for tattooing and other such expressions to occur. With the incorporation of sub-cultural styles of music into worship in the late 1960s, as well as the reception of certain elements of the hippie culture (bare feet, blue jeans, beads, and so on), Calvary Chapel set a precedent of cultural acceptance and appropriation for that generation as well as for those to come.

Although within these churches there are definite generational differences regarding preferences for or against religious tattooing, it nevertheless is an accepted form of religious expression. According to Rob Silva, although some Calvary Chapel leaders would not personally have a tattoo, they accept those who do. He remarks, "Okay, like Chuck Smith [and] Don Stewart [on] *For Every Man an Answer* on the radio, and also through Jennifer and Sid, you know, being [related to] Chuck Smith—we asked him if there's anything wrong, and he totally agreed with us. . . . He totally don't like tattoos himself, he doesn't like them. Why? Because that's his preference; he does not like them. But there's nothing wrong with them." Thus we do not believe that it is a coincidence that Sid's shop has strong ties to Calvary Chapel, and that many of its clientele whom we encountered are from various New Paradigm–type churches.[7] The cultural space encouraged by the institutional precedent as exemplified by Calvary Chapel explains much about why there is an opportunity for evangelical religious tattooing.

Finally, within the general space of evangelicalism and the specific institu-tional room of New Paradigm churches that allows for tattooing, the next question is, Why are certain groups within this generation of evangelicals get-ting tattooed? We believe it is significant that this is (at least in part) a gener-ational issue. According to Karl Mannheim ([1927] 1952), individuals in any given generation share a common social and historical location that limits their potential range of experience, "predisposing them for a certain charac-teristic mode of thought and experience, and a characteristic type of histori-cally relevant action" (291–92). Thus the difference in cultural expression between Chuck Smith Sr. and his grandson-in-law, Sid, is not surprising. However, it is beyond the scope of this paper to determine the social and his-torical factors that separate the generations; suffice it to say that there is an obvious difference based at least in part on generational experiences. And although we cannot answer with empirical certainty this question of *why* these people within this specific generation are getting religious tattoos, we would like to offer three reasons that characterize our findings.

1. *Group Identity.* Tattooing is a signification of identity to a larger group, be it secular or religious. According to Rob and his observations of his clients, "If you're punk rock, you'll get yourself the skull or the cross-bones, or black widow, you know. If you're *cholo,* you're gonna get the

26

Old English [writing] or the Mexican girl with the hat. And if you're rockabilly, you're gonna get your Elvis, your dice, and your flames. And if you're a surfer, you're gonna come in and get your waves and your dolphins. It's to identify yourself, you know, where you're from. . . . The Christian group, they come in and get their ichthus [fish], you know, their little Calvary dove, their crosses, their scripture, you know, they come and get all kinds of stuff." This echoes Durkheim's (1915) analysis that tattooing "bears witness to [a group's] common existence," and that it is a permanent mark of one's communal identity (136–37). One young Biola woman whom we interviewed, who thought the reason people are getting tattooed is as an act of conformity, put forth an extension of this concept. She said, "I mean, I hate to admit this, but it is really kind of conforming, you know, just 'cause everybody is doing it so you do it."

2. *Individual Expression.* Tattooing also can be an artistic tool to express a unique self. According to Rob, "Some are doing it for the love of it, you know, because it's awesome and beautiful." He refers to Jason's Moses/Yoda backpiece, and how that is expressive of how "he's a *Star Wars* freak" and at the same time how "he loves the Lord." This is suggestive of Georg Simmel (1950, 339–40), who describes tattooing as part of one's bodily adornment that outwardly expresses one's inner self. A further example of Simmel's "fulguration," or spiritual flash, that adornment expresses is found in Michelle, another Biola student with a religious tattoo. For her, tattoos can be an expression of a very personal religious commitment. She says, "I felt that I always wanted [a tattoo] that was religious and that would remind me of who I was in the Lord and who I am in Christ. . . . I just wanted something to remind myself all the time that it's going to be there forever and hopefully I'll be serving the Lord forever." As such, religious tattoos are a mark of individuality and an expression of individual belief and commitment.

3. *Mutual Attraction.* Generally, tattooing is thought to be deviant, stigmatizing, and a permanent mark of difference. Although it is often condemned by the larger society, tattooing is unashamedly "out there," confronting anyone and everyone who happens to gaze upon it (cf. Blanchard 1994). There is a marked similarity to the form of evangelical Christianity practiced in New Paradigm churches: an encompassing Christian identity that confronts "the world," and high moral demands coupled with a conservative theology, sectarian in content but not in form. Such Christians are, in their terms, "in the world but not of the world," often feeling scorned and mocked because of their faith in Jesus Christ, and

27

encouraged to leave their previous lifestyle upon conversion. Thus, it is conceivable that people who embrace radical spiritual commitments may be more likely to embrace radical physical commitments. Moreover, given the nature of these churches to adapt various cultural expressions, is it any wonder that youth within New Paradigm churches would go after the more extreme forms of expression of that faith, including religious tattooing?

Material Christianity Embodied

We would like to frame our final thoughts about sacred tattooing within the framework set up by Colleen McDannell in her insightful work *Material Christianity* (1996). McDannell argues that material products and representations are indeed important in the lives of "average Christians." Because people need objects to help establish and maintain relationships with the supernatural as well as the natural, such artifacts help create "religious landscapes" through which Christians tell themselves and others who they are. Moreover, as religious meaning is constructed and reconstructed, it is through external practices and products that the "inner experience" of religion comes. Indeed, McDannell argues, "the sensual elements of Christianity are not merely decorations that mask serious belief; it is through the visible world that the invisible world becomes known and felt" (272).

Thus, it is useful to view religious tattooing as another—perhaps ultimate?—example of material Christianity. It is here that the spiritual is indelibly marked upon the flesh, and sacred images are inscribed upon profane surfaces. Rather than religious representations being depicted in the public stained-glass windows of the local church, these images are instead indelibly placed upon one's body, one's own private "temple of the Holy Spirit." It is a personal, individualized (bri)collage of images, mixing sacred and profane images (skulls with crosses, demons with angels, evil with good) of the spirit inked on the flesh. Religious tattooing blurs the sacred/profane, spirit/flesh, public/private dichotomies of evangelical Christianity, redefining the boundaries of orthopraxy in the articulation of orthodoxy. As a symbol of identity and individuality, an extreme expression of an extreme faith, religious tattooing among young evangelical Christians embodies—literally—their beliefs in a new, innovative, and radical way. And for a generation of young Christians who are testing both spiritual and physical boundaries, sacred tattooing provides a tangible, permanent means of expressing an intangible, transcendent faith.

Notes

1. All quotes taken from personal interviews unless otherwise noted.
2. We also drew on Mitchell Duneier's (1992) notion of, in this particular case, the cafeteria having greater significance than just a food establishment—it is a meeting place encouraging sociability, intimacy, and community.
3. Elaine Gale, staff writer for the *Los Angeles Times*, informed us that over 230 newspapers picked up her January 11, 1999, story on the emerging network of Christian-run tattoo parlors across the United States.
4. Durkheim (1915, 264) also makes reference to early Christians having a cross or name tattooed on their arms.
5. *Fulguration* is defined as "radiating like a flash of lightning."
6. As coined by Donald E. Miller (1997). Among other things, New Paradigm churches (which include movements such as Calvary Chapel, Vineyard, and Hope Chapel) are marked by openness to and adaptation of mainstream, secular cultural practices. Writes Miller, "Rather than calling their members away from cultural engagement, they actually appropriate many aspects of contemporary culture, transforming these aspects for their own purposes" (154).
7. These include Calvary Chapel, Costa Mesa; Vineyard Fellowship; True Vine Fellowship; Committed Fellowship; and an evangelical Anglican church.

References

Blanchard, Marc. 1994. "Post-Bourgeois Tattoo: Reflections on Skin Writing in Late Capitalist Societies." In *Visualizing Theory: Selected Essays from V.A.R., 1990–1994*, edited by L. Taylor, 287–300. New York: Routledge.

Christian Tattoo Association. 1998a. Home page, http://home.dwave.net/~hoss/cta.htm.

———. 1998b. *Eternal Ink*, pamphlet. Willmar, Minn., and available online, http://home.dwave.net/~hoss/cta-newsletter1.html.

Delio, Michelle. 1998. "Psychobilly: When the New and Old School Styles Collide." *Tattoo* 110 (October): 50–53.

Durkheim, Emile. 1915. *The Elementary Forms of the Religious Life*. New York: Free Press.

Duneier, Mitchell. 1992. *Slim's Table: Race, Respectability, and Masculinity*. Chicago: University of Chicago Press.

Flory, Richard W. 1996. "Maintaining 'Christian Manliness' and 'Christian Womanliness': Controlling Gender in Christian Colleges, 1925–1991." Chap. 5 in *The Power of Gender in Religion*, edited by GeorgieAnn Weatherby and Susan Farrel. New York: McGraw-Hill.

Gilbert, Steve. 1996a. *Tattoo History Source Book: Jews and Christians*. Tattoos.com.

———. 1996b. *Tattoo History Source Book: U.S.A.* Tattoos.com.

Hunter, James. 1987. *Evangelicalism: The Coming Generation*. Chicago: University of Chicago Press.

Mannheim, Karl. [1927] 1952. "The Problem of Generations." In *Essays on the Sociology of Knowledge*. London: Routledge and Kegan Paul.

McDannell, Colleen. 1996. *Material Christianity: Religion and Popular Culture in America*. New Haven, Conn.: Yale University Press.

Miller, Donald E. 1997. *Reinventing American Protestantism: Christianity in the New Millennium*. Berkeley and Los Angeles: University of California Press.

Sanders, Clinton R. 1989. *Customizing the Body*. Philadelphia: Temple University Press.

Simmel, Georg. 1950. *The Sociology of Georg Simmel*. Edited by Kurt Wolff. New York: Free Press.

Steward, Samuel. 1990. *Bad Boys and Tough Tattoos: A Social History of the Tattoo with Gangs, Sailors, and Street-Corner Punks, 1950–1965*. New York: Harrington Park Press.

2

Spirituality Bites

Xers and the Gothic Cult/ure

Julia Winden Fey

Monique is rather typical of the Goths I have encountered. I had arranged to meet her at a coffeehouse in San Francisco's Haight-Ashbury district, and although we had never met before, I identified her as soon as she walked through the door. At three o'clock on a sunny afternoon, this tall, extremely pale-skinned, raven-haired woman was dressed entirely in black—hat, shirt, vest, skirt, tights, and shoes. Her fingernails too were coated with glossy black polish, and her eyes were heavily lined with kohl. The starkness of her appearance was relieved only by her blood-red lips and the large quantity of silver jewelry that adorned her hands, ears, and neck. She was a striking figure, even in a neighborhood where unusual garb is the norm.

Monique had responded to my posting on the Internet newsgroup alt.gothic, in which I asked for subjects willing to discuss their involvement in the Gothic subculture. As we talked over hot cider, she told me that she was twenty-five, and a student in the Bay Area. A self-described army brat, she had spent much of her childhood in Europe, and had only returned to San Francisco in the late 1980s. Although aware of the Gothic subculture as a child, she says that her involvement in the movement only developed after her move back to California. Since then, her participation in San Francisco's Gothic community has provided her with a way of hooking up with others who share her love of Gothic literature, architecture, music, and costume.

When I asked Monique about her religious background, she said she had attended church up until the age of five, when her parents divorced. From that point on, she was raised primarily by her father, a nonpracticing Presbyterian, who "thought that it would be more fun to see the castles [of Europe] than to go to church." Consequently, she and her father often spent weekends touring through French and German castles, as well as cathedrals and art museums. While these excursions may have removed structured

31

religion from her life, they did instill in her an ongoing fascination with medieval architecture, art, and cultures—interests that continue to influence her perception of life and its meaning. Although she describes herself as having no strong religious ties, Monique has nevertheless developed a belief system of her own out of the hodgepodge of religious and secular ideas she has encountered over the years. Identifying herself as "spiritual" rather than "religious," she says, "I'm interested in religions from around the world, but for me, spirituality is more of a personal sense of connection with the universe. It's more of a personal development of my own morals or ethics." She builds her "personal sense of connection" by selecting from among the beliefs of the various faiths she has experienced or at least read about, ultimately creating her own, unique spiritual collage. Importantly, she recognizes Gothic as a central, even unifying part of that collage. She notes that being part of the Gothic world has become an integral aspect of her worldview and her own identity. "Gothic" interests and "Gothic" values delimit the outlines of her passions and provide a context for her ongoing self-development. Being Gothic for her is an important part of "becoming who I am," as it enables her to do so within a community in which she feels free to explore her ideas and indulge her interests.

I have heard Monique's views on the spiritual nature of the Gothic world echoed by other Goths, former Goths, and even outside observers. Based on these perceptions, I offer the following discussion of the Gothic underworld as an introduction to one form of Generation X spirituality. After considering in some detail various aspects of the Gothic scene and its history, I will explore the manners in which this particular subculture provides its inhabitants with a unique, if loosely defined, worldview that is rich in spiritual resources, and perhaps typically Generation X in form. This discussion is drawn from one-on-one interviews, questionnaires, and observations conducted primarily in San Francisco and Los Angeles in the mid- to late 1990s. Although the Goths quoted below are real individuals, I have changed their names so as not to "out" anyone. Ultimately, based on these interviews and observations, I have come to think of the Gothic world as a *cult/ure,* a term I use in order to speak of Gothic as something existing somewhere between, or perhaps beyond, the traditional concepts of subculture and cult. As a cult/ure, Gothic can be understood as one more example of Xers' refusal to fit into predetermined categories or to trod solely on an already beaten path. Gothic Xers, while mostly rejecting traditional means and modes of spirituality, nevertheless seek out and seem to find spiritual elements within the shadowy realms of Gothicdom. As such, an exploration of those realms is in order.

Gothic Club Culture

For many Goths, the hub of the Gothic world is located in the various late-night clubs primarily scattered across the United States, the United Kingdom, and Germany. With names like the Bat Cave, Vampire's Kiss, and Helter Skelter, these clubs are found mostly, if not exclusively, in metropolitan areas, where the concentration of Goths, or at least the Gothicly inclined, is high enough to support a weekly nightclub. Like contemporary dance clubs in general, Gothic clubs tend to come and go with the popularity of the music—or, more precisely, with club owners' perceptions of the music's popularity. Today music fashions change rapidly, and so do their venues. However, while Gothic rock first made its appearance in the early 1980s, it has remained—or perhaps is again—trendy, keeping newer clubs, as well as older ones open.

Although the clubs differ in appearance and size, the experience they offer tends to be similar, with dim lighting, loud, droning music, and plenty of clove cigarettes. Now approaching its twentieth year in operation, Los Angeles' Helter Skelter is typical of such clubs. Located in a warehouse in a slightly run-down business section of the city, it is unmarked except for the street number over the door. The surest way of locating it is to wait until eleven o'clock on a Wednesday night, after which the line of people dressed in black, and the two or three hearses parked out front, serve as reliable guideposts. Before entering, you must present proper identification and pass through a security inspection. Although the guards are looking for concealed weapons, they are quick to admit that Goth Night at Helter Skelter generally involves fewer fights or problems than any other night. Goths, they have told me, tend to be introspective and nonviolent.

Having passed through security, those over the legal drinking age are given a plastic bracelet. Once inside, you face a long dark hallway filled with cigarette smoke, with a desk where each person signs a membership book and pays the cover charge. The hall ends with a long stairwell leading to a balcony overlooking the dance floor. From here, you might watch people on the dance floor swaying to the sonorous drone of an early David Bowie song. Video screens on the side walls will flash black-and-white images of people in various sexual positions, including several stills of women in bondage chains. You might also be able to discern fifty or so people scattered about the edges of the dance floor, standing in the gloom with drinks and cigarettes in hand, watching those dancing or, occasionally, trying to make conversation above the din. By midnight, the room fills with another three hundred people or more, and the smell of clove cigarettes becomes suffocating. On the dance floor, people sway in the serpentine, self-absorbed manner that characterizes

Gothic dance, and the noise level becomes deafening. In the nearly nonexist-ent light, made even dimmer by the smoke, it is difficult to distinguish one body from another. The room is reduced to a crush of black velvet dresses, satin skirts, lacy shirts, shiny polyvinyl chloride pants, fishnet stockings, com-bat boots, and black high heels, all topped by beautifully eerie faces, with uni-formly kohl-rimmed eyes, blood-red mouths, and white faces.

Central to the Goth club experience is the music, known as Gothic rock. The term *Gothic* in reference to a genre of music was first used by the manager of the band Joy Division. In a 1978 BBC interview he described Joy Division as "Gothic compared with the pop mainstream" (Wake 1994). Although Gothic aficionados generally do not include Joy Division in the Gothic cate-gory, the term was quickly picked up by the U.K. music media, and "they applied it in a nasty sort of pigeonholing way to a number of bands that were around in the early 80s." Bands such as Bauhaus, Siouxsie and the Banshees, the (Southern Death) Cult, the Cure, and the Sisters of Mercy eventually became leading representatives of this new genre, acquiring the Gothic tag in part for the style and mood of their music and lyrics, but also because of their look, most dressing solely in black.

Despite its disparaging origins, the term *Gothic* has now been embraced by bands, record companies, and fans alike. The typically Gothic sound, if one exists, is similar to its punk roots, yet darker in both tone and content. Retaining some of punk's anger and its expressive driving beat, Gothic emphasizes bass guitar and deep vocals. One online Goth lists the following as technical earmarks of Gothic music: "At least one layer of thickly distorted, chorused, flanged, or otherwise heavy and ethereal electric rhythm guitar. . . . Musical construction suggesting a blend of gregorian chant, baroque minuets, and [heavy] metal on morphine. Melodies produced by old world instru-ments, be they real or synthesized, such as harpsichord, viola, cello, pipes, and ESPECIALLY cathedral organ. And vocals which are thick, smooth, ephemeral, and riddled with angst" (Couchman 1995).

The overall effect is dark, sensuous, and eerie. Fans of Gothic often men-tion the emotional reaction they have to this music as the reason for its appeal. Another online Goth says he sometimes likes industrial music, which has a hard, mechanical sound, but at other times prefers Gothic because it "speaks more to the heart" (Neely 1995). Club dwellers at Helter Skelter also point to the emotional tones or mood of Gothic music as a primary source of its appeal. One woman summarized her attraction to Gothic music by saying, "It puts me into a deep, dreamy, contemplative state. I consider myself a very thoughtful, introverted person, so I identify with the lush sounds." Another clubber said he liked Gothic music, "because it is the most beautiful music anywhere. The songs have more meaning relating to our lives and the way most of us feel in the Gothic scene. I like the music's down tone and depressing feeling which is more true to life." An online Goth perhaps best summarizes the overall emotional effect of Gothic music as consisting of three words: "MELANCHOLY, MELANCHOLY, MELANCHOLY," and then suggests that while at first Gothic music can be frightening, its melancholic tone becomes comforting with familiarity (Couchman 1995).

As is suggested above, sound is only one aspect of Gothic music. For many, lyrical content is equally important in distinguishing Gothic from other genres of rock music. As with punk, much of the music produced by Gothic bands has been "angst ridden but all the hatred is turned inwards and the music is typified by introspective lyrics" (Gothic FAQ 1994). Where punk deals with anger, Gothic lyrics tend toward absorption in the singer's quieter or more internalized emotions and personal desires, and frequently concern loss, sadness, and death. Because of its occasional use of vampiric imagery and themes, and because of many musicians' vampiric appearance, it is also sometimes referred to as "Vampire music." The band Bauhaus's 1979 release "Bela Lugosi's Dead" is probably the most famous of the early Gothic songs dealing with death and vampires. Its fame is in large part due to the movie *The Hunger*, in which this song accompanied the opening shots of a very gaunt, pale, and literally vampiric David Bowie. However, its monotonous lyrics, while fitting the stereotypical content of Gothic, do little justice to the greater lyrical depth of later Gothic songs. The refrain of the Bauhaus song, which actually constitutes most of the song and is sung in a low drone, accompanied by a steady, driving beat, is as follows: "Alone in a darkened room, the Count. Bela Lugosi's dead. Bela Lugosi's dead. Bela Lugosi's dead. Undead, undead, undead. Undead, undead, undead." In comparison, songs from contemporary bands, such as Los Angeles' London after Midnight (LAM), more poetically incorporate the standard Gothic themes of death, pain, and suffering: "Is this life this degradation—this pointless game, humiliation. Born to die, we're born to lose—and not one choice we make we choose. And when this life is at an end we find that Death's our only friend. Must we suffer through your games, oh Lord? Can God really be so bored?" (London after Midnight, 1998). Themes such as these abound in Gothic songs. Even the names of bands pick up this dark focus, as in Black Tape for a Blue Girl, Love Spirals Downwards, Thanatos, and Bleak.

Although Gothic music is often equated with punk, heavy metal, and industrial, it should be seen as occupying its own niche within the music world. Punk has traditionally been seen as an expression of youthful anger and frustration over social conditions, while heavy metal has been regarded as an effort to evoke raw power in order to empower its listeners (Walser 1993). In similar fashion, industrial music's cacophony of sound has been understood as an attempt to represent its creators' (and audience's) sense of chaos and meaninglessness in the world. Departing slightly from these other genres, Gothic rock encourages its listeners to address and embrace the darker aspects of their inner selves and of life. Indeed, many Goths believe that this embracing of "the dark as well as the light" is what Gothic and Gothic music is, finally, about. Carlos, whom I interviewed, explains this by saying,

> To me, personally, it means being . . . I don't know, like I guess enjoying the darker sides of life, you know? Like, when you think about it, there's happiness, there's sadness, there's life, there's death, there's joy, there's agony, you know? It's like everybody usually tries to go out in this happy little world or whatever. I'm not saying that it's bad. I like to be happy. But the way I see it, we try to, in order to get a better experience in life, it's kind of best to see both the light and the dark. You know, the happiness and the sadness. Life and death. Just try to experience both of them in order to maybe appreciate the other one.

Serving as a conduit to life's darker side, Gothic music thereby seeks to uplift its listeners rather than depress them, as many non-Goths, or "Casuals," might think. Echoing findings about the cathartic nature of heavy metal for alienated young people, Gothic music's affirmation of death and darkness serves to reinforce Goths' own beliefs about the value of all aspects of life, providing both reassurance and comfort to its listeners (Arnett 1995).

Gothic music, however, is not all there is to Gothic club culture, for the music does not exist in a vacuum. Gothic is as much an experience, a look, and a way of life as it is a genre of music. It is produced by, and in turn produces, an international community of people who share an interest in the music, the look, and the lifestyle. For most, the music remains the hub of this culture, yet it does not constitute its entirety. The bands and their music, the bands' promoters, the clubs that play Gothic music, the record companies and distributors who make it accessible, the online "Net Goths" who keep up a running conversation about the merits of the music and the culture, and the many fringe retail operations—Gothic clothing stores, catalogs, art and paraphernalia vendors—all exist in a complex relationship that results in what my interviewees call "the scene." The Gothic sensibility that is explored in and promoted by the music manifests itself throughout this scene that also overlaps and is sometimes indistinguishable from the industrial crowd, as well as S/M culture, vampire culture, the tattoo and piercing worlds, and many more.

The scene, referring primarily now to those who frequent the clubs and keep up with the newest bands, had its beginnings in a London nightclub called the Bat Cave in 1981. After its initial popularity faded in the U.K., the Gothic craze moved to the United States, primarily to Los Angeles and San

Francisco, although Gothic clubs and bands have a strong presence in New York and Seattle and can even be found in places like Atlanta and Cleveland, as well as many smaller urban areas. Almost two decades after Bauhaus's release of "Bela Lugosi's Dead" and the early Siouxsie and the Banshees albums, Gothic rock continues to thrive in the United States, the U.K., and Germany, a survival directly attributable to the development of the larger scene. As Deena Weinstein notes in her study of heavy metal music, while most musical genres tend to follow a process of formation, crystallization, and decay, some, like heavy metal, and here I would include Gothic, have "persisted in large part because of the development of a supportive subculture." This subculture not only provides a venue for music to be played (the clubs) and a group of consumers to buy the music but creates a fertile breeding ground for the emergence of new groups and new fans. Additionally, in the early 1980s, and again in the late 1990s, this subculture has provided a base population from which fashion designers, fiction writers, and others have been able to commercialize and popularize "the Gothic look" and attitude within the broader culture. The explosion of interest in vampires and vampire fiction, as well as the promotion of Gothic designs in 1990s fashion and cosmetics, while temporarily making Gothicdom "in and trendy," much to the disgust of those who consider themselves "real" Goths, nevertheless must be credited with assisting in the continuation of the Gothic scene. Clubs only remain open as long as there are sufficient numbers of patrons crossing their thresholds, and marketers of Gothic items have greatly increased the number of people looking for somewhere to go wearing their new Gothic fashions.

Gothic Online

There is another aspect of the scene that is not as visible as the fans, the bands, the music and retail industries, and the clubs, but which also contributes to the vitality of the Gothic world. Coexisting with the real world, Gothic culture is a flourishing virtual community. Many are introduced to the Gothic culture by the Net Goths who post on the Internet newsgroup alt.gothic. With messages being sent from countries worldwide, this online site averages almost one thousand postings per week. Topics of conversation on this site include postings from people who "delurk" (post) for the first time to ask, What's really Gothic? and lamentations by rural Goths over their isolation from real Gothic culture, which generally means clubs and clothing or music stores. Responses to these lonely Gothic teenagers, stranded in the wilds of Arkansas or Minnesota, with no other Goths in sight, generally include welcomes, but also a lot of warnings not to fall prey to the "Goth police," or any other semi-authorities, such as some of the slicker Gothic magazines who might pretend to define what is Gothic and what is not Gothic. Gothic, the newcomer is told, is *whatever you feel it is*. End of discussion.

While such threads reappear on alt.gothic with reliable frequency, other topics that regularly show up include discussions of new and old bands, favorite songs, characteristics that make a song Gothic, club openings and closings, and finally, discussions about why someone feels Gothic. Questions about where to find a new black hair dye or a clothing or record catalog also appear frequently, although some of these are shunted to alt.gothic-fashion. And then there are the endless lists of the best Gothic albums, and movies, and numerous jokes—the latter invariably poking fun at stereotypes of Gothic dress and attitudes. For example:

What do you store your heavy velvet cape in for the summer?
Goth balls.

Why is it so hard for Goths to get work?
Because all they can do is mope the floors and depress the buttons.

In spite of their reputation for moroseness, Goths, or at least Net Goths, seem to have a sense of humor.

Perhaps surprising to many outside the Gothic world, these Goths also reveal a social conscience. Despite the results of my survey, which showed that less than half of the respondents vote regularly, and even fewer are registered with a specific party, the online discussions generally entail a few threads concerning current social and political issues. For example, during one particular week in June 1997, alt.gothic contained discussions of various efforts in the United States to ban handguns, as well as calls for a counter-boycott of Southern Baptist–owned businesses in retaliation for their boycott of the Disney Corporation and its same-sex-partner-friendly policies. Discussion of these issues was lively and well informed. Past threads have also touched upon feminism and sexism—both within Gothicdom and the larger culture—and issues surrounding sexuality and sexual identity.

Not limited to the alt.gothic newsgroup, this active online community also cross-posts to many other newsgroups—such as alt.vampyre, and alt.AnneRice—and also creates and maintains a staggering number of websites or home pages dealing with everything Gothic, or even remotely Gothic. The elaborate designs of personal Gothic home pages by persons with names such as "Cryptie" and "Vulture Miranda" often include advanced graphics such as flames licking around the edge of the screen, or blood dripping down the screen as you scroll through the site. Such pages often contain lists of the favorite songs and lyrics, poetry, and photographs (sometimes sexually explicit) of the page's webmaster. These webmasters are obviously technologically adept; it is not surprising that almost all of the Net Goths who responded to my survey claimed to spend more than five hours per week online, many even indicating that their web surfing time usually exceeds fifteen hours each week.

Gothic Style

The third aspect of the Gothic scene to be considered, and generally the first one most people notice, is the appearance and attire of many Goths. The Gothic look, while admittedly open to variation, tends toward a pale, preferably gaunt face, with heavily lined eyes and red or black lips, and, of course, black clothing. Although I have been assured that one can be Goth without dressing the part, Gothic garb seems to play a key role for many in feeling Gothic.

According to Generation X scholar Tom Beaudoin, this emphasis on clothing and appearance clearly marks Goths as members of their generation. In his book *Virtual Faith: The Irreverent Spiritual Quest of Generation X* (1998), Beaudoin notes that Xers have used fashion as a means of expression ever since they were old enough to determine their own style. He suggests that clothing is an important means by which members of Generation X have been able to work through their experiences of hardship and suffering. Among the earliest fashion trends to be created and adopted by this generation were the military look and grunge, both styles expressive of what Beaudoin calls an "emerging bunker mentality among Xers." He further suggests that grunge, with its unkempt and ragged look, expresses much about Xers' feelings of neglect and need. Reputedly survivors of parental and social disregard, and sometimes abuse, the teens and twenty-somethings of the 1980s and '90s, he says, have hid their bodies and spirits within the protective camouflage of oversize flannel shirts and ripped jeans.

Beaudoin notes, however, that it is another such fashion trend, found particularly within metropolitan areas, that is the quintessential expression of Xer suffering, loneliness, and need. In its emphasis on death, decay, and darkness, Gothic, he says, is the starkest expression of Xer suffering. Whether dressed in the traditional, romantic Gothic look of black velvet, flowing white lace, and rich brocade, or in the more contemporary look of black leather, glossy polyvinyl chloride (PVC), and chains that shares much with industrial fashion, Gothic attire always has intimations of suffering, pain, and death. Within their elaborate costumes and makeup, Goths give tangible form to Xer experiences of separation and aloneness through an irreverent mimicking of death: "The gothic style is excessively funereal. Survival, it seems, is only possible by hyperbolizing death, by making an entire wardrobe out of bleakness"

(Beaudoin 1998, 104). In appropriating a deathlike wardrobe and mask, Goths attempt to overcome what seems so daunting. Their social, emotional, and physical suffering is cathartically faced, allowing Goths to empower themselves to move beyond feelings of loneliness, repression, and unimportance.

Beaudoin's observations certainly provide an important insight into Gothic fashions, but my interactions with Goths suggest that there is more to their garb than simply catharsis. From their perspective, their attire and makeup more importantly serve as means for creating and then communicating who and what they are. For many, adopting Gothic clothing enables them to feel comfortable with themselves by allowing them more fully to reveal their inner selves. As one twenty-four-year-old woman writes, "I see black as absorbing all color, all emotions. It is a metaphor or symbol for the vast universe and the unknown. It is also quiet and contemplative at times. Also, I have a deep love of travel and exploring unusual cultures (compared to my own mainstream [Mormon] culture). I always felt like a minority in personality, and now I choose to be comfortable with my unusual tastes [rather] than die trying to conform. Expressing myself with clothing and jewelry feels *freeing* and natural [emphasis hers]." Another woman comments that Gothic attire "makes me feel real. It makes me feel like myself." Finally, one Gothic man says, "It makes me feel good. I wear it almost every day because it says something about me to everyone."

For these and others, Gothic fashion both liberates and validates. Indeed, one woman announces, "It doesn't make me feel anything to be dressed in the goth garb. However, it makes me feel plain SILLY to be dressed in anything else. I can't stand to wear colours anymore; they slide off me like an oil slick. It would drive me insane." For this woman and many others, the black garb becomes essential for expressing and affirming identity. In fact, some Goths even have two separate wardrobes, one for work and one for comfort. Kyla, who works as a special education instructional aide, says that while her daily wear is "totally black," her work wardrobe, unfortunately, "has color." Still, she limits the color of her work clothes to darker tones such as navy blue, often accessorizing with black shoes and nylons.

Beyond the clothing, however, Kyla also points out another aspect of her preferred self-presentation that work requires her to do without—the elaborate makeup so cherished by most Goths, male and female. Generally involving white face powder, black or blood-red lipstick and nail polish, and a dark kohl eyeliner, Gothic makeup, like Gothic garb, becomes a defining element in many Goths' appearance and self-perception. Without it, they feel lost and exposed. Kyla, whose daily look includes what she terms "Cleopatra eyes," notes that the first thing she does after work is to remove her work clothes and reapply her makeup.

I come home, and I actually have to go "bbbllllll" and take [my work clothes] off. Run to my bathroom, and scrape my makeup on, and go "aaaahhh." Seriously, I feel like that's who I am. That's who I am. . . . I need to put all my black on, and I need to get out of here and go to school. When I go to school, to my college, when I've just got off of work, I feel so weird. I'm like so, I'm like so totally self-conscious, because I don't wear makeup to this other thing, and it drives me nuts. It's still taking a bunch of my friends to convince me, "You look OK without your makeup. You're still a pretty girl." I'm like NO. I can't stand it.

Other Goths relate similar sentiments regarding the role and importance of makeup in their lives. One woman says she wears makeup because her "gypsyesque alter-ego" loves captivating faces and drama. Another said she uses it "as another way to be creative and express my inside on the surface, though I'm sure I hide behind it also the same as many other things." For men, too, elaborate makeup and dress serves the dual purpose of hiding and revealing their inner selves. Michael, who showed me Polaroid photographs of himself in full makeup and wearing an evening gown, alluded to the ways in which the wearing of makeup reflects the way the Gothic culture encourages both men and women to get in touch with their emotions: "I think a lot of Gothic men are more in touch with themselves because they are able to express their emotions. They're able to get in touch with the other side of life [the 'feminine'], while a macho jock would be too afraid to put on lipstick."

In addition to makeup and dark clothing, the Gothic look increasingly involves accessories such as colored contact lenses, fangs, piercings, and tattoos. The newest of these fads—the colored or even cat's-eye contact lenses—is largely a product of Hollywood. Contact lenses in vivid red, green, and yellow have been used by characters in recent shows ranging from the television production *Babylon 5* to the wildly popular (among many Goths) syndicated vampire detective show *Forever Knight* and the screen adaptation of Anne Rice's *Interview with the Vampire*. In each of these, nonhumans, including and especially vampires, are shown to have senses and abilities superior to that of humans, as suggested by the catlike shape or dramatic color of their eyes.

Hollywood is also responsible, at least in part, for the growing number of Goths with altered orthodontics. While always popular with Gothic's vampire-loving crowd, fangs have become increasingly so with the development and availability of professionally designed incisors. Initially created for use in movies, these are a far cry from the plastic teeth popular among children at Halloween. Often custom-made, these fangs can be either temporarily or permanently adhered to one's real teeth, much like a corrective cap. When someone wearing these smiles, the fangs produce an eerie and highly realistic effect.

Finally, in addition to these more temporary artifices, the Gothic look today increasingly involves more permanent markings, primarily tattoos and piercings. Like other Xers, Goths appear to be infatuated with this ever-growing trend of "body modification." Although cost again is often cited as prohibitive, especially for tattooing, many Goths sport intricate designs as well as rather imaginatively placed piercings. Of those who responded to my survey, nearly 80 percent of the women and a third of the men have piercings, while half of the women and a third of the men are tattooed. In response to the questions of whether or not they have tattoos or piercings, here is a sampling of the replies I received from women:

> Yes, [I have] two tattoos. One is an arm band and the other [is] on my ass, and [I have] seventeen piercings: my septum, earlobes, labrette, lip, two traguses, two stretched earlobes, navel, two clit piercings, tongue, five in my ears.

> Two [piercings] in my nose (left side); two in my tongue; eight in my left ear; two in my outer labia; a tattoo of a winged horse on the back of my right shoulder; [and I am] planning more of both.

and from men:

> I have four holes in my left ear, two in the right, and both nipples pierced. I have a tattoo of Giger's alien on the back of my right shoulder and a tattoo of a large rose on the left side of my chest.

When asked to explain why they adorn their bodies in these ways, most talk about finding meaning through controlling, pleasuring, and/or beautifying themselves. The man mentioned above writes that

> The piercings were purely ornamental, although the nipples were also for the sensation (which is exquisite) and have made them more sensitive than before. The tattoos have meaning: the alien played a large part in my life and Giger's work is just wonderful. The Rose is a reminder of the pain I went through when I separated from my wife and my family. It's to remind [me] never to allow myself to get into that situation again.

A woman with five piercings in her right ear, one in her left nipple, and a navel pierce replies,

> I feel that piercings help me to regain a sense of reality through pain. When I've completely lost control of my life, or when things seem to get out of control, it is quite therapeutic to get a needle shoved into your flesh. It's like, if you can handle having a thick needle shoved into your body, and

watch it and not flinch, then you could take on [anything] anytime. For me, piercings are not for show, but for personal gratification and emotional stability.

And finally, another woman, who is in the process of "starting an industrial project (big bars through my ear cartiledge [*sic*])," argues,

> I think the least you can do to liven up your short lifetime is to make your sort of beauty wherever you can, starting with yourself (unless you find something better to do), and I find little bits of metal and dermal pictures to be nice additions to the strange body I've picked up.

For this woman, and other Goths, tattoos and piercings, in much the same manner as Gothic clothing and makeup, are a means of establishing control over the only thing many Xers feel they can control—their own bodies—while also being a conduit for self-exploration and expression. Through these external accoutrements Goths, and Xers in general, are able to develop themselves into a self that is uniquely their own, reclaiming and delineating their own physical and spiritual boundaries.

Gothic Vampires

Finally, no discussion about Gothicdom is complete without direct mention of the figure whose spectral image lurks beneath much of Gothic music, fashion, literature, and art. Beloved by the majority of Goths I have encountered, the vampire makes its haunting presence known throughout most elements of Gothic culture. In hundreds of novels, comic books, films, and poems, all avidly read and sometimes written by Goths, these dark kin of humankind skulk and suffer their way through time. In the plush velvets and elegant laces of high Gothic fashion, they receive homage from adoring fans who are eager to emulate their antiquated (and obviously wealthy) style. Particularly notable members of this undead race have had songs written about them, and some even have their own fan clubs. In Gothicdom, it is good to be undead.

Gothic admiration of these creatures is significant, as it marks a notable departure in Western attitudes toward the vampire. Europeans in the Middle Ages spoke fearfully of these creatures, whom they saw as putrefied, corpse-like monsters, able to return from the grave to suck the blood of the living. Nineteenth-century audiences shuddered in horror as vampires moved up the social ladder and drained polite society of its females, one by one. Even certain types of contemporary treatments of the vampire, especially low-budget horror flicks, continue to represent the undead as fiends. Like their many predecessors, these films suggest that the only good vampire is a truly dead one. Goths, however, seem to disagree. Where others have seen only a horrifying beast, they see a tragic hero. Instead of a monster who brings death, they see the promise of eternal life. Rather than the bearer of a curse, Goths perceive vampires as beings who are immensely powerful and highly erotic. But why this shift?

According to several scholars of popular culture (Auerbach 1995; Dresser 1989; Gelder 1994), vampires have always served as mirrors capable of reflecting their society's particular fears and desires. Nineteenth-century vampires, like their human counterparts, existed in a sex-segregated world. In this context, vampires were creatures who formed "special friendships" with individuals, and then drained the life out of them. In Bram Stoker's notorious work, written in 1897 as the Western world saw women increasingly entering the public domain, Dracula threatens to vampirize (read: sexualize) Mina and destroy the harmony of the Harker home. Now, as this millennium comes to a close, vampires have become powerful, rich, sexy, and of course eternally young. They have attained the American dream. Or have they? In the midst of their success, it seems they have begun to doubt the dream. They have begun to question the meaning of it all.

The vampires whose charisma and angst most pervade Gothic culture are undoubtedly the brood created by Anne Rice in *Interview with the Vampire*. Led by her beloved Lestat, these children of the night have come to define the late twentieth-century image of the vampire, much as Stoker's Dracula did for earlier generations. However, whereas Stoker portrayed his vampire as a cold, ruthless, and nonhuman character, driven solely by bloodthirst, Rice has indelibly stamped contemporary vampires as creatures possessing sarcastic wit, devilish good looks, and most interesting, spiritual burdens that could be said to make Judas Iscariot look carefree. The movie version of *Interview*, featuring a blond Tom Cruise as Lestat and Brad Pitt as the angst-ridden protagonist, Louis, only serves to reinforce these characteristics. Unlike the older image of the cool, aloof vampire, Lestat and Louis struggle with the guilt and extravagances of possessing an eternal life that is based on repeated killing and the consumption of blood. They spend centuries in search of the answers to their questions on the origins and meaning of their undead existence. Endlessly searching for the truth of their existence, and even for God, these millennial vampires have reached a spiritual crisis, one perhaps matched only by that of their fans.

Gothic as a Religion?

Although a "spiritual crisis" might seem too harsh a description of the current status of religion in Western culture, few observers of the religious scene will deny that significant changes that have occurred in the twentieth-century religious landscape pose new dilemmas and difficulties for the study of contemporary religion. A complete discussion of these issues and their relevance to Gothicdom is beyond the scope of this particular work, but in brief, several scholars of the baby-boom generation have described boomers as "religious seekers," noting that members of this generation frequently seek out their religiosity within a variety of traditional and nontraditional venues (Roof 1993). Often choosing self-guided exploration over inherited dogma, boomers have created a climate in which faith involves actively selecting beliefs and practices from among an array of sources. As children of boomer parents, Xers are now following the older generation's lead, perceiving "spirituality"—as they more often call it—as something to be shaped and practiced however and wherever one chooses. Significantly, this distinction between *spirituality* and *religion* is more than mere semantics, for it reveals a distinction among both boomers and Xers between established, organized religion and what many perceive to be a more genuine or more "real" faith. Religious subjectivism, like subjectivism in general, is key with members of Generation X.

Of the Goths I have contacted, the majority tell me they were raised in a religious tradition, but only a few describe themselves or their parents as having been very involved with a religious group during their childhood. When asked if they consider themselves to be religious or spiritual now, more than half say yes, but few affiliate themselves solely with mainstream Protestant, Catholic, or Jewish denominations. Instead, they identify their spirituality as consisting of beliefs and practices drawn from Christianity, Judaism, and a variety of other faiths, including Buddhism, neopaganism, Taoism, Santeria, and Scientology. Even those who continue to identify with their parents' religious tradition say they are very selective as to which elements of this tradition they continue to observe. Others, believing that no religious tradition offers them anything of value, define themselves as not religious or spiritual, or they take the approach of a woman who says, "I worship me, and now I'm much happier."

When I have asked Goths if they see Gothic as a religion, the most common response is a laugh and a quick no. A few have said yes, it is for them religious, but for most, Catholicism and Judaism are religions, while Gothic is just Gothic. Upon further consideration, though, many have conceded that Gothic, while not a religion, certainly has spiritual aspects. Building upon such comments, I offer the following exploration of Gothicdom's potentially spiritual elements. To do so, I have utilized Joachim Wach's three forms of religious expression—theoretical, practical, and sociological—as a framework for teasing out and examining these religious, or at least spiritual, aspects of the Gothic world.

Wach argues that it is human nature to give expression to that which we experience, and says that religions traditionally enable us to do so in three specific ways (Wach 1958; Ellwood 1999). The first of these is the theoretical, which concerns the ideas and theories we develop about our experiences, and how we then convey these through the use of words, pictures, statues, or symbols. For most religions, this aspect seeks to communicate information about our encounters with the sacred, our experiences of reality, and our interactions with one another. From my observations, Goths do not share any explicit notions about God or the sacred. Some speak of God, others do not. They do, however, often share a specific understanding of the world, one that portrays the cosmos as consisting of complementary forces that must be kept in balance. Some will even mention the Taoist concepts of yin and yang in their discussions of these forces. It is typically thought among these Goths that Western culture has failed to obtain or even to seek such a balance, instead focusing on attaining happiness while desperately avoiding or denying pain, suffering, and death. As Carlos explains above, while not disparaging the pursuit of happiness, Goths perceive the importance of contemplating life's bleaker aspects. As a result, they devote what some consider to be an inordinate amount of attention to the darker things in life. Their poetry, literature, and songs become purposeful celebrations of the fearsome, the dark, and even death. "Life and death," says Carlos, "just try to experience both of them in order to maybe appreciate the other one."

I believe this is the aspect of Gothic culture that accounts for Goths' avid fascination with the vampire. As portrayed by Rice and others, the vampire is no longer merely loathsome or frightening. Instead, it has gained a humanity that brings nobility and pathos to its struggle with its own nature. When Louis denounces Lestat's viciousness in killing, asking if there is not more to vampire nature, the reader's sympathies no longer lie solely with the victims.

> "Why did you become a vampire?" I blurted out. "And why such a vampire as you are! Vengeful and delighting in taking human life even when you have no need." . . . He shook his head. "Louis!" he said. "You are in love with your mortal nature! You chase after the phantoms of your former self." . . . I objected to this at once. "My vampire nature has been for me the greatest adventure of my life; all that went before it was confused, clouded; I went through mortal life like a blind man groping from solid object to solid object. It was only when I became a vampire that I respected for the first time all of life. I never saw a living, pulsing human being until I was a vampire; I never knew what life was until it ran out in a red gush over my lips, my hands!" (Rice 1976)

Suddenly, there is an eerie similarity between the plight of the vampire and that of humanity. In the vampire, late twentieth-century human concerns and fears become visible. It rails against its own kind and God in search of meaning. It experiences life's pleasures, while also tasting its bitterness. It recognizes that it is caught in a web of ceaseless violence. In this being, then, coexist the same darkness and light, or good and evil, found in humanity. For Gothic Xers, such vampires have become archetypes of their own experiences of the world.

Beyond such theological and cosmic concerns, the theoretical expression of Gothicdom also includes issues surrounding individuals' interactions with one another. As in nearly all religious traditions, the Gothic scene has its ethical codes, proscribing some behaviors while encouraging others. When asked about these, Goths generally point to two injunctions: respect for the rights of all persons, and tolerance for individual creativity and diverse lifestyles. Monique and others say that most people in the movement emphatically denounce sexist, heterosexist, or racist behavior and try to make the clubs a "safe" environment, one in which women and sexual or racial minorities will not be harassed, segregated, or oppressed. Any degrading treatment of others, they say, is "un-Goth."

This focus on respect and care for others can often be found in the lyrics of Gothic songs. Themes dealing with the lack of, or loss of, love in a world dominated by violence and oppression run throughout the music. For example, in "The Ghost in You," Siouxsie and the Banshees lament over the tragedy of events such as occurred in China's Tiananmen Square. Love, Siouxsie sings, is not only forgotten in such instances but is destroyed and betrayed. Using their music to comment on the frequent and often overpowering immorality of the world in this way, Gothic musicians express their frustration and outrage with the world, while also acting as conduits of Gothic mores.

In addition to such illustrations of support for basic human rights, Gothic music and culture also emphatically embrace individuals' rights to develop and express themselves, particularly through explorations of their identity and sexuality, and encourage people to accept—even appreciate—others who are doing the same. Vampire scholar J. Gordon Melton suggests that Gothicdom, in taking an "explicit nonconformist stance vis-a-vis the dominant establishment," is similar to other countercultural forms in its advocation of androgyny and experimental forms of sex play (Melton 1994). The tangible effects of this nonconformist attitude within Gothic culture include experiments with anything from makeup and dress to same-sex sex and S/M. As long as no one is physically or emotionally endangered, such searches are considered enriching. Indeed, the majority of women I have encountered in Gothicdom describe themselves as bisexual, or at least as "bi-curious." Some say they understood themselves in this way prior to their involvement with Gothic, but for others, it is the Gothic culture that has made them more open to the possibility of a relationship with another woman. Even Goths who identify as straight are mostly supportive of same-sex relationships.

Most Goths also see other so-called deviant sexual practices, especially S/M and blood drinking, as acceptable avenues of sexual exploration, again with the stipulation that all parties must be fully consenting. One man summarizes this requirement by saying that, while S/M is personally not his cup of tea, "If all parts are in, then why not!" Of those who engage in S/M, most say they use such practices only occasionally, as a form of "spicing up" their sex life. One woman compares S/M to action movies, arguing that a nice romantic movie is good, but sometimes she likes something a little more exciting. While much less common than S/M among Goths, blood drinking is also gen-erally tolerated, if not encouraged. Many express concern over the obvious risk involved in this behavior, in light of the AIDS epidemic, but among those who regularly, or even occasionally, drink a partner's blood, all I have spoken to say they are careful to practice "safe sex." Ultimately, Gothic sexual ethics, like the Gothic worldview, encourage individuals to embrace the darker pleasures of sex, but to do so in full awareness of the dangers involved.

The second form of religious expression that Wach discusses is the practi-cal, or what is more commonly understood as the ritual aspect of religious traditions. The most notable rituals found within the Gothic club culture are the rituals of dance and costuming. While the music itself is central to the club experience, it is the act of dancing that connects the dancer with, or better yet, involves the dancer in the music. Swaying in a serpentine man-ner, Goths unite their bodies with the keening, mournful sounds of the music. While yet part of the larger crowd, dancers in Gothic clubs generally dance alone. Their movements, sometimes "voguelike," vacillate between the contemplative and the ecstatic. As they move around the floor, their bodies seem to give silent testimony to things intoned by the music but otherwise inexpressible.

In addition to the dancing itself, it is important to recognize the role played by the dancers' costumes. Costuming performs a key part in creating the proper ambience within a club. Without the sea of black, the scene would lose its mysterious, mesmerizing aura. Without the clothing and the painted faces, and the fangs and piercings, the appropriate spirits and beings are not present for the ritual gathering. In order to experience the world as a Goth, one must "feel" Gothic, and while this can be done without the garb, it is often facili-tated by Gothic accoutrements and the rituals involved in donning them. As in the act of putting on religious vestments or wearing one's "Sunday best," applying makeup, or even putting on a black skirt or a leather collar, can alter one's self-perception and sense of time and space. As Kyla comments above, putting on the garb and makeup is an experience of "aaahhh"—of reentering the realm of Gothic.

Although speaking about piercings, rather than Gothic attire, Elias Farajaje'-Jones has argued that various forms of "body modification" can also be redemptive (1995). He suggests that such things constitute an "act of de-colonizing our bodies" from a culture that is erotophobic and heteronormative, by enabling us to bring the spiritual and the erotic together once again. These alterations serve as reminders to the one pierced of his or her erotic nature, both at the time of piercing and each time a piece of fabric, a hand, a tongue, or a stranger's gaze touches the hoop or stud embedded within them. I would extend his argument to the acts of costuming and applying Gothic makeup. Each time a Goth sees a Casual look at her on the street and do a double take, or each time he is admired in his long black skirt, a Goth has her or his self-perception of being someone mysterious and dark confirmed. The makeup and fashion along with piercings and tattoos become a means to transcending the world of the Casuals and their mores for Goths who have chosen to demarcate themselves from the ordinary world through their bodies.

Finally, Wach's third form of expression concerns the ways in which a movement expresses itself through social structures and organization. The obvious beginning point for such an analysis of Gothic is the club scene, for it is in the clubs that Gothic originated, and it is there that the Gothic world most clearly becomes visible to observers and participants alike. One of the first things to note about the Gothic world is that it provides its members with something sought through most religious traditions: community. As Monique says earlier, in the club scene and its various extensions, she readily finds others with whom to associate who share her interests. In Gothicdom, she and others find a group in which wearing black lipstick, for both women and men, is not only not strange, it is the norm. They find people who have read all of Anne Rice's works, including those she wrote under her various pseudonyms. They even meet others to whom it is generally acceptable to introduce your same-sex partner. Because of these things, many people who have not been able to fit in elsewhere find a haven. They find somewhere they actually belong.

As for the particular groups that give structure to Gothicdom, as indicated above, the heart of Gothic culture is found in the bands who perform at the clubs and record the albums, and the fans who attend the clubs and buy the albums. However, as also noted, the Gothic scene is a much more complex structure than this implies, with record producers, club owners and promoters, publishers, authors, and vendors of various items each playing their part in creating the scene. To further complicate things, the Gothic world also exists within the murky territory of the Internet, as well as within the private lives of Goths themselves. Determining where Gothic begins and ends, therefore, is nearly impossible. It has its visible and invisible social structures, as well as its quasiclergy, its laity, and its many supporting groups and industries. As already discussed, it also has its beliefs and practices.

In the end, I think it is clear that Gothic has spiritual elements. However, it is less clear how we should categorize and label this world. How, exactly, do we define this movement? Is it a religion, or merely one more youth subculture? One man I interviewed, who had been in the Los Angeles Gothic scene since its beginnings, said that originally many people he knew understood being Gothic as being opposed to traditional religions, and as such, it was almost an "'anti-religion' religion." For this Goth, like others, it appears that Gothic, if not a religion per se, nevertheless functions as a religion, or at least an "anti-religion." But what does this mean? Is an "anti-religion" a religion?

Merely conceptualizing Gothic as a youth subculture, where *subculture* refers to "the blueprint for behavior of a smaller group within the society" (Sebald 1968) is, I think, inadequate. Gothic, as a blueprint, includes much more than just its adherents' behavior. But is it a religion? Ultimately, I think to affirm that Gothic is an established or organized religion would be to go too far, particularly as most of its members do not themselves perceive it as such. But if it is not a religion, yet functions in religious ways for many Goths, how might we best describe it? The sociology of religion offers the construct of a cult, with which I think Gothic has much in common. Conventionally understood, a cult is a group disenchanted with common religious forms (as many Goths claim to be), that tends to be urban in nature (which Gothic is, except on the Internet), centered around a charismatic figure or figures (such as the musicians), which develops its own terms and symbols to describe reality—in this case, the use of vampire imagery (Johnston 1983). Usually more concerned with the needs of the individual rather than the collective, this form of religious group also tends to be loosely organized (Dawson 1997). One difficulty that arises in applying this term to Gothicdom, however, is that cults, like subcultures, have generally been perceived as being geographically located and institutionally distinct. The Gothic realm is not located within one geographical area, nor does it follow one leader or even an identifiable hierarchy of leaders. Recent discussions within the sociology of religion, however, have begun to expand the cult typology in an effort to reflect the more fluid, unstructured nature of many contemporary groups. Such endeavors have resulted in the generation of new cult types, such as "audience" cults and "client" cults (Stark 1985; Dawson 1997), as well as the introduction of new constructs, such as "correspondence religion"

(Deitrick 1997). Although none of these yet describe Gothic adequately, I believe that this recognition of the increasing fluidity and creativity of form occurring within the modern religious realm opens the door for considering movements such as Gothic religious.

Ultimately, I have concluded that I will have to be satisfied with describing the Gothic world as a movement existing somewhere between, or maybe beyond, a subculture and a cult—something I have dubbed a "cult/ure" for my own purposes. As a cult/ure, Gothic, like many other current movements, points to the increasing difficulties of separating religion from other aspects of contemporary and popular culture, and of defining exactly what is meant by the term *religion*. Members of Generation X, like their boom generation parents, are breaking the old rules and seeking meaning far beyond the confines of churches and synagogues. While admittedly not typical of a large number of their peers in certain respects, members of the Gothic cult/ure clearly exemplify a yen within their generation for meaning and community, as well as a willingness to seek—or even a preference for seeking—these in nontraditional venues. I believe that Goths, like most of their peers, are searching for an environment that supports creativity and difference, as well as a perspective from which to make sense of a fast-paced, enjoyment-based, homogenizing, and potentially isolating world. For Gothic Xers, an affirming community and a tenable worldview are found within the clubs, myths, music, and makeup of Gothicdom. In demarcating themselves from those of us who generally favor the day over the night, or the light over shadows, Goths create and sustain a haven and a worldview that is uniquely theirs. One particularly poetic and insightful Net Goth succinctly captures these aspects of the cult/ure in describing her own understanding of Gothic: "To me, 'Gothic' is rather an aesthetic and sometimes, a collective worldview. A lot of people sharing the same tint on their glasses realized each other and said, 'Hey, y'know we could have some fun with this sad world, or at least on it, before we shuffle off, and we could do it our way.'"

Her message is signed, "A completely anonymous, utterly guessable soul."

References

Arnett, Jeffrey Jensen. 1995. *Metalheads: Heavy Metal Music and Adolescent Alienation.* Boulder, Colo.: Westview Press.

Auerbach, Nina. 1995. *Our Vampires, Ourselves.* Chicago: University of Chicago Press.

Bauhaus. 1986. "Bela Lugosi's Dead." *Bauhaus, 1979–1983.* Atlantic Recording Corporation.

Beaudoin, Tom. 1998. *Virtual Faith: The Irreverent Spiritual Quest of Generation X*. San Francisco: Jossey-Bass.

Couchman, Stephen. 1995. "What Makes a Song Gothic?" Online posting, January 25. Retrieved from alt.gothic December 30, 1998.

Dawson, Lorne L. 1997. "Creating 'Cult' Typologies: Some Strategic Considerations." *Journal of Contemporary Religion* 12, no. 3.

Deitrick, James E. 1997. "Who Needs Church when You Have a Mailbox? Correspondence Religion and the New Spirituality." Paper presented at the Society for the Scientific Study of Religion Annual Meeting, San Diego, Calif., November.

Dresser, Norine. 1989. *American Vampires: Fans, Victims, Practitioners*. New York: Vintage Books.

Ellwood, Robert S., and Barbara A. McGraw. 1999. *Many Peoples, Many Faiths: Women and Men in the World Religions*. 6th rev. ed. Englewood Cliffs, N.J.: Prentice Hall.

Farajaje'-Jones, Elias. 1995. "Piercing Analysis or in-to Body Travel." Paper presented at the American Academy of Religion Annual Meeting, Philadelphia, Penn., November.

Gelder, Ken. 1994. *Reading the Vampire*. London: Routledge.

Johnston, Ronald L. 1983. *Religion in Society: A Sociology of Religion*. 2d rev. ed. Englewood Cliffs, N.J.: Prentice Hall.

London after Midnight. 1998. "A Letter to God." *Psycho Magnet*. Available from London after Midnight, P.O. Box 1377, Hollywood, CA 90078-1377.

Melton, J. Gordon. 1994. *The Vampire Book: The Encyclopedia of the Undead*. Detroit: Visible Ink Press.

Neely, Neil. 1995. "Gothic Music." Online posting, November 28. Retrieved from alt.gothic November 1995.

Rice, Anne. 1976. *Interview with the Vampire: Book I of the Vampire Chronicles*. New York: Ballantine Books.

Roof, Wade Clark. 1993. *A Generation of Seekers: Baby Boomers and the Quest for Spiritual Style*. New York: HarperCollins.

Sebald, Hans. 1968. *Adolescence: A Sociological Analysis*. New York: Appleton-Century-Crofts.

Siouxsie and the Banshees. 1991. "The Ghost in You." *Superstition*. Geffen Records.

Stark, Rodney, and William Sims Bainbridge. 1985. *The Future of Religion: Secularization, Revival, and Cult Formation*. Berkeley and Los Angeles: University of California Press.

Wach, Joachim. 1958. *The Comparative Study of Religions*. Edited with an Introduction by Joseph M. Kitagawa. New York: Columbia University Press.

Wake, Peter, comp. 1994. "Gothic FAQ." Online posting, May 31. Retrieved from alt.gothic September 14, 1995.

Walser, Robert. 1993. *Running with the Devil: Power, Gender, and Madness in Heavy Metal Music*. Hanover, N.H.: University Press of New England.

Weinstein, Deena. 1991. *Heavy Metal: A Cultural Sociology*. New York: Lexington Books.

Part 2

GenX Multicultures

3

An Urban Mosaic in Shangri-La

LaDawn Prieto

As I peered inside the nightclub door, the darkness was pierced by white votive candles that lay before me. Each candle, placed intentionally on every step, helped guide my way into the popular Los Angeles nightclub. When I reached the top of the stairway, I was overwhelmed by loud, thumping music and tawdry lights. Hypnotically my eyes followed the lights until they met a dance floor below.

A smile came to my face when I realized that my expectations of a burnished environment had been met, evidenced by silver countertops, shiny couches, and sequined footstools scattered throughout the club. I had heard rumors that this club was built by the artist formerly known as Prince. Behind the stage hung a huge checkered backdrop that hovered above a wooden dance floor. Peering through a maze of microphones, cords, monitors, and guitars, I saw a large drum set that read "BIG DOG, SMALL FENCE," the name of a Christian ska band that originated from Mosaic, and prodigiously placed above the center of the dance floor, among the latticework of lights, spun a mirrored ball that cast small flecks of light onto the crowd below. "This is going to be interesting," I thought, and let out a small laugh as I began making my way to take a closer look at the sea of people that glowed under the black lights.

I continued to walk down another set of stairs, passing a large display of José Cuervo tequila bottles, until I stood comfortably by the bar. Here I had a great view of the dance poles that sat on top of silvery pedestals near the stage. Gathered beneath them was a small crowd, each person smiling, talking. I was becoming more intrigued by my surroundings. My eyes, skimming over the smiling crowd, were drawn to various pieces of art that hung on the club walls. And suddenly the music stopped, the house lights turned on, and I noticed the crowd turning its attention toward the stage.

I was startled when a six-foot-four-inch man wearing bell bottoms and an Afro wig bolted onto stage and began dancing to disco music. The crowd roared with laughter. At the end of his dance routine he stepped to the microphone, pronouncing that he was the fourth member of classic 1970s rock band Earth, Wind, and Fire, and that his name was Water. After making these claims, the young man welcomed the crowd. Then, he asked us to join him in prayer. Prayer?

Urban Mosaic

I had come that night fully aware that an established church, called Mosaic, held its night service at Club SoHo, located in the heart of Los Angeles.[1] According to its pastor, the church, known for innovation, has a long history of media interest and growth. For over one year the service, named "Urban Mosaic," has met in this nightclub each Sunday night at 6:00 P.M. The services bring upward of 200 twenty- and thirty-somethings together to sing, pray, and listen to biblical messages inside these club walls.

Urban Mosaic, with its unique personality, began as a response to the rapid growth rate the church has been experiencing since the arrival of pastor Erwin McManus in 1993. At one point Mosaic membership had nearly tripled, resulting in a need to increase the number of services from two to four to accommodate the number of persons attending each Sunday morning. Feeling that the number of services he was conducting took away from his family life, Pastor Erwin requested that the church find a larger facility that would hold all of the congregation in one or two services. Not too much later, the morning service would be held in the auditorium at East Los Angeles College (ELAC) and the night service would meet at a club in downtown Los Angeles. Since January 1998, each Sunday roughly seven hundred persons gather to worship at ELAC and at least two hundred young adults attend Urban Mosaic. With the help of its charismatic pastor, this Southern Baptist church has managed to create a new church language for a generation that has been turned off to Christianity by the religious rites of their parents. Mosaic, with its unique focus on community, leadership, and an aesthetic church experience through art and symbolism, has become an example of a New Paradigm church.[2]

In six months' time, through observation and interviews I breathed in the texture of the church through the lives of sixty-four different attendees of Urban Mosaic as I collected their personal demographics, followed their attendance at services, and traced their current involvement and commitment at Mosaic. I also conducted several in-depth interviews with pastoral staff and various Urban Mosaic churchgoers. Through their stories, I gathered a greater understanding of how one Southern Baptist church has managed to attract a Generation X population while exemplifying the changing face of mainline denominations moving into the next millennium.

The Service

Immediately after Water's short prayer a band entered onstage and stood prosaically behind their instruments and microphones. The drummer's long chunk-bleached hair swayed like a metronome as he counted the band into their first song. Soon the room echoed, heavy with drum riffs, demanding that the crowd begin clapping. Original song lyrics flashed on a giant screen next to the band, and it felt as though the designated worship time had become a corporate concert. With eyes closed and a swaying hand or two lifted, the crescendo of voices and music emphasized the lyrical intensity. "Rain down on me, Lord from above, Pour out on me, the depth of Your love."[3] Slowly, evidence of religiosity emerged. While the lyrics and song arrangements were original, I no longer doubted that I had stepped into an evangelical church that evening. The lyrics were directed toward God and Christ but lacked the familiar "Christian-isms" of the modern church that hold little to no translatable significance for those persons outside that culture. For example, such typically evangelical phrases as "Lamb of God," "Sanctified by the Spirit," or "Redeemed by the blood" were noticeably absent. However, the song lyrics seemed to embody a poetic, yet more literal alliteration, as in, "Open my eyes so I can see all You want to show to me, open my eyes, open my eyes and hold me in Your arms."[4] Most important, these lyrics presented a new church language, which I easily understood.

When the singing time ended, the lead singer asked the crowd to move away from the dance floor. After the floor was cleared and all house lights dimmed, a lone figure crouching in the center of the dance floor was captured by a spotlight. Slowly the music drifted from the speakers across the assembly, causing the figure to move. Rolling, crawling, the figure revealed her anguished face. Her hands, outstretched and reaching toward the heavens, grasped empty handfuls of air. Meanwhile, another figure emerged from the darkness. Smiling, the new figure moved across the floor with a lengthy train of white following her like rippling waves. Soon others joined the dance until the first dancer was engulfed by waves. One by one the waves moved away from the hidden figure until she emerged smiling. The crowd clapped robustly as the dancers bowed and exited the dance floor.

I was a little confused after watching the dance, as I held the assumption that Southern Baptist churches generally disapproved of dance. This concern was later clarified through a conversation with one of the dancers that night. She explained that dancing to glorify God, as a form of worship, was seen as biblically prescribed for followers of God. She contrasted the dance with nightclub-style dancing that promotes sexual lust and focuses more on pleasuring the self instead of bringing pleasure to God. One life group leader stated that he refrains from club dancing, "not because it makes [him] lustful" but because his motives are never questioned if he does not participate in dancing. He stated that the church leadership strongly urges the congregation to refrain from dancing if their intent is other than to glorify God.

Life Groups

The dancer also explained that many of the dances, scripts, and original music lyrics for Urban Mosaic had originated in the creative arts "life groups." Although there are several types of life groups, creative arts are the most represented at the Urban Mosaic service. Primarily, life groups are considered to be the base source of church social interaction, as well as a method of introducing non-church-attendees and potential converts into the church. "Anna," a thirty-year-old Chinese-American dentist, stated that through the life group setting, she "initially started connecting with people and started understanding what the church was about."

According to Mosaic church literature, life groups function as a source of community that provides "gospel-true, rich deep Christian soul-fellowship." All of the life groups within the church are centered around specific commonalties as a method of increasing community and connectedness for the overall church body and are viewed as the primary vehicle to assist in drawing new converts to the church. For example, students from the University of Southern California gather together in a life group every week near the campus. These students, bonded by geography, college culture, interests, and similar economic status, assemble to establish stronger bonds of friendship, increase their biblical knowledge of God, and present their beliefs to classmates.

These commonalties shape each life group experience for the life group attender, resulting in distinct personalities and a slightly different focus for each life group. For example, the university life group tends to focus more on college-type activities and discussions, while the creative arts life groups focus on creative growth and expression. More simply stated, while the university life group attends the college football game, one of the creative art groups is writing dramatic scripts. Although the life groups' primary function is to draw in new converts while creating a Christian community, the creative arts life groups have become the creative sources for most multimedia presentations, artwork, dance routines, and performance art pieces for the church, and most of their time is spent working on commissioned art pieces or dramas.

Every Tuesday night, one creative arts life group gathers at an "art house" on the main church site. Each week they share their creative art ideas and are supplied with brushes, oils, canvas, and various other artistic materials to complete their projects. The art products of the life group time are displayed each Sunday in the main entryway of the nightclub and in the foyer of the main church site in East Los Angeles. Often their art coincides with sermon themes or the individual's personal spiritual experience. Each life group is intended to be established within a naturally drawn community, such as artists, actors, young professionals, and the like.

Creating this kind of community is a distinctive feature of Mosaic as it seeks to secure a place for persons to belong. Although most Urban Mosaic churchgoers come from Christian backgrounds, many have found Mosaic's strong community unique and inviting. According to several members I interviewed, Mosaic has become a place of "healing and restoration" for believers who have been hurt or jaded by other church experiences. Anna, who is also a life group leader, stated that Urban Mosaic churchgoers are drawn because "they have been hurt by traditional churches, so they are looking to get away from tradition and try something new." She continued by saying that she often counsels those who have been hurt by their previous church's expectations. Anna explained that this feeling of bitterness stems from rigid church standards: "You can't dress like this, you can't look like this." She explains that these standards come "from a segregationalist attitude that some churches have," struggling with how to be set apart from the secular world.

Cindy, a twenty-one-year-old Japanese-American college student, described her previous church experience as "dry and lifeless. " This "shallow spirituality," as she called it, left her feeling lonely and isolated from the rest of her congregation and even her family. Like many others from Mosaic, she was invited to a life group activity where she met one individual who demonstrated joy and genuine friendship. "He had so much joy and excitement about his faith, I wanted that too." As she spoke she conveyed that her search for true Christian community was over because she had found a place where she could belong.

If we assume that Generation X is characterized by loneliness and isolation, Mosaic's focus on genuine community becomes inviting. The Urban Mosaic community is 82 percent drawn from a previous Christian church experience; almost half of them had initially walked away from the church because they had felt like an outsider in that community. Just as Cindy did, many of those I spoke with felt they finally had a place to belong, and that in turn, the community looked to them as individuals to contribute their own uniqueness.

The Crowd

Soon after the dance was finished, the crowd grabbed chairs and began placing them near the stage. And although the clanking chairs were somewhat distracting, I was impressed by the overall ambience of the service. Glancing at the large screen again, I noticed that the sermon topic for the evening would be "water." My eyes began to follow one man, Pastor Erwin McManus, as he walked up to the stage. He smiled and asked the crowd to turn to chapter 1 in Genesis. As he began reading, I surveyed the faces that filled the room. As I looked closer, I was bombarded with images that fused the sacred and profane worlds. Behind the open Bibles I saw shelves filled with alcohol. Scripture was read from a stage where pop star Ricky Martin had performed and filmed a provocative music video overflowing with sexual innuendo and partial nudity. I wondered if I was the only one to catch the irony of that evening—worshiping within the walls of a room that would otherwise appear void of God.

Looking for the answer, my eyes began to search the room until I noticed a unique and distinct quality of the congregation; the myriad of faces around me appeared to paint a colorful mosaic of ethnic diversity. I would later discover that approximately 48 percent of the congregation was of European descent, with 27 percent Latin, 18 percent Asian, and less than 1 percent African-American. The worship band members evidenced the most obvious sign of this diversity. The band consisted of a thirty-two-year-old Mexican-American female lead vocalist, a twenty-six-year-old Caucasian female vocalist, a twenty-six-year-old Caucasian male guitarist, a thirty-year-old Chinese-American female bassist, and a thirty-three-year-old Japanese-American drummer.

Overall, the crowd looked young. Originally, I had guessed the age of the churchgoers to fall between eighteen and thirty-eight. After several months of observation and interview with service attenders, I discovered that one-third of the congregation were in their mid-twenties. Even the pastor looked under forty, and almost half of the congregation ranged between twenty-three and twenty-nine years old, with the average age being twenty-seven years. The gender split was almost equal; 47 percent female and 53 percent male.

Appearance and clothing seemed to be represented by two distinct styles. The first, I will call the college prep look. This look—khakis, cargo pants, or jeans, purchased from the Gap, Banana Republic, Express, or similar stores—was usually accessorized by a linen shirt or college-name-bearing sweatshirt. The second style I will tactfully label the "individualized artist" look. This look is diverse, but the person falling under this category would probably own a black leather jacket, a few T-shirts bearing the name of underground or vintage clothing stores, small record labels, or independent film labels, have an assortment of possible hairstyles and/or colors, and carry a cellular phone. The point of this style is to be an individual. While speaking with one church member, I commented on the uniqueness of his shoes. He proudly displayed his new slip-on shoes while pointing out how comfortable they were, and added that a friend had purchased them for him while in Holland. Indeed, no one else in that room owned a similar pair of shoes.

Service Participation

I later discovered that almost half of those in the room were directly involved in the arts and entertainment industry of Los Angeles. I spoke with screenwriters, independent film directors, producers, theater and film actors, muralists, architects, a clothing designer, photographers, a model agent, professional musicians, and lighting and sound technicians, who used their professional skills to add to the aestheticism of each Mosaic service. Professional scriptwriters and actors are responsible for the opening acts and dramatic sketches, musicians are responsible for promoting and writing culturally relevant music, and artists are commissioned to create pieces to display at each service. According to the pastoral staff, all these creative contributions are viewed as supplemental and necessary to the main biblical teaching time. Songs, art, or drama not only illustrate the sermon topic each week but also preserve a unified theme throughout that evening.

When speaking with those associated with creating service aesthetics, I was surprised to learn that many of these professionals felt as though their skills were being refined, which restored their creative passion while involved with Mosaic. Nathan, a twenty-two-year-old independent film director, said, "I am inspired when I feel like my contributions are important to God." He continued by stating that he experiences personal growth while assisting at Mosaic, which is directly translated into running his film production company; "I am always learning what it means to be a leader," which refines "the vision I have for the company."

This refinement does not exclude those without professional experience in the arts and entertainment industry, but instead has facilitated an explosion of creativity and personal career growth for other members of the Urban Mosaic church body. Blaine, a twenty-three-year-old Ph.D. student, explained that through his involvement at Mosaic he has discovered other areas of creative interest in his life. While maintaining his graduate studies he began assisting with the multimedia crew at Urban Mosaic. He is considered by the other crew members to play a significant role in increasing the quality of the services' different multimedia presentations. His responsibilities include artistic displays of sermon points, song lyrics, and announcements of church information on the screen next to the band, as well as the overall organization and flow of these media presentations. After a few months at Mosaic, Blaine was approached by two music video directors, both members of Mosaic, who asked him to coproduce two music videos for Aslan Productions.

Soon after, this independent film company aired a music video on the Black Entertainment Television (BET) cable channel. While continuing his studies in a graduate program for physical therapy, Blaine attributes his newfound vocation, associate producer for Aslan Productions, to his participation in the creative arts life group and the multimedia crew at Mosaic; this outlet for creativity adds balance to his overall life, he explains.

The Sermon

As the sermon proceeded, I realized that all five of my senses were at work. Visually, I was stimulated by flashing images on the screen next to the stage as my ears took in the sermon words, accompanied by background music. I smelled the wicks of burning candles while drinking bottled water that had been passed out to the congregation earlier that evening. And on cue, in the middle of the sermon, another young man walked onstage and asked the crowd to begin tapping our hands on our legs. He then asked us to slowly hit our legs harder and faster and eventually asked us to tap our feet at the same time. "Slower," he demanded, until the noise again came to a soft sound and he told us to stop. The leg slapping, foot stomping, speeding, and slowing resulted in a sound much like the rain slowly dropping to the ground until the cloud released stronger streams of water. And as I sat with my stinging hand, I thought how clever and creative it was to demand a multisensory experience of the audience.

While Pastor Erwin explained that offering a multisensory church experience was important, it was always checked against the church's overall mission, vision, and supporting core values, all of which he described as biblically based. Mosaic's mission statement is to function as "a spiritual reference point to Los Angeles and a sending base to the world." This mission is said to be accomplished through the church's vision, which challenges all members and attendees to "live by faith, to be known by love, and be a voice of hope" to their communities and the world.

Supporting the overall church mission are five core values, which Pastor Erwin describes as aiding the church through cultural issues. The five values for Mosaic are: (1) Mission is why the church exists, (2) Love is the context for all missions, (3) Structure must submit to spirit, (4) Relevance to culture is not an option, and (5) Creativity is the natural result of spirituality. These core church values are examined when dealing with issues like gathering in a nightclub for a service.

According to those I spoke with, meeting in a nightclub does not compromise the first or second core values, which are based on the belief that through love "Jesus came into the world declaring He had come to seek and save that which is lost, and He established a Church to take His gospel to the very ends of the earth." One member stated, "There is no verse in the Bible that says we can't meet in a club." In fact, many of those I spoke with referred to the early church in the Bible as a defense, claiming that it met in homes or public gathering places. According to an article printed in the church's membership booklet, church buildings are viewed by Mosaic as a "witness to our inflexibility, our immobility, our lack of fellowship, our pride, and our class divisions." This article is heavily based on the church's third value, that structure must submit to spirit.

The fourth value, "Relevance to culture is not an option," is based on the biblical passage of 1 Corinthians 9:22, in which the apostle Paul states that he has "become all things to all men so that by all possible means I might save some." Mosaic leaders view this passage as support for the importance of cultural relevance in order to gain converts at Mosaic. Pastor Erwin stated that his goal is "to have a biblical church that effectively reaches the postmodern context." He describes the postmodern context as experiencing a collision of worldviews, which demands a new way of relating biblical messages in a relevant way. This new way of relating includes flexibility in trying new things, such as moving services to popular public gathering places like a nightclub.

Most of what sets Mosaic apart from other churches appears to be the result of their fifth core value: "Creativity is the natural result of spirituality." Not only has this value supported meeting in places like a nightclub, but it also, as mentioned previously, has given license to experiment with original forms of music and dance worship for the church. It has also opened the door for Mosaic pastoral staff to include names like Kurt Cobain, Douglas Coupland, and Depak Chopra to illustrate biblical messages in sermons, church literature, and multimedia presentations at Mosaic.

Mosaic Faith

At the end of the sermon, Pastor Erwin looks through the crowd, pauses, and begins to speak directly to those seeking a personal relationship with God. There is no formal altar call, but instead, moments of challenge as he calls for the congregation to examine their life and commitments. He concludes by directing those wishing to learn more about Christianity to a lime green card inside each church bulletin. As he explains how to fill out the card, its image appears on the large screen next to him. Soon there is a prayer for the offering, church announcements, and a closing song by the worship band.

To me, this congregation's commitment to Christian faith seemed uniquely intense. According to a Mosaic congregational audit, conducted by the Gallup organization, 95 percent of people attending Mosaic believe that their religious faith is the most important influence in their lives.[5] All of those I spoke with labeled themselves as Christians but felt compelled to explain that the term is a definition of their spirituality. Each gave me a slightly different definition of the term, but included Jesus as a defining factor. Markus explained that a Christian is "someone that has accepted Christ as their personal savior and allows Him to change the thing that keeps you distant from Him." Another member stated that being a Christian is being in love with Jesus, which, he explained, requires obedience to His commands. Finally, Pastor Erwin summed up the term as "knowing God through the transforming power of Jesus Christ." It is after the announcement of belief in Christ that the individual is asked to profess her new commitment as a Christian to the entire church body. Since the nightclub does not have a place to conduct full-immersion baptisms, special services are held at various places like a college swimming pool, the beach, or at the main church site in East Los Angeles. The various geographical locations also reflect the church's overall rejection of established structures for their religious rites.

Leadership

Mosaic continues to explore new ways of relating its message to a changing society, but it has managed to find a charismatic leader who it believes will guide Mosaic into the next millennium. Pastor Erwin, a native of El Salvador, initially came from Texas to Los Angeles in 1992. Having been in other church ministries with the leaders at Mosaic, then called "the Church on Brady," he and his family felt comfortable with the community and began attending services. He stated that he began volunteering as a consultant to the church to assist in strategizing to raise the falling church attendance numbers. Erwin's contributions were seen as significant to the church as he brought experience as a national and international consultant and speaker on issues of leadership development, organizational change, church planting, and urban and global issues.

It was not long after his arrival in Los Angeles that the pastoral staff approached Erwin with an offer to pastor the church. He describes the decision as difficult and said to me, "I can honestly say that I didn't want to be pastor but I felt like God wanted me to be the pastor." He said that he felt he could bring the church into a more multicultural experience and desired to "do something that either no one else will do, or no one else can do." Most of those looking for change in the church were eager to participate in the new vision for the church, although McManus describes being met with serious opposition as he began to help the church transition culturally.

Some of the changes in the church services were met with extreme resistance. McManus recounts that when he first arrived, the church met the needs of a modern churchgoing congregation. He described the use of overhead projectors to display song lyrics of "seventies and sixties Scripture songs and hymns," and he spoke from a stationary pulpit that was elevated above the entire congregation. All these things had been identified as innovative for a previous time, but Pastor Erwin had a vision to begin changes that would entice a pluralistic society. As he moved toward change, he included movie clips that would illustrate certain points of the sermon topic. "I had horrific feedback, I mean, it was like 'You are bringing the world into our church!'" He describes being reprimanded for moving the offering from the middle to the end of the service. To some, this change was considered a violation of Scripture and demeaned the value of giving. Another point of rebuke came from a member when Pastor Erwin asked another member to do the congregational welcome and was quickly accused of destroying the culture of the church. Pastor Erwin describes that time as growth—but "growth is painful." Through this painful growth, the church has experienced changes in church leadership, particularly within the Elder Board of the church. However, despite these conflicts, church attendance and membership continue to grow, as do the number of new converts (measured by baptisms) to Mosaic each year.

Through interviews I discovered that many Urban Mosaic churchgoers who were originally from out of state had been initially drawn to the church because of the leadership of Pastor Erwin. One twenty-six-year-old told me that after graduating from college, he decided to move from Missouri to attend Mosaic because of the leadership and vision of the church. He gave specific credit to Pastor Erwin, whom he describes as a great teacher and illustrator of biblical messages. Aside from his academic background, McManus demonstrates a great understanding and ability to communicate to the postmodern, Generation X culture. He explains that the first time he felt a "huge win" for the church was when he decided that he needed to cut down on the number of services so he could spend more time with his family. "People never really experienced pastors who put their kids over growth, you know, I think it helped bring me some credibility with people, especially in their twenties, who felt neglected by their parents." Indeed, Pastor Erwin has gained significant trust from his congregation, over 90 percent of whom say they trust church leadership. It seems that McManus has brought a unique quality to a unique church that attempts to find relevancy in a pluralistic culture.

As I continued my observations over several months, I noticed two more unique qualities of the church: literal interpretation of biblical text and the use of symbolism combined with audience participation as means to explain Scripture.

Literal Interpretation

Through individual stories, church literature, and sermon topics, the Bible is seen by the Mosaic community as a source of truth on which all courses of social interaction are, or should be, based. Gallup's congregational audit revealed that an overwhelming 98 percent of those at Mosaic believe in the full authority of the Bible. According to Pastor Erwin, this percentage is overwhelming; most pastors contend that an extremely healthy church would fall into the sixtieth percentile range. But what is more intriguing is how this strongly biblically based church has maintained its core of values and beliefs over the years and at the same time changed the language in which this is communicated to reach a new and younger audience. Unlike churches such as Calvary Chapel, whose founder walked away from denominational ties during major social change, Mosaic has managed to target a similar audience without compromising either its doctrinal stance or its denominational association.

It was not out of place for a passage of Scripture to be read, or even sung, at some time during the course of each Urban Mosaic service. The passage would remain the main text of the evening, explicated for literal meaning, principle, and personal application. One familiar form of adaptation for mainline churches is evidenced by the moving away from traditional stands on issues, like homosexuality being a sin, into more liberal interpretations of text that allow for homosexual church leaders. However, Mosaic has maintained its traditional messages with literal text interpretation while growing in church numbers and converts, and at the same time has attracted those from the homosexual or bisexual communities.

One church member, a twenty-four-year-old African-American man called Markus, revealed that as a Christian, he struggles with having an attraction toward men. Originally he came to Los Angeles to pursue a career in acting, but he describes the town as "an incredibly lonely place to be" and recalls losing track of his career goals as he experimented with drugs and became involved in his first homosexual relationship. As he continued to experiment with homosexuality, he told me that he always felt a tension between his desire to know God and his sexual tendencies.

Markus described how slowly God worked on him until he began to seek out a Christian community. Through his involvement in a life group, he said he finally got to a point where he prayed, "God, I can't live if it is not real for me, if it isn't real this time. You gotta show me how to make it work." The "it" Markus wanted to work for him was being able to walk away from his homosexual lifestyle and pursue a relationship with God, a concept embraced by the Mosaic community. Markus claims that today, at times, there are still "very real struggles," but that God "just showed me to focus on Him and my relationship with Him . . . not the things that made me feel 'not good enough.' . . . I'll never be good enough, it's not about deserving [a relationship with God], because I don't." Throughout the interview Markus spoke about the love of God, his grace on humanity, and how the Mosaic community reflected those attributes to him while maintaining that homosexuality is a sin that separates man from God.

Drinking, dancing, gambling, premarital sex, and divorce are among the other issues that are disapproved of at Mosaic, through the lens of literal biblical interpretation. I encountered one couple who shared their love story and how Mosaic leaders played a significant role in guiding their relationship by helping them set dating standards until they became married.

Bea, a twenty-five-year-old fashion designer, explained that she and Mike, a twenty-five-year-old pre-med student, met in a nightclub during their first semester of college. Mike explained, "I thought she was beautiful!" He confessed his immediate attraction to Bea, and they began living together after a courtship of two weeks. Mike claims his lifestyle at the time involved all forms of self-indulgence—drinking, partying, and sex—which ultimately resulted in his expulsion from a major university. With Bea continuing her studies and Mike's lifestyle adding stress to their relationship, they both decided to take a road trip out of state for a break. Gesturing with her hands, Bea showed me how their car had been in an accident. "It just kept rolling, we should have died," she said, staring intently at me. "We both knew there had to be a God."

Through their involvement in a life group, they were counseled by Mosaic church members to stop living together. The reasoning, they were told, is that God designed long-lasting relationships to be established on a foundation of purity. Wanting to have a strong relational foundation, Mike and Bea took the counsel and promised each other that they would not have sex, kiss, or even hold hands until they were married. It was not until four years later that they would walk down the aisle. During their courtship they had also been advised to wait to be married in order to honor their parents' desires for them to finish college. During their four years of dating, Mike returned to school, while Bea received her bachelor's degree in clothing design from Otis School of Design. After the honeymoon Bea said to me with a big smile, "You have to get married . . . it's awesome!" The four-year wait was difficult, according to the couple, but Mike stated after their honeymoon, "Praise God, it was worth the wait."

I also spoke to "Jim," who was going through engagement counseling at Mosaic. He said of the pre-engagement counsel, "I resisted the concept of dating her like she was my sister. . . . I thought it was strange." He went on to describe that his counsel was to treat his girlfriend with the same respect he would give his sister. The dating guide that remained in the back of his head was, "Do not do anything with her you wouldn't do with your sister." He stated that this type of dating allowed him the opportunity to get to know his fiancée as a good friend. He added, "It's a good foundation for a lifetime."

To ensure that all members of the Mosaic community have access to "a good foundation," pre-engagement and pre-dating standards are listed and explained in a church informational booklet. This booklet, given to each new member after the completion of membership classes, explains that each new member should date only other believers, date to find a marriage partner, be aware of timing (marriage between two persons who have known each other less than one year is discouraged), and maintain sexual purity before marriage. Couples wishing to be married must take part in a four-part counseling period before announcing their engagement. The purpose of pre-engagement counseling is to assist the couples in getting to know each other better before committing to the promise of marriage. And although the church has a strong influence in the counseling period, it states, "We will not tell anyone whom to marry, but will act as a check point to confirm wisdom and timing in the establishment of any plans for marriage in which we are to participate."

Mosaic Symbolism

Although Mosaic has managed to maintain its biblical views, at the same time it has distinguished itself from other churches by creating a new church lingo intended for, and understood by, the new generation of churchgoers. Primarily, this new language is seen as the result of the church's focus on creativity and takes the form of the use of symbolism in combination with audience participation. This is evidenced in the overall aesthetics of each service, the desire to find culturally relevant church locations, and the original art and music.

Often, the congregation is given sermon props, like a piece of coal that symbolizes man being created from the earth, or a package of seeds representing spiritual growth in Christ. During one sermon, artists were asked to paint, sculpt, draw, and so on while Pastor Erwin was speaking. According to Pastor Erwin, the overall purpose of creating this new form of church experience is to "push people to a level of uniqueness . . . a push of human creativity" that does not take away from God but adds to his glory. As an individual you are seen, in the Mosaic community, as having purpose and significance. And when the individual joins that with "God in intimacy, [they] begin to discover both [their] uniqueness and the unique contribution that God wants to make through [them]."

I see this new language of art, creativity, and symbolism, which originates from each individual's spiritual experience, as being modeled by the Mosaic community and thus difficult to consider hypocritical, fake, or boring. The church has chosen to take on the ultimate form of symbolism and express it through the church body as a means to cultural relevance. This is done specifically through the symbolism of the church name and the history of mosaic art itself. With its name, which drops all forms of mainline church identity, Mosaic chose to shroud its image in an art form. I saw this image as I walked throughout the club that first night. I found the church logo, a mosaic-style cross bearing the church name inconspicuously placed around the room. It was carefully pasted to each glass candle container near the entrance, so that light shining through them acts as a small reminder of sacred stained-glass windows. Again the logo appeared on the church bulletin and in the corner of each sermon point that flashed across the screen next to the stage.

According to Pastor Erwin, the name was chosen in a little-known incident. He prefaced the story by explaining that many of the leaders at the church are visionaries and creative minds, which results in moments of "daydreaming" together. In one of these moments three of the pastoral staff were talking about products they would like to invent. One stated she would like to invent "a drink that tastes different with every sip." Playing off the idea, another chimed in, "I know what you could call it! Mosaic!" Erwin exclaimed, "That's the new name of our church!" He told me that what he meant to say was, "That is the new name of our night service," but he felt deep inside him that this would soon be the new name of the church.

As the elders of the church continued to discuss changing its legal name, First Southern Baptist Church of East Los Angeles, Pastor Erwin described the need to have a culturally relevant meaning behind the new name. He said that the night that the new name was to be revealed to the congregation, he chose the carrier of this message carefully. As the young woman he had chosen to deliver the message stood behind the microphone, she uttered the words that had been thoughtfully passed down to her from the pastor: "Mosaic represents broken and fragmented pieces of humanity that, when brought together by the light of God, reflect His image" (McManus 1998, 2–9). According to Erwin, the young woman, open to discussing her painful and difficult past, was chosen to convey the new name because it would cause others to think, "You know, we're all just broken people."

Symbolically, the church has strategically used mosaic art to unify its congregational community in the midst of a pluralistic culture. But the name also provides a key to understanding how this church really views its ability to exist within this culture. Given the loneliness and isolation of Generation X, the image of the mosaic takes on a greater significance. This image likens the individual to broken and fragmented pieces of glass. Alone the piece finds no beauty, no purpose, and is easily overlooked. But when put together with others, it becomes part of a whole and beautiful picture. Each piece has found not only purpose, but also collective aesthetic beauty, which provides a sense of community and belonging. Through this analogy Mosaic finds relevance to everyday life by offering the "broken" person a community in which to belong. We see this reflected in the stories of those drawn to the Urban Mosaic service. People who were previously disillusioned by the church community have found a place of healing and restoration. And with it they are offered a new set of symbols to express their faith.

Not only are churchgoers offered a new symbolism, but according to Pastor Erwin, they are also given the opportunity to create "a more artistic expression of faith [based on] . . . a core value of 'creativity is a natural result of spirituality.'" As in a mosaic, each person's beauty is seen as she contributes her uniqueness through the creative expression of her faith. A tie between human creativity and spirituality appears to be the pervasive language of this church. "God was not jealous of the genius of Einstein . . . the artistry of Picasso . . . He's for it," states McManus; "he wants that to be expressed to give Him glory." This language of creativity has become an important method of "democratizing the sacred" at Mosaic (see Miller 1997, 80).

Urban Mosaic has compelled hundreds of GenXers to give the church another chance. Through its trademark use of creative arts, symbolism, and a strong focus on community, Mosaic has managed to converge the sacred and profane without compromising denominational doctrine or literal interpretation of biblical text while reaching a new generation of churchgoers. At the same time, it has created a new church language, led by a charismatic leader, that appears to empower the churchgoer and explain traditional messages in a new way. In its own right, Mosaic has become a model for mainline denominations attempting to convey their messages to a new generation.

Notes

1. Club SoHo, also known as the Shangri-La, is located on 333 Boylston Street, Los Angeles.

2. See Warner 1993; Miller 1997.

3. "Rain Down on Me," written by Erwin McManus, 1999.

4. "Open My Eyes," written by music director David Files, 1998.

5. Percentage is taken from information disclosed during a sermon in June 1999 based on a congregational audit conducted by the Gallup Organization in April 1999. The data/report was not publicly released.

References

Berger, Peter L. 1969. *The Sacred Canopy: Elements of Sociological Theory of Religion.* Garden City, N.Y.: Anchor.

McDannell, Colleen. 1995. *Material Christianity: Religion and Popular Culture in America.* New Haven, Conn.: Yale University Press.

McManus, Erwin. 1998. "Fulfilling the Vision." *Heart and Mind.* Bethel Seminary, San Diego, fall.

———. 1998. "Engaging the Third Millennium." *Shout* 2, no. 4. (winter).

———. 1999. "Taking on Postmodernism." *Religious Herald* (Virginia), January 4.

Miller, Donald E. 1995. *Reinventing American Protestantism: Christianity and the New Millennium.* Los Angeles: University of California Press.

Warner, R. Stephen. 1993. "Work in Progress toward a New Paradigm for the Sociological Study of Religion in the United States." *American Journal of Sociology* 98, no. 5.

4

Slipping into Darkness

Popular Culture and the Creation of a Latino Evangelical Youth Culture

Arlene Sánchez Walsh

On any given Thursday evening, Victory Outreach's ministry to gang members, "Barrios for Christ," meets at their La Puente, California, headquarters, on the grounds of an old elementary school where they gather to worship and share testimonies. On this particularly hot summer evening, GenX leader Manuel Alvarez invites a new convert to give his testimony to the crowd of about a hundred. Alvarez describes Juan, the former gang member, as "rough," and intimates that the gathering should not expect a polished speech. Juan is in his late twenties, and tattoos cover his arms. His hairstyle and clothing represent a past era of gangster, late 1970s, old guard—*veterano*. Clearly Juan is too young for this style, but he bears the marks of a serious gang member, not the shaved-head, baggy-pants-wearing wannabe typical of many young gang members today. Juan is nervous, he gestures with his hands, and his testimony is peppered with several "y'know's." He speaks about how grateful he is to Alvarez for taking the time to help him and lead him to God. Juan receives warm applause and sits down. The next testimonial is from a young girl who does not dress in any particular style, does not look like a gang member, but as Alvarez tells the crowd, this "wild" kid has made progress. The young girl spoke briefly and was not very forthcoming. She thanked people and sat down, obviously uncomfortable with the idea of sharing her testimony.

The music, a mixture of classic Victory Outreach worship songs and R&B-tinged numbers, resumed after the testimonies. The meeting, which began at 7 P.M., lasted past 10:30 P.M. There were simultaneous meetings of nearly every ministry group on campus that night, as there are nearly every evening. The specialized nature of these meetings symbolizes the desire of Victory Outreach to meet the needs of all its constituents—from hard-core gang members like Juan to at-risk girls and any other people who find that the church's brand of fiery evangelism, drama, and worship is what they need at

74

the time to help mend broken lives. Keeping both Juan and the young girl within the Victory Outreach fold depends heavily on the use of specialized ministries and within that, using popular culture as an evangelistic tool.

Such outreaches to disaffected youth are not new. Youth have always been a difficult group to reach and even harder to keep in the church. In the mid-1940s, Youth for Christ was fronted by an up-and-coming evangelist dressed in flashy clothes and Day-Glo socks. Billy Graham presided at hundreds of rallies that catered to teenage audiences with "snappy choruses, instrumental solos, magicians, and Bible trivia contests." Graham would later ask youth of the 1960s to "tune into God" (Eskridge 1998, 85, 86). Graham's risky endorsement of the Jesus movement in 1971 before the National Evangelical Association was the parental approval that the movement never sought, but accepted because it symbolized a shift from Graham's era to the era of John Wimber and the Vineyard.

Evangelical Christianity has an almost limitless ability to harness its message to nearly every facet of popular culture: bobby-soxers, hippies, *cholos*, tattooed, body-pierced college students searching for God—if there is a song to be coopted, a style to be transformed, a ministry will seek to do just that. In the twenty years that the Vineyard has been planting churches and attempting to bridge the gap between the evangelical and Pentecostal worlds, it has never been a concerted effort to reach out beyond its Euro-American baby-boomer base. Such work has been left to a small group of Latino pastors and sympathetic church leaders.

A worship service at the "Lord's Vineyard," in Pico Rivera, California, begins with music and a small group of about fifty worshipers that will grow to over seventy-five as the service continues. The youth group begins worship with the adults, but as soon as the music is over, they leave for their own informal time of fellowship outside on the lawn. The Lord's Vineyard has been meeting in various locations and under different leadership for the last fifteen years, and has been pastored by Richard Ochoa for the last fourteen years. The church is one of the few English-speaking Latino Vineyards. The worship and music are quintessentially Vineyard—upbeat and emotional. Church members range from youth to seniors, and many are converts from Catholicism. During the time that I visited the church during the summer and fall of 1998, the sermons covered familiar themes: surrender, raising good kids, perseverance, avoiding temptation, and a series of messages about the need to reach out to youth at risk in the neighborhood. Ochoa spent several Sundays discussing the problems of gang violence that plagued the city when several drive-by shootings occurred over a month-long span. Ochoa began asking for prayer for the city council to approve his plan to teach character development at a nearby continuation school for at-risk youth—and the congregation responded. The autonomous nature of the Vineyard's churches creates the opportunity for each church to develop whatever programs it deems necessary to evangelize the communities around it. Therefore, discussing how the Lord's Vineyard, and the Spanish-speaking Vineyards, called La Viñas, reach and retain GenX Latino youth requires moving beyond examining ministries to examining the ministers themselves and how the philosophy of ministry of the Vineyard appeals to Latino youth. Looking for an atypical GenX Latino youth culture is not possible until one examines the varieties of culture evident just in these two churches.

This chapter examines several forms of popular cultural expression by youth and ministerial styles in two charismatic/Pentecostal groups: Victory Outreach and the Vineyard. In order to evangelize to the unchurched, and to retain youth in church, these disparate groups use various popular cultural forms: dramas, rap, and rock music. They also tailor their ministerial styles to suit the very specialized communities they serve. In doing so, popular culture serves several purposes: (1) it sacralizes secular forms of entertainment, (2) it re-creates the notion of "dangerous" youth by providing them with the religious cover of legitimate expressions of worship, and (3) it creates an atmosphere of comfort where different social classes can have their ministerial needs met through peer representatives.

In particular, the use of gang and hip-hop culture by Victory Outreach reorients this African-American cultural form from "attempts to negotiate the experiences of marginalization" (Rose 1994) in a socioeconomic context to a spiritual one. In the context of the Latino church, hip-hop helps young people denounce drugs, gangs, premarital sex, violence, racism, and other evils as overwhelmingly spiritual problems. The Latino Vineyards, through their pastors and leaders, have sent a clear message to youth as well. Using relational, casual, and confessional methods of doing ministry along with contemporary worship music, the Vineyard seeks to create an environment of comfort. Having sacralized contemporary music and reformed the "dangerous" and rebellious youth of the sixties into many of the Vineyard's pastoral staff, the Vineyard, through its Latino leadership, is grooming its youth to take part in the church using whatever means it believes will work to retain youth.

Examining these two groups allows us to compare and contrast the evangelistic methods of the predominantly Latino Victory Outreach and their targeting of marginalized youth: gang members, drug addicts, prostitutes, and the homeless; and the predominantly Euro-American Vineyard and their targeting of unchurched Generation X. The specific expressions covered in this chapter are Victory Outreach's drama and youth ministries and the Vineyard's Latino churches: their youth ministries, and profiles of Generation X church leaders. Interviews and fieldwork conducted between 1998 and 1999, and audiovisual materials comprise the majority of primary source materials. Secondary sources were comprised chiefly from historical analyses of popular culture and the postmodern church.

Victory Outreach: Street Life Dramas

Victory Outreach's drama ministry began before it officially broke away from Teen Challenge in 1967. Since its days of performing street theater in New York, dramas have been an integral part of the church's evangelistic outreach. One of its first plays was called *The Junkie*. The playbill announces: "The most shocking portrayals of the dope addict ever witnessed by any audience. Once you see this drama, you will be able to better know the horrors that a drug addict goes through." The playbill also features the actors, Latino men and women, one of whom is shooting heroin. The play was performed at Pioneer High School auditorium in Whittier, California, in 1968. Nearly all Victory Outreach dramas to this day focus on the harsh realities of inner-city youth, use realistic props to demonstrate drug and alcohol abuse and gunplay, and use church members as actors.

Dramas became very important to Victory Outreach when it moved from its first headquarters in Boyle Heights to Montebello, California, in the mid-1970s, and soon after that to the International Club in Pico Rivera. Evangelist Philip LaCrue notes that dramas were held regularly at the latter locations. The dramas succeeded as no other evangelistic technique did in bringing in young people and expanding church growth. The churches' first drama to reach a wider audience was written by church elder Pastor Ed Morales, and entitled *The Duke of Earl*.

The Duke of Earl, like all of Victory Outreach's dramas, is laced with references to popular culture, particularly to the Chicano gang subculture. An analysis of the drama illuminates what role the drama ministry of the church plays in re-creating the notion of "dangerous" youth and how the popular culture of Chicano gangs can be used as an evangelization tool.

Duke, a young Latino gang member, leaves prison to rejoin his gang. He is posturing, dressed in the style of a Chicano gang member of the late 1970s and early 1980s. The Gene Chandler oldie "Duke of Earl" plays over the first few scenes of this teleplay version of Morales's drama. The gang life is not glorified. The party scenes are rife with alcohol and drug use. The discussions between gang members focus on violence and retaliation over various past offenses. The only consistent attempt to convince Duke that there is no future in gangs comes from his grandmother, who prays for Duke without success.

Duke's gang is shopping at a local Army-Navy surplus store when Morales enters, breaking up a fight that began when the rival gang attacked Duke's gang in the store. Morales's attempts at Christian witness fall flat, but not before he preaches Victory Outreach's quintessential message in a few short lines: "Ask God to come into your heart right now . . . Jesus died on the cross for all of you . . . We need to get together and fight against the Devil . . . it's about the barrio [mockingly] . . . it's about God! Homeboy! God loves Toker's Town, God even loves Fifteenth Street . . . Can't you handle God's love?" The gangs then return to their hangouts to party and plot retaliatory strikes against each other.

After a series of fights in which rivals are killed, Duke returns home, and his grandmother "lays hands" on him. Duke finally realizes that the gang life is not for him and goes to see Morales. Morales and his wife Mitzi lead Duke in prayer, Duke cries and converts, and Mitzi asks the Holy Spirit to come.

This drama accomplishes several things: (1) it inscribes a Pentecostal notion of religious expression and conversion (laying on of hands and inviting the presence of the Holy Spirit), and (2) it allows a negative portrayal of the gang life without condemnation of the individuals. In effect, all future and current gang members watching the drama are taken to task for their actions, but their unconditional acceptance into the church and profound conversion experience as portrayed by Duke signals that the "outlaw" has become a child of God. Recapturing the menacing gang member from the margins and placing him in the mainstream of charismatic/Pentecostal Christianity creates and reinforces both the social and the new spiritual reality of Latino youth who respond to the altar call that occurs after every performance. Gang culture transcends generations through geographic space, dress, language, and music. Music that reflects the era of the *veterano* is used to reach the *veterano*, but that same blend of oldies rock and roll and rhythm and blues reaches some of today's GenX gang members as well.

Victory Outreach's evangelistic techniques serve as a "refiner's fire" to the *cholo* subculture the church views as part of its own special dominion (Arguinzoni 1995). The church did not stop producing dramas that resonated with some gang members a generation ago. Members have written new dramas such as *Cry of the Young* in attempts to evangelize in new quarters of the gang subterranean. Part of the reason the dramas continue to draw such large crowds—six thousand in Riverside, California, in June 1996 (Carnline 1996)—is because the church makes modifications to its dramas and to its youth ministries in general, based on the prevailing trends of urban youth culture. Hip-hop instead of "old school," sports jerseys, tennis shoes, and baggy pants instead of pressed khakis and flannel shirts—all help welcome the second generation into the church.

Victory Outreach makes concessions to popular culture because unlike other, perhaps more traditional Pentecostal denominations (Assemblies of

God, for example), it has not seen the need to demonize certain cultural practices. The church neither seeks to endorse secularism nor has the same historical animosity toward dancing, various hairstyles, clothing, and other cultural expressions the Assemblies (Victory Outreach's foundational denomination) have had throughout their history. Legalism is not a part of Victory Outreach's prescription for spiritual health. Rather, desiring to seek out the most desperate people trapped in the inner city, the ministry attempts to carve out a familial, cultural, and religious space for them within the church.

Another drama, *Street of Dreams,* illustrates how the church modifies its message and appearance to meet the needs of GenX hip-hop youth. *Street* debuted on the West Coast in the summer of 1998, as it closed out Victory Outreach's weeklong youth convention. This drama focuses on a young man saved from a life of drug dealing at a Bible study held by his brother. In contrast to *Duke, Street* chronicles the violent lives of a crew of drug dealers. *Street* is multiracial and features rap and soul music. Its props and characters are more reminiscent of its East Coast origins (the cast is from the Bridgeport, Connecticut, church). There are walk-up brownstones, and distinct East Coast accents. Not marked by any distinctive fashion features, the actors dress like young adults.

The treatment of women as party companions in *Duke* is duplicated in *Street,* in which women are called "hoochies." In *Duke,* there is physical violence against women, but none occurs in *Street.* Both dramas reinforce the idea that women are lost without men. In *Street,* they are discouraged from attending college and reminded that without their boyfriends or brothers to care for them, they may revert to lives as "tramps" and "ho's."

Trappings of urban youth culture abound: pickup basketball games, parties, dating, drug and alcohol use, and violent gunplay. Violence, unlike in *Duke,* is not limited to knife fights and occasional gunfire. *Street* features extensive use of guns, and several characters die, including the pregnant girlfriend of a treacherous crew member.[1] The life of a drug dealer, like the life of a gang member, is never glorified. The crews describe their lives as filled with uncertainty and back stabbing. Loyalty to the crew depends on one's success as a dealer; territorial loyalties are not as strong as in *Duke.*

Victory Outreach's diversification of its style and message reflected what many church growth specialists and theologians began saying over eight years ago, when a small industry within the larger industry of Christian publishing focused on attracting GenX youth to the church.[2] Theologian Leonard Sweet defines the process of specialization: "Traditional 'youth ministry' won't work any longer. Nor does the entertainment/message mode of the '60s and '70s. . . . No one 'group' is 'in' anymore; groups have demassified into affinity communities. There is no one 'youth ministry' possible anymore because there is not now one 'youth group' anymore . . . church warfare in the postmodern era is less over theological issues than social and stylistic issues" (Sweet 1999).

Victory Outreach's ministry cannot be characterized as traditional, but its youth have broken into several affinity communities: party crews, gang affiliates (wannabes), gang members, drug users (casual and addicted), and second-generation members, who have little experience with any of these communities. These groups are bonded by their common experiences and tend to affiliate with each other. All have common ties through popular culture that allow the church's evangelical message to resonate to every community. Adding to these specialized ministries, Victory Outreach attempts to find specific peer representatives to minister to each community. However, the youth ministry serves all communities, though the dramas are written to appeal to the specialized needs of party youth and gang members. To examine how hip-hop culture helps to reorient marginalized youth's anger toward a collective "enemy," a description of the church's youth ministry, GANG, and its extensive use of rap helps illuminate this process.

Sacralizing Gangs and Hip-Hop Culture

Wednesday is youth ministry night at Victory Outreach in La Puente, California. Over seven hundred young people meet to hear Victory Outreach worship standards and rap, and also socialize with friends. After an hour of worship music, Tim Arguinzoni delivers a message. He and worship leader Mando Gonzales Jr. typify the second-generation leadership. They must guide the church through the process of change that seeks to retain second-generation members without diluting the original vision of the founder, Sonny Arguinzoni. The founder's son, Sonny Arguinzoni Jr., is charged with negotiating this delicate balance. How does one incorporate this new generation into the church while not alienating older members? How does the church retain its second generation, who for the most part do not suffer from the same pathologies that their parents did? More important, for a church that rarely experiences and does not encourage transfer growth (Arguinzoni 1995), how does Victory Outreach ensure its survival into the next millennium? Part of the answer lies in the brilliant, if unintentional, coopting of the emblematic expressions of inner-city youth gangs to sacralize their social purpose and reclaim the idea of "gang" for a generation marred both by the violence of gangs and by the constant stereotyping of all Latino youth as gang members.

Arguinzoni Jr. serves as assistant pastor of the La Puente church. He is a graduate of LIFE Bible College, former semi-pro baseball player, and graduate student at Fuller Theological Seminary. Arguinzoni Jr. rebuilt a moribund youth ministry program over two years ago that attracted only a few dozen youth. Nearly two years ago, he reports receiving word from God that this was "God's Anointed Now Generation"—GANG.[3]

By naming the youth ministry GANG, Arguinzoni Jr. has reoriented the concept of a gang from a violent, predatory entity toward a sacred, familial entity that provides an alternative identity for GenX and millennial Latino youth in the church. Such coopting must also bring with it the popular cultural expression that pervades urban youth culture—hip-hop. Historian Tricia Rose describes the role of the crew for inner-city youth and its cohesive bond with hip-hop: "The crew [is] a local source of identity, group affiliation, and support system. . . . Identity in Hip-hop is deeply rooted in the specific, the local experience, and one's attachment to and status in a local group or alternate family. These crews are new kinds of families forged with intercultural bonds that, like the social formation of gangs, provide insulation and support in a complete and unyielding environment and may serve as the basis for new social movements" (Rose 1994).

GANG serves as an alternative to street gangs, and also as an alternate family for those who want or need that, but for the purposes of creating and maintaining an evangelical identity, the GANG youth ministry is crucial. Being in this "gang" creates a sense of local identity and secures often tenuous intercultural and interracial bonds, but more important, it insulates youth from the harsh environment of the inner city. It places that environment and its residual ills—poverty, crime, gangs, drugs, and familial dissolution—in a religious context in which youth feel spiritually empowered to fight such ills.

GANG has its own merchandise, conventions, retreats, and a website. The 1998 convention held at the La Puente church lasted three days, with nearly three thousand attending. Some attendees raised the $60 registration fee by holding fund-raisers: food and bake sales and car washes. Others had to raise significantly more money to travel from Europe and Latin America to attend the convention. Local GANGs were acknowledged at the beginning of the conference when church leaders asked: "Is Fresno in the house?" "Is Spain in the house?" Each group responded with enthusiastic shouts reinforcing their local identity. The stage was cloaked with all the trappings of a youth rally: graphic posters warned youth to avoid drugs, teen pregnancy, gangs, and graffiti. The stage looked like a basketball court, and the crowd cheered wildly when Arguinzoni Jr. entered the stage on a motorcycle. Worship then began and lasted over an hour. The music was distinctly tinged with R&B, soul, and rap. Three rappers performed that evening to the delight of the crowd. Tim Arguinzoni preached for over an hour following the music. The message was a familiar message to youth to give up their partying and follow Jesus, and a warning that if they were attending this conference for socializing, they were attending for the wrong purpose. In the crowd, African-American youth intermingled with Latino youth, who also intermingled with the Europeans. The audience was overwhelmingly Latino with small pockets of Europeans, African Americans, and Euro Americans.

Two church members, from Connecticut and London respectively, performed rap, as did a well-known Christian rapper named Deezer-D. Deezer-D's rhyme, "Ain't no party like a Christian party, 'cause a Christian party don't stop," is a play on a popular secular rap song. As simple as this rhyme may sound, Deezer-D's rap reflects a theme crucial for convincing youth to see Christianity as a substitute for the party life. The act of partying, characterized by music, dancing, and drinking, is reoriented toward the idea that if you are a Christian, the partying never stops, Christianity is fun. GenX religion appears intent on stripping Christianity of any vestiges of what one of my informants called "that Orange County" look—a buttoned-down, stuffy Christianity that does not resonate with dyed hair, nose rings, goatees, baggy pants, and espresso breaks during service. Young people do not have to stop socializing, and can have healthy relationships provided they abandon the ubiquitous drinking, drugs, and sex. As long as it reinforces a Christian message, hip-hop culture remains a powerful evangelistic tool for reaching GenX Latinos and African Americans, thus creating and securing intercultural and interracial bonds.

As the church appears willing to use hip-hop and its GANG youth ministry to attract a new generation, Victory Outreach has also seen the benefits of what the larger world of evangelical Christianity has been engaged in for a couple of decades—marketing its own line of merchandise. The GANG youth convention is where old-school Victory Outreach converts and new GenX and millennial converts meet, and where the overarching framework of evangelical marketing culture is most prevalent. Manning the security and walking among the crowd are older *veteranos* dressed in old-school style. Others are dressed more casually with "O.G." (Original GANGster) sweatshirts. The majority of the crowd is young, fifteen to thirty-five, including both men and women. Many have Bibles, key chains, and other paraphernalia with evangelical messages. There is a prevalence of WWJD (What Would Jesus Do) items that are very popular among the attendees. Some have the WWJD neckwear, some write it on their Bible covers or on key chains. Victory Outreach simply grafts on its own merchandise in an attempt to separate it from the generic items. There are GANG T-shirts, sweatshirts, hats, CDs, Bible covers, dog tags, and wallets. One young man had engraved GANG into his hair.

The practical successes of these conventions and dramas are difficult to assess. The church has made some concerted efforts to do follow-up on those who answer the altar calls, and on those visitors who choose to fill out information cards. The church rarely discloses such information, so based on journalistic accounts and a few candid assessments, success appears mixed. The youth conventions of the past three years have been well attended: three thousand in 1998, two thousand in 1996, and six thousand for a drama in Riverside, California, in 1996 (Hendrix 1996, 1; Carnline 1996, 1). Journalists who reported on the conventions and dramas, and my own fieldwork for both events confirm my initial observations that there was more interest in the La Puente conference by those youth at the front of the auditorium than in the back, where I sat. The journalist who reported on the Riverside performance found some attending with an ulterior motive. A young woman opined that her friends attended the Riverside drama to socialize and hopefully meet gang members.[4] I too noticed pockets of socializing and many youth walking around, especially at the *Street of Dreams* presentation. Every church member I have spoken to over the last two years lauds the effects of the dramas as evangelistic tools. However, one member doubted the long-lasting effects of dramas if follow-up did not include church attendance and Bible study.[5] However, there should be no doubt that at the convention and the drama performance, there were altar calls that drew hundreds of youth who answered the preachers' call to give their lives to God.

One final example of how GANG hopes to broaden the church is its website, which advertises merchandise and provides a schedule of upcoming events and a detailed guide to GANG initiation. Initiation begins with acceptance of Jesus. The rules for this gang include bringing their "weapons"—their Bibles—with them to church and reading them every day. They are also advised to pray every day. GANG members should find and attend a Christian church and seek more recruits by witnessing.[6] That no one need attend Victory Outreach or recruit others to the church is a remarkable statement considering the importance of conversion for the growth of the church. A website also connotes an outreach to youth in a different class than the first generation, and even some in the second. The GenX leadership of Victory Outreach appears ready to reach out beyond their traditional base of inner-city drug addicts, gang members, prostitutes, and the homeless, even if it means that those who convert will find another church. The strategy hopes to broaden the appeal of the church to a more middle-class, better-educated, committed Christian constituency. In short, the second-generation leadership appears to be looking to bring in more of its peers.

The Vineyard

In contrast to Victory Outreach, the Vineyard began over twenty years ago with the goal of reaching baby boomers. By sacralizing popular cultural forms such as rock music and re-creating the notion of sacred space to include school auditoriums and coffeehouses, the Vineyard positioned itself as a pioneer in innovative forms of worship. The Vineyard's musical tastes offer more diversity than Victory Outreach. When one visits a Vineyard, depending on where it is, you can hear balladlike hymns like "Mercy, Mercy," or soft rock sounds of "Light the Fire Again." Alternatively, if you are at La Viña, you can hear uptempo versions of Latin American evangelical music, or translated Vineyard classics—many accompanied by the beat of a tambourine. Then again, if you visit a youth meeting you may hear nothing but infectious beats of rap or industrial-techno music reminiscent of the Chemical Brothers. There is a perception of class difference when one examines the Vineyard's Latino youth, who do not suffer from the same cloud of delinquency that stereotypically marks Victory Outreach youth. Class divisions within La Viñas are demarcated by geographical location of the particular church. What do these churches do to attract and retain youth? (1) They cultivate a relational atmosphere with specialized ministries that attract varying classes of youth, (2) They serve as a bridge between U.S. and immigrant Latinos, and (3) The church itself supports the growth of GenX ministry through its support of GenX leadership.

Creating a Relational Atmosphere

The Vineyard cultivates relational atmospheres by creating a sense that whatever class or familial background youth come from, the church is an accepting place. In the church youth can find relationships based on trust, friendship, and common faith. The Vineyard creates this atmosphere through outreaches like inner-city ministry to at-risk youth, outreach efforts to immigrants, and ministry to unchurched youth. The success of the efforts depends on how adept the various churches are at developing leadership composed of peers who serve as authentic translators of the faith. The outreach, worship style, and even location of service tend to be determined by where the church is and who attends. Two examples of inner-city ministry emanate from an English-speaking church called the Lord's Vineyard, located in Pico Rivera, a Latino working-class suburb of Los Angeles.

This emphasis on inner-city mission is the work of Pastor Richard Ochoa, a high school dropout, ex–gang member, and longtime Pico Rivera resident. At a recent service, Ochoa passionately described how he presided over a funeral of a gang member who died during a particularly bloody month of drive-by shootings in Pico Rivera. His solution to such violence is twofold: Ochoa actively participates in a character development program at a local continuation high school. He invites his students to church and hopes that conversion will help stem the violent lives of these at-risk youth. Ochoa has been teaching character development since late 1998. Though he cannot preach in the school setting, he uses the time that he has with these youth to invite them to church, and on several occasions, they have attended. One time, a group attended and sat together, unsure of what to expect. When the worship began, they stood but did not sing. When many of the people raised their hands in praise, they did not. They looked uncomfortable and waited for a suitable moment to sit down. By the end of the service, Ochoa attempted to signal to the congregation, with these young men in mind, that anyone wishing to accept Jesus should make a private statement. Ochoa continues his teaching/ministry to this day.

Music at the Lord's Vineyard is almost exclusively Vineyard worship standards, with the occasional traditional gospel song added for emphasis. Unlike Victory Outreach, the music does not appear to resonate with gang members, and aside from Ochoa's outreach, there are no other formal programs that the church supports. GenX gang members attend the Lord's Vineyard in large part because the pastor is an ex–gang member who does not bother to hide his tattoos, invites them, and tells them that he understands what caused them to become what they are, and most important, that there is an answer. However, gang youth are not the only group ministered to by this church; a large percentage of their youth are unchurched. For this ministry, Ochoa delegates to GenX youth pastor Teresa Arce.

Arce is in her early thirties and has spent a little over two years in the Vineyard. Though aware that she cannot relate to every experience that her group of about eight to twelve youth discuss with her, Arce seeks to communicate empathy by being relational and confessional—talking about her father's death, her unwed pregnant niece, and her own personal problems when necessary.

Arce's group began as a traditional Bible study, which she soon abandoned when she discovered that none of her students had even the most rudimentary knowledge of the Bible, or evangelical Christianity. Instead, Arce made the biweekly meetings an informal time when her group could discuss relevant personal issues and what the Bible had to say about those issues. She stresses building trust, counseling, and being inclusive. Very informal, she is an encouraging voice to youth facing what she believes are social problems multiplied many times over: "We don't say you can't do this, you can't do that . . . you can be yourself . . . we can talk about anything."[7] Sermons on behavior are not the purpose of Arce's get-togethers; she seeks to open the meeting to any of the youth who wish to speak, with confidence that she will listen and that the group will help each other. Arce also emphasizes that she is not above reproach; she is a sinner and does not allow herself or others in the group to judge others because she says that should be left to God. Inclusiveness and a nonjudgmental approach appear to be essential to propagating the faith from GenX to millennials and beyond.

Becoming an indistinguishable part of the group is Arce's goal, which is part of what attracts GenXers to the Vineyard—an egalitarianism based on shared faith and equality before God. Such attitudes should not be viewed as concessions to liberal views on morality. To the contrary, Arce, and many others I interviewed for this study, see the decline of morals in America as a major reason why youth are seemingly surrounded by the social ills of drugs, gangs, and sexual promiscuity. The Lord's Vineyard, through Ochoa's character-development class and Arce's teaching, attempts to counter what they both see as Latino youth's worst enemies—a moral relativism and lack of religious foundation that have made youth uneasy with the absolutes offered by evangelical Christianity.

La Viña: A Bridge for Immigrant Latinos

Another way the Vineyard is seeking to attract and retain youth is by serving as a bridge between U.S. and immigrant Latinos. Such a bridge is occurring at several Vineyards, most obviously at La Viña in Downey, California. At La Viña, a half dozen different Latin American countries are represented with generational, cultural, and linguistic differences that make youth ministry challenging. According to Pastor Joe Castaños, La Viña seeks to "create a contemporary environment where [youth] . . . can identify with and dwell in, in a sense." Castaños sees the problems of Latino youth as compounded by a lack of opportunity and a pervasive sense of isolation. He notes that they have "a lack of identity in feeling that they are part of this society. I think there is a real strong sense of rejection [and] that is why we have gangs . . . we're not part of this society, so we create our own . . . subcultures." To counter these feelings, Castaños bridges the worlds of traditional Latin American Pentecostalism and contemporary charismatic Christianity, combining traditional Latin American gospel with contemporary Vineyard standard worship songs. Examining how La Viña deals with some of these issues and creates its contemporary environment illuminates how an evangelical Latino youth culture is shaped in this denomination.

For Spanish-speaking young adults, the Sunday service provides contemporary worship music mixed with Latin American gospel standards like "*Jehova Es Mi Guerrero*" (Jehovah Is My Warrior). The congregation is well dressed, some more formally than others, in dresses, suits, and ties. Those not wearing their Sunday best are nonetheless made to feel comfortable. Castaños notes that one of the generational and cultural gaps that he is trying to mend in the church is the legalistic tendencies of some older, newly arrived Latino immigrants who come from countries where not dressing formally for Sunday service was considered disrespectful. Castaños is trying to change that by dressing casually—jeans, loafers, and a casual top without tie or jacket. He would love to make the service more informal, copying other Vineyard styles that interrupt worship with a coffee break—but he fears that may be too informal for his church. Informality is important because it is Castaños's style, and the style of many of the second-generation young adults that attend La Viña.

As the young adults and youth of the church become more acculturated to life in the United States, they need to find something for themselves: English services, rock music, drama, and dance ministries are used at La Viña to keep them interested in church. They also provide the added benefit of keeping the second generation in an immigrant church rather than losing it to an English-speaking, Euro-American church. Paul Castaños, Joe's son and youth pastor of La Viña, presides over the youth service held in the main sanctuary on Wednesday nights. Dimly lit, and attended by fifty to seventy-five youth and young adults, it begins with praise and worship—and very loud rock music. The music is a mix of Vineyard standards, Christian rock, and slower ballad-like hymns. Paul follows with a message relevant to youth, and the service ends with a ministry time when people pray for each other.

The music, this evening, is a rendition of "We Wanna See Jesus Lifted High." People lift their hands, and many sing. There is an overhead projector with the lyrics displayed, but few need to look—these songs are familiar throughout the evangelical Christian church. Occasionally the music is accompanied by a dance performed with flags. In the past, Paul has spoken on the potential danger of secular music, but instead of condemning secular music entirely, Paul singles out music that he believes supports occultism and perversion, like the rock group Marilyn Manson. Part of creating and maintaining an evangelical youth culture, Latino or otherwise, means that coopting rock music has its drawbacks. How do you sacralize music you believe accomplishes your religious purposes, while at the same time warning of the dangers of rock music? Lyrical content becomes the standard by which La Viña measures the extent to which they will coopt music for worship. Rock, rap, industrial, and techno can all be reoriented and used by churches, provided the content conforms to the goal of proclaiming the gospel.

La Viña seeks to help GenX Latino youth find their identity in the larger American society through spiritual transformation. The rejection that Castaños believes Latino youth face emanates from the isolation they feel as nonparticipats in mainstream society. What charismatic/Pentecostal Christianity provides is a place where youth can come and have a personal experience with God—a supernatural experience that nearly all of my informants claim to have experienced. Sharing such beliefs and experiences in fellowship creates a community that the isolated immigrant or the disaffected youth needs. Spanish services, familiar Latin American music, weekday English or Spanish services, rock music, acoustic Spanish worship songs, after-service prayer groups—GenX religion makes you feel comfortable with the traditional notions of conservative Christianity because it speaks your language and can sing the song you want to hear.

GenXers Ministering to GenXers

This last example demonstrates that one of the most effective methods of ministry to GenXers is from one of their own. Ryan De la Torre is a twenty-five-year-old youth pastor at the Vineyard in Monrovia, California. His hair is dyed blond, and he wears several earrings and tattoos. He prefers to minister over barbecues, or at a coffeehouse. He is also of mixed ethnicity: a Mexican father, and an Irish mother who raised their family in the American Baptist church. De la Torre began searching for a church more accepting of charismatic experience when his American Baptist church attempted to discourage such experiences from breaking out in his church. The Vineyard's nondogmatic approach to charismatic experience and their evangelistic bent appealed to him. He attends LIFE Bible College and hopes to pastor his own church in the South Bay area of Los Angeles within a few years.

The Monrovia Vineyard meets in an elementary school auditorium. The congregation is 95 percent Euro-American, and numbers between 100 and 150 adults and young people. De la Torre begins services as part of the larger congregation; then, when worship ends, he leads his youth groups outside to continue their service. De la Torre's stint as a youth pastor began a little over two years ago and has grown from a few high-school-age kids to include more of them and also a growing college group. There are between 35 and 45 in his group.

De la Torre's philosophy of youth ministry mirrors that of many others in the Vineyard. Youth must be accepted unconditionally and should not be judged. The focus should be on making church a place where youth find and cultivate a relationship with Jesus. The presentation of the Gospel needs to be appealing as well—De la Torre uses multimedia presentations for his messages, and he also mixes in music that ranges from alternative rock and rap to industrial-techno music. His groups meet as often as they can outside church, as church can be seen as intimidating and uninspiring. They meet at coffeehouses, at the beach, in parks, and in each other's homes. De la Torre empathizes with his "kids," and that appears essential to being able to work with this often rebellious and difficult group. He says, "Kids aren't evil. They do evil things. . . . God created them in His image. They're no different. I mean, they might not know who God is. They might not know exactly who they are. But God created them in His image and I see them that way. I see them as kids who need help."[8] Like Arce, De la Torre does not want youth to think that he does not sin: "I have never put any kid down for anything they've ever done. . . . I've done a lot worse than a lot of them have." De la Torre appears to value authenticity—if God is not active in the lives of his youth, superficial growth in attendance is irrelevant. At the same time, if the ministry becomes too gimmicky and the message diluted to the point of "compromising who Jesus is," then De la Torre wants no part of that.

One of the reasons why specialization appears so important to attracting and maintaining GenX youth in general is because tastes in music and in worship style are linked to issues of race, ethnicity, and class. For example, De la Torre sees his coffeehouse ministry as an "Anglo" thing that will not work with youth of color. Similarly, certain music, like rap and old-school R&B, may be put to better use in urban settings with Latino and African-American youth. Such specialization runs the risk of being labeled as blatant pandering. To counter such criticism, De la Torre relates a story. A friend of his in his early thirties who dresses in a more straitlaced, conservative style—an "Orange County kind of look"—attempted to implement a youth program in Los Angeles that never worked. Youth felt out of sorts with someone who did not look like them. However, De la Torre concludes, his friend found success in the more conservative, homogeneous city of Columbus, Ohio, where his friend's youth ministry is thriving. One tends to believe that the mixed ethnicity, dyed hair, and tattoos of De la Torre do better in Los Angeles because he looks like the people in his group. Such specialization might upset those distressed by the marketing of Christianity, but for pragmatic GenX ministers, the threshold of acceptance and cultural accommodation appears to be limitless.

In the inner-city ministry of Victory Outreach, what is attractive to GenXers is the acceptance of gang members—the idea that their music and culture are worthy of grafting onto Christian culture. Especially noteworthy is the GANG youth ministry, in which youth can use the language and culture of the gang subculture and dress styles as a form of outreach. The Vineyard's bridge to immigrant youth is attractive because the church becomes a place to find community, hear the sounds of the home country, and provide an instant community of believers. Ministry to the unchurched attracts youth for a whole host of reasons: not having to meeting in a church and especially having pastors like De la Torre who look like them. Vineyard churches may meet in school auditoriums, private homes, warehouses, or coffeehouses, or they can hold meetings over barbecues or at the beach. Sacred space is wherever two or three are gathered together to worship, a simple biblical verse that GenX ministers like De la Torre have taken literally—churches are not and should not be the only places where people can find solace.

What is innovative about Victory Outreach's inner-city outreach is that it is singularly focused on the inner city. Victory Outreach re-creates the notion of "dangerous" youth by providing the marginalized youth of Victory Outreach with the religious cover of legitimate expressions of worship through rap, R&B, and dramas. What is innovative about the Vineyard's efforts to reach GenX is their contemporary worship, which, rooted in the Jesus movement of the 1970s, can be modified and translated to largely immigrant Latinos in La Viña while at the same time assuring immigrants that their language and culture can be retained in a Euro-American denomination.

Critics of a more fundamentalist bent might lament this "watering down" of the Gospel, but according to the ministers and lay leaders, the stridency of the past simply does not resonate with this generation. Some mainline Protestant denominations may express disappointment that very little is said in these charismatic circles about political solutions to the problems of gangs, drugs, or familial dissolution. The solution, say the informants, lies in the power of charismatic Christianity to reshape and re-create the interior life, and to affix those changes to a young person's cultural surroundings. The role of the church, then, is not to echo the sentiments of the past and condemn culture but to encourage youth to reclaim culture by affixing an evangelical seal of approval on their culture.

Notes

1. *Crew* is rap slang for a group of rappers, gang members, or graffiti artists.

2. Since 1992, of the nearly fifty-five books published by Christian publishers such as Zondervan, Baker, and Eerdmans, on various aspects of Generation X, fifteen of them focus specifically on the problem of evangelization.

3. Arguinzoni related this prophetic word in an interview held on July 13, 1998.

4. "They come looking for cholos because they know what kind of play it is and they know they'll be here." Crescencia Pacheco, quoted in Carline 1996.

5. Over fifty pastors and members of the church voiced positive responses about the dramas and conventions. The lone dissenting voice, "Joe" (a pseudonym), is a longtime church member.

6. The website address is www.victoryoutreach.com/youth.

7. All quotations in this section are from interviews conducted with members of the Lord's Vineyard, from November 1998 to January 1999.

8. All quotations in this section are from an interview with Ryan De la Torre, conducted June 1998.

References

Almaraz, Roberto. 1968. *The Junkie*. Playbill.

Arguinzoni, Sonny. 1995. *Internalizing the Vision*. La Puente, Calif.: Victory Outreach Publications.

Carline, Pam. 1996. "Christian Anti-Gang Play Draws 6,000." *Riverside Press Telegram*, June 30, B1.

Eskridge, Larry. 1998. "'One Way': Billy Graham, the Jesus Generation, and the Ideal of an Evangelical Youth Culture." *Church History* 67 (March): 83–106.

Hendrix, Anastasia. 1996. "Gang Bangers Find Salvation with Ministry." *Fresno Bee*, July 26, B1.

Kelly, David. 1998. "Inland Gangs: Solutions." *Riverside Press Telegram*, December 15, B1.

Morales, Ed, dir., 1982. *Duke of Earl*. Produced by Victory Outreach. 90-min. video-cassette. Trinity Broadcasting Network.

Rose, Tricia. 1994. *Black Noise: Rap Music and Black Culture in Contemporary America*. Boston: Wesleyan University Press.

Sweet, Leonard. 1999. *Soul Tsunami: Sink or Swim in the New Millennium Culture*. New York: Zondervan.

5

Creating Campus Communities

Second-Generation Korean-American Ministries at UCLA

Sharon Kim

On the second day of fall semester, as I walk up UCLA's Bruin Walk, a narrow uphill stretch of campus, I glance at the two rows of small bolted-down wooden tables lined up along both edges of the walkway. Eager, smiling students sit like vendors behind tables cluttered with pamphlets, flyers, and photographs advertising their particular campus group. A young Korean man, holding a stack of quarter-sheet neon green flyers, selectively passes them out to Asian individuals. Passively and without saying a word, he thrusts a card out in front of me. I take one while most of the other Asian students around me smile politely and wave their hands to communicate their disinterest. Continuing to make my way up the walk, I glance down at the card, which reads "Little Spark at UCLA," and even before I could finish reading all of the printed information, I am greeted by another Korean man, this one much more animated. He says to me in a playful tone of voice, "Hi, I'm from KBS, and I know you are dying for one of these" as he hands me his flyer. He then points to the direction of the KBS (Korean Bible Study) table with an almost dancelike gesture, using both of his extended index fingers, and says in a salesmanlike manner, "If you want more info, you can ask those two friendly girls at the table." By the time I reached the end of Bruin Walk, I have in my hand five different flyers advertising five different Korean Christian ministries at UCLA.

There are currently fourteen Korean Christian ministries at UCLA,[1] and 54 percent of the Korean undergraduate population at UCLA is involved in them.[2] Past studies have noted the high involvement of Korean Americans in evangelical ministries on college campuses across the nation (Busto 1996). However, my study is the first to explore the following two central issues in examining and analyzing the relationship between Korean-American college students and campus evangelical ministries. First, I examine the forces that draw Korean-American students at UCLA to join evangelical ethnic ministries. Second, I discuss the manner in which these ministries reflect, reinterpret, and respond to the changing dynamics of race, ethnicity, and religion on college campuses.

Parachurch campus ministries first emerged on college campuses across the United States during the 1940s. During the 1970s, there was a rapid growth of evangelical campus organizations, "fueled by the personal spiritual vacuums left in the wake of cultural upheavals late in the 1960s and a generation of post-1960s university students in search of meaning and values on which to build their lives" (Busto 1996, 135). At about the same time, due to the enactment of the 1965 Immigration Act, there was also a dramatic increase of Korean immigrants from the professional classes to the United States. Immigrating to the United States with dreams of a better future for themselves and for their children, Korean immigrants, viewing higher education as the primary vehicle for upward mobility, have encouraged their children to study hard, make good grades, and attend elite universities. As a result, there has been a steadily growing presence of Korean-American students at elite universities throughout the nation. UCLA provides an interesting case example of the intersection of and attraction between evangelical campus ministries and Korean-American college students. I found that a significant percentage of Korean-American students at UCLA do not join secular, political, cultural, or social clubs. Rather, they join and are actively involved in religious, namely evangelical, Christian clubs at UCLA.

For this research, I interviewed twenty-three Korean-American undergraduate students at UCLA who are involved in campus ministries.[3] I also attended weekly Bible study meetings and fellowship gatherings, as well as a number of campuswide joint group events.[4]

Forces of Attraction

A variety of interrelated factors influence Korean-American students at UCLA to join evangelical ethnic ministries. Among them, I found the following three to be the most powerful: racially structured friendship networks and campus environment, a high level of momentum and vitality among campus Christian groups, and a search for a meaningful, supportive, and empowering community where their racial, ethnic, generational, and religious selves intersect.

First, as at many other campuses across the nation with high percentages of minority students, friendships at UCLA are largely divided along racial lines. Universities currently serve as sites where differences in lifestyles, values, and cultures are embraced, celebrated, and reinforced. These differences serve as the boundaries for numerous student organizations. Korean-American students' decisions to join a Korean ministry are shaped by the racial realities of UCLA's campus culture. Second, there is a high level of momentum and activity among the Korean campus ministries. Their size, resources, energy, and vitality draw many Korean Americans to join them. They have highly organized and effective methods of outreach and recruitment, with each group catering to different niches of the Korean-American student population. In addition, there is a constant new inflow of Korean students who have grown up in the church and enter college with intentions of joining a campus ministry. Finally, in a large university such as UCLA, students find, at the campus ministries, a supportive and caring community where their religious, ethnic, and racial selves come together. At these ministries, they are no longer perceived and treated as racial minorities. They are surrounded by other students who have had a similar set of experiences growing up as racial minorities and as children of immigrants. These groups provide an atmosphere in which second-generation Korean Americans are affirmed and recognized. It is at these campus ministries that many students reclaim and/or reconstruct their identity as Korean-American Christians.

Racially Structured Friendship Networks and Campus Environment

Friendships at UCLA are drawn largely along racial lines. A large majority of Korean-American undergraduates, 87 percent, state that most or all of their friends are either Korean or other Asian Americans (Park 1996, 44). At UCLA, where students live, eat, and study together, racial diversity comes together in the closest possible way. Although students of different races and ethnicities may sit side by side in formal settings such as the classroom, they choose to associate with coethnics in primary encounters, a trend widely observed in campuses across the nation. The existence of numerous ethnic evangelical groups at UCLA is both a reflection of and a contributor to this reality.

As freshmen, Korean Americans quickly learn that UCLA is a racially segregated campus and that most individuals stay within their respective ethnic communities throughout their entire college term. According to an American-born student who grew up in a predominately white suburb of Los Angeles, "In high school, all of my friends were white. There were a few other Koreans in my school but we didn't hang out with each other. It's totally different here at UCLA. Somehow most all of my friends are Korean now . . . they are all my ministry friends."

Upon entering college, Korean Americans reconstruct their interpersonal space. This reconstruction is motivated by both internal and external factors. Both personal choice and racial marginalization shape Korean-American students' decisions to join ethnic ministries at UCLA. The ministries provide institutional settings and regular opportunities for social interaction between individuals with similar experiences, values, and lifestyles. According to the students I interviewed, UCLA's cultural and racial environment is radically different from that of their high schools. The push toward Anglo-conformity and assimilation is much stronger in high schools, particularly those with smaller populations of Asian Americans. Students found less stigma attached to ethnic identification and solidarity at UCLA, and many had experienced culture shock upon arriving at UCLA, where it was more "cool" to associate with coethnics. In fact, according to one student, "We Asians outnumber other racial groups at UCLA. There is power and security in numbers." Many students I spoke with chose to join an ethnic ministry because they wanted to connect with and embrace their "Koreanness." Others said that one of the main reasons why they joined a Korean ministry was because they had felt marginalized, self-conscious, and unwelcome at various "mainstream" campus organizations. In other words, their involvement was in reaction to racial marginalization.

Nonetheless, I found that Korean campus ministries are not just reactions or responses to racial discrimination. One approach to ethnic identification has been to focus on intergroup hostility and discrimination. According to George Simpson and J. Milton Yinger (1972), "A sense of group identification is, in fact, to a greater or lesser degree an almost universal result of discrimination." In characterizing ethnic group identification as primarily a defensive response to discrimination, scholars have often overlooked the inventive, viable, and empowering facets of minority group solidarity. Many students I interviewed commented on how coming to UCLA and joining a Korean ministry enabled them to gain a newfound security and pride in their Korean identity and heritage. In other words, it was not so much a defensive reaction as one of empowerment, liberation, and choice. One male student who grew up in a suburb of Orange County recalled his embarrassment over his ethnic identity during his high school years: "I used to be so ashamed whenever I heard a bunch of other Korean students at my school speaking Korean to each other. They looked so nerdy and out of place. I used to pretend that I couldn't understand them. . . . all of my friends during high school were white. I wanted to be popular so I tried to make all white friends. I tried really hard to be as white as I could. . . . I wanted to be popular." After joining a Korean Christian group at UCLA, he finally felt free to embrace and express his Korean identity.

Sharon Kim

The Draw of Momentum:
Aggressive Outreach Strategies and Niche Marketing

There is a high level of competition, enthusiasm, and activity among the different Korean-American campus ministries. In their study of American denominations, Roger Finke and Rodney Stark (1992) argue that religious groups in pluralist America exist in competition with one another and that this competition increases the overall participation in religion. Pluralism, they find, encourages diligence in recruitment efforts. They quote Francis Grund, writing in 1837, who in contrasting the American and European religious situations stated, "Not only have Americans a greater number of clergymen than, in proportion to the population, can be found either on the Continent or in England; but they have not one idler amongst them; all of them being obliged to exert themselves for the spiritual welfare of their respective congregations" (Finke and Starke 1992, 19). There is a tremendous level of diligence and aggressiveness in outreach strategies at most of the Korean ministries at UCLA. The outreach fervor is seen most vividly during the first two weeks of the fall quarter, when new students arrive and returning students, if they haven't yet joined a group, are looking for one.

Each group that I visited had some type of outreach strategy, which most often included advertisements in the campus newspaper, flyers posted on the walls of dormitories and classrooms, hand-distributed flyers, information booths at Bruin Walk, and specially planned welcoming events. In addition to these approaches, many of the groups also implemented various innovative and creative methods of recruitment. Outreach and evangelization begin on the day when freshmen first move into the dorms. On the Saturday before the first week of classes, I saw representatives from two different groups waiting in the parking lot and front entrance of the dormitories to help freshmen carry in their luggage. I observed one Korean representative of a campus ministry approach an Asian freshman as he was making his way through the double glass door entrance with his parents trailing a few steps behind. After warmly greeting the freshman with a smile, introduction, and handshake, the representative proceeded to help carry some of the luggage up to the room. Then, in the elevators up to the fourth floor, the freshman was invited to attend the group's orientation party. After phone numbers were exchanged, the ministry recruiter then found another prospective member in the parking lot of the dormitory to introduce himself to.

Another group encourages its sophomores and juniors to live in the dormitories so that they can develop friendships with incoming freshmen. During the first week of school, a group of two or three of the older classmates will then make visitations to different freshmen in their dorm rooms.

There they will share advice about which classes to take, how to find the financial aid office, and the importance of finding a good group of friends. Then, in a very casual manner, they will invite them to visit their on-campus Bible study.

All of the groups realize the importance of friendships. Several leaders that I spoke with acknowledged that friendships are the greatest draw for prospective members. If the prospective member finds friends within the group, he or she will most likely join that particular group. According to a member of Kyrie Catholic Fellowship, "The best time to get them is during the freshman year when they haven't yet developed their set of friends." In the same vein, a Korean-American sophomore remarked, "I decided to join because the first friends that I met in college were from the group. I remember it was during the first week in the dorms. I had a white roommate and she was busy rushing for sororities. I didn't want to get involved with the sorority stuff so I was in the dorm room by myself. Two members who lived down the hall from me came into my room and invited me to their meeting. I started to go and the people there were really friendly so I decided to join."

The groups also persistently call and meet with first-time visitors. The existence of many groups targeting the same pool of people causes each to be diligent and aggressive in its outreach efforts. The first few weeks of the fall quarter are when groups are most active in attracting prospective members. Established members of the groups invest large sums of money, energy, and time in promoting their groups.

The aggressive outreach efforts have led to an overall growth in the number of students involved in campus ministries. In 1985 there were four Korean ministries (Korean Bible Study, Little Spark, Ascension Ministries, and Korean Christian Fellowship), and only 8 percent of the Korean undergraduate population was involved in a Korean Christian group.[5] Now, with fourteen groups, the total percentage has risen to 54 percent, over a 600 percent increase.

Along with aggressive outreach practices, the groups also offer different subcultures to cater to the various tastes of the student population. Each group possesses distinctive features that either attract or deter prospective members. This further increases the overall participation in religious groups because there are more choices to meet the different preferences among the Korean student population. The primary differences among the eleven groups are neither theological nor denominational but rather reflect variations such as the level of "Americanization," worship styles, attitudes on gender roles, level of strictness, level of friendliness, and degree of intimacy.

At most of the groups that I attended, the meetings lasted one to one and a half hours, with similar formats. The meeting began with a time of praise followed by a Bible message and ended with discussion and prayer groups. At the larger groups, praise bands complete with guitars, bongo drums, keyboards, and vocalists led the members in worship, while at the smaller groups praise songs were sung with a single guitar accompaniment. At some groups, members stand, lift their arms, and clap while they sing, while at other groups, members sit and sing unenthusiastically. However, all the groups sing the same types of praise music. Along with the contemporary praise music from the Vineyard, Integrity, and Hosanna music groups, there has also been an increased attraction to new praise music emerging from Great Britain and Canada. Some of the new artists that are becoming increasingly popular among the students at these groups are Delirious, Matt Redman, Paul Oakley, and Passion Worship. This new breed of contemporary Christian music targets itself to Generation Xers and is characterized by a heavier, grunge-style beat and lyrics that challenge young people to envision a new season of spiritual revival. For example, in describing this coming revival, praise leader Paul Oakley sings,

> It's a thousand guns all firing, buildings crashing, bombs exploding
> Like a burning furnace, roaring fire. It's like a live volcano blowing.
> Thunder lightning, hurricane warning
> Revival sounds, revival sounds.
> You can't stop it.
> Can you hear it? Can you believe it? Can you receive it? The sound of revival.

The recurring theme in the music of these new artists is the coming revival ushered in by the "Revival Generation"—"Imagine a generation that passes on a passion for Jesus to a new generation. Imagine a generation of history makers. A revival generation is arising around the world."[6] Korean-American students at UCLA are attracted to the message of these new artists because it resonates with their desire to witness spiritual revival on their college campus.

Each group caters to certain segments of the Korean-American student body at UCLA. When asked why they decided to join their particular campus ministry, students always answered that their group met their needs in ways that the other groups were unable to. Their answers always included references to the inadequacies in the other groups that they had visited. Korean Americans evaluate these different ministries in essentially the same way that they evaluate all other objects of choice. After visiting several of the different groups and weighing the pros and cons of each, Korean-American students choose the organization that best meets their personal needs and tastes.

The attendance at all the groups during the first two weeks of school is at least three times higher than during the rest of the year because students are attending several groups at the same time. Nearly all the groups hold special welcoming meetings where they offer dinner, games, gifts, exciting music, and other special attractions to impress and encourage students to join. After shopping for several weeks, most Korean-American students settle down at the group that they feel best suits them. This process of finding a campus ministry mirrors, in many ways, the rushes that the Greek sorority and fraternity system offer during the same time to a largely white segment of the student population.

I spoke with a sophomore and asked her how she decided to join KBS (Korean Bible Study), and she told me how she "shopped" for a ministry during her freshman year. She had entered UCLA wanting to join a Christian group.[7] She had been a Christian for as long as she could remember, and her father is an elder at an immigrant Presbyterian Church. She heard from many people how important it was to keep strong in her faith during her college years. She moved into the dorms and during her first week determined to visit different groups and choose one to join. On Tuesday night, she attended the Little Spark meeting, which was held in a lecture hall that fits around one hundred. She noticed that most of the fifty or so people were quite serious about their faith, for they had their notebooks wide open as they rapidly scribbled notes on the Bible study. However, she was taken aback by the teaching, which focused heavily on sin and repentance, and felt that the atmosphere was too serious. She also heard from others that Little Spark was very strict about dating. She decided to continue her search, and on Wednesday night she visited KBS (Korean Bible Study) and was excited about the size of the group, which numbered over a hundred Korean students. Her church did not have a college group, so she was thrilled at the chance of meeting and becoming friends with so many other Korean college students. But before she made her decision, she wanted to visit a few more groups. On Thursday night, she went to KACF (Korean American Christian Fellowship). The group was about half the size of KBS, and the people there were also very serious about their faith. She liked the fact that the people all seemed to know each other well, but she felt that they were too conservative about the role of women in the church. After thinking and praying about her decision, she chose KBS and has been an active member of the group for nearly two years.

In my interviews with the members of the different groups, I learned that each group prided itself on its distinctive and unique subcultures. The large size of KBS draws many who want the excitement of belonging to a big social group without the pressure of having to conform to a certain lifestyle. According to one KBS member, "Me and a couple of my other KSA (Korean Student Association) friends go to the KBS meetings sometimes. The other groups are too strict and look down on KSA people because we party, drink, smoke.... I feel kind of guilty about going to both groups because I feel like a hypocrite but something within me tells me not to give up on God."

The Korean American Christian Fellowship (KACF) is smaller, with fifty active members. They boast a more Americanized membership, along with conservative or "Bible based" teachings. According to a female member of KACF, "I like KACF because we are very Bible based.... Some groups try to reinterpret scripture but the truth is the truth.... Our group has the courage to not water down the truth." Growing in their faith is an important value among KACF members, and they feel that the other groups are too social and too concerned with worldly affairs. A personal relationship with God and uncompromised biblical living are high priorities among the members of this group.

The smaller groups, such as KCCC (Korean Campus Crusade for Christ), Students for Christ, Upper Room, Little Spark, and Agape, offer what the larger groups cannot, a close-knit, familial environment. A member of Upper Room said, "I chose Upper Room because it is small and intimate. It's so easy to get lost in the large groups. I'm kind of an introvert and I've always liked small groups. The big groups intimidate me. Upper Room's size is perfect for me. Everyone knows each other."

I asked several leaders of smaller and more recently formed groups why they had decided to start their groups when there were already so many Korean ministries at UCLA. Each of them answered that his or her particular group offered something that the other groups did not offer, such as "more connection to the Korean culture and language," or "a strong tie to an ethnic church," or "more emphasis on evangelism to the larger campus." The market had not yet been saturated, and as long as there were still people who needed to hear the gospel, the campus would always need more groups to fill the gap.

In addition to aggressive outreach methods and a distinct subculture, many of the groups also are a part of a larger network of groups much like mainstream groups such as InterVarsity and Campus Crusade for Christ. The leaders of several of these groups betrayed a distinct entrepreneurial spirit and pride in the existence of several Little Sparks or Korean InterVarsities or Korean Bible Studies in numerous campuses throughout the nation. There is tremendous fervor for starting up more new branches of campus ministries. The president of Korean InterVarsity came to UCLA primarily with the vision of beginning a new chapter there. The groups benefit from name recognition; one member decided to join Little Spark because she had heard so many good reports from her older sister, who attends Little Spark at UC San Diego. For many members, the highlight of the year is when the different campus chapters come together for joint meetings, retreats, revivals, and sporting events.

With each new school year, the groups have a new pool of prospective members from which to recruit. Many Korean-American students at UCLA have attended church with their parents since their childhood, and they come to college with the desire to continue in their faith. It has been widely documented that Korean immigrants exhibit a high level of church participation. According to a survey conducted in 1988, nearly 70 percent of Korean immigrants in Los Angeles attend church weekly (Kim and Hurh 1990). This high level of church participation among the immigrant generations has shaped the church participation rate of the 1.5- and second-generation children.[8] Among the college-aged, English-speaking Korean population, 61 percent attend an ethnic church weekly (Park 1996, 20). For the most part, a strong foundation of faith has been laid for Korean Americans who grew up in the church, and they hunger for a sense of spiritual continuity upon entering UCLA.

A large percentage of the members I interviewed said that they entered UCLA wanting to join a Christian group. I spoke with a sophomore and asked her why she joined her ministry and she explained, "I have been a Christian for as long as I can remember. My father is an elder at his church. I heard from everyone that it's very important to join a campus Christian group because the college environment is very secular. I heard stories of how people became atheists after coming to college." One of her top priorities after coming to UCLA was to find a strong campus ministry to join. Others indicated that one of the primary reasons that they decided to come to the UCLA was because they knew that UCLA had strong Christian groups. Thus, the high level of momentum and vitality among the Korean Christian groups at UCLA serves to draw even greater numbers of Korean students to join, the forces of attraction from campus ministries far outweighing the forces of attraction from other voluntary student organizations.[9] Among the different types of student organizations and clubs, the campus ministries have the greatest effect in keeping Korean-American students' personal associations within the boundaries of the ethnic community.

Creating Communities around Hybrid Identities

Large universities such as UCLA can often be intimidating and alienating places where students are left to independently navigate through their four years of college. The campus ministries are places where students can enter into an all-inclusive subsociety that provides them with friendships, identity, recreation, networks, status, and support. The primary reasons why second-generation Korean Americans choose to attend a Korean ministry revolve around the issues of acceptance and belonging. The informal community of believers, which provides individuals with a sense of belonging, is a very important part of campus ministry life. There is still a sense among many of the Korean Americans that I interviewed that mainstream organizations do not provide the closeness and comfort that a Korean organization does. Particularly during the college years, Korean Americans gain a stronger awareness of their ethnic identity and, lacking a sense of belonging at other social outlets, choose to associate with other coethnics in religious organizations. The Korean church and other parachurch campus organizations offer second-generation Korean Americans an opportunity to join a group in which they can feel a sense of belonging and validation. According to Judy Kim, a junior at UCLA, "When I began my first year at UCLA, I was really excited about making new friends but I had the hardest time making Caucasian friends. My roommate in the dorm was white and during the first few weeks of freshman year, we tried to join the same clubs. Both of us joined a sorority together but after one semester, I just knew that it wasn't for me. My friend and I were treated differently because she was white and I was Asian. Especially at the parties. The only type of guys that showed an interest in me were the strange ones who had some sort of Asian fetish or something. I felt that I just didn't fit in because I was Asian." Judy now is an active member of a campus Korean Christian group and finds that the majority of her close friends are Korean American; the sense of belonging and comfort that she had so eagerly sought after is much easier to gain in a Korean organization.

Many students state that their college years have been centered around their campus ministries. According to a senior member of KBS, "All of my friends during my college years have been KBS members. I've lived, eaten, and studied with them. I've spent many hours at KBS meetings and events." These students live, study, and interact primarily with other members of their campus groups. More than just extracurricular clubs, these groups serve as surrogate families.

The campus ministries, entirely student run and led, also provide Korean-American students with opportunities to hold positions of power. Their structures are modeled after immigrant churches, with lines of hierarchy often drawn along age and gender lines. Many of the members of the groups attend first-generation churches, where all of the decision-making power rests with the immigrant leadership. There is a general sense among several people I interviewed that their spiritual and social needs are met primarily at the campus ministries. According to one student, they get "fueled up" spiritually during the week at their campus ministries in order to serve as Sunday school and youth group leaders at their first-generation churches during the weekends.

What is distinctly Korean American about these ministries? What sets them apart from mainstream evangelical campus ministries? The distinctiveness is forged around the multiple overlapping worlds in which the majority of Korean-American students exist. As children of immigrants, many students are caught between the culture and value systems of American society and the Confucian society of their first-generation parents. A recurring theme at these ministries is the generational struggles that students face in meeting their parents' expectations, particularly for educational and economic mobility. Repeatedly, students are reminded to focus on pleasing God rather than pleasing their parents. There is an evident emphasis on combating societal and parental pressures to attain worldly success. According to many leaders I interviewed, worldly success is driven by self-centered ambitions, whereas Godly success is driven by God-given vision.

The campus ministries are developing an ideological second-generation Korean-American Christian culture around shared experiences, accomplishing this by attempting to pick and choose positive aspects of American, Korean, generational, and evangelical cultural values to formulate a new hybrid "Korean-American Christian" culture and value system. This newly emerging value system reflects a desire to retain selected aspects of the Korean worldview. For example, many comment on the dangers of American individualism and the ways in which it promotes self-centeredness and undermines collective efforts. Korean ministries noticeably emphasize the importance of involvement and commitment to the group. Members are taught to look out not for their own personal interests but for the interests of the group. For example, they teach, using biblical text, that one person's sins affect not only the individual but the entire group.

In addition to a reclaiming of group centeredness, the Korean ministries also find themselves moving away from the traditional Korean perspectives of absolute submission to authority, yet at the same time they have not embraced an entirely egalitarian structuring of relationships. Sermons also appeal to common experiences, shared struggles, and values as second-generation Korean Americans.

These groups practice a Koreanized version of Christianity. One Korean woman who used to attend InterVarsity before she joined a Korean ministry remarked on the differences she noticed between Koreans and Caucasians at InterVarsity: "White people pray differently. They are much more informal and chatty with God. It's probably because they speak with their own parents in that way. . . . For example, they'd start their prayers with, 'Hi God, how ya doing? It's me, Susie.' I felt really uncomfortable with this kind of praying. For some reason, it almost sounded blasphemous to me. Koreans are different. I was taught to respect authority figures. This carries over to my relationship with God. Sure the Bible says he's my friend, but he's still an authority figure. I think that's why we Koreans pray differently."

Of the fourteen Korean-American ministries at UCLA, nine retain their "Korean" boundaries while the other five have widened their boundaries to include other Asian-American groups. Among the exclusively Korean ministries, there is an attempt at incorporating selected aspects of what it means to be "Korean." For example, Korean Bible Study (KBS), the largest Korean ministry on campus, has a reputation among the student population as being the most "Koreanized" group. According to an American-born male student, "I used to attend KBS during my freshman year but decided to quit because the people there were too Koreanized for me. I had to call all of the older people *unni* or *hyung*. I don't even call my own brother *hyung*. This really bothered me. I don't buy into the Korean way of respecting people just because they are older. Some of those older guys were real jerks. Also, people would always drop in Korean words here and there during their conversation and I couldn't understand them. This made me feel really left out. I decided to join another group because the people there are more like me . . . more Americanized."

During the first week of classes, KBS holds a *sunbae* and *hubae*[10] banquet where upper classmen are assigned as mentors to the younger classmen, and members are expected to address one another with honorary Korean titles. On my first visit to this group, I arrived fifteen minutes late and asked the woman at the door if the meeting had started yet. She casually remarked in a matter-of-fact tone, "Oh, not yet. We're always on Korean time."

During the messages, which are given in English, Korean words and phrases are often mentioned. KBS offers Korean Americans, the majority of whom immigrated to the United States as young children, a context in which they can explore and connect with their "Koreanness." Several KBS members I interviewed said that upon entering college, they for the first time felt free to explore and embrace their ethnic and racial identity. Developing close friendships with coethnics at KBS enabled many students to develop newfound pride and connection with their ethnic identity. Several members of KBS whom I interviewed remarked, "I've become more Koreanized since I joined my fellowship." What they meant by this statement was that they have intentionally embraced and incorporated aspects of the Korean culture such as food, language, relationships, and values into their everyday lives. They often spend their recreation time doing what they consider to be "Korean" activities. They eat at Korean restaurants, drink coffee at Korean cafés, sing at Korean karaoke clubs, and play pool at Korean billiard halls. According to one male student, "I know Koreatown like the back of my hand now. I used to never go there, only once in a while to go to the Korean market or a restaurant with my parents. Now I go there all the time to eat with my buddies or to the *Noraebangs* [karaoke clubs]. It's actually a fun place to hang out."

At KBS, Korean Americans are able to carve out unique spaces in which their ethnic and religious identities intersect. There is a strong sense among the leaders as well as the members of these groups that Koreans should retain their ethnic identity and not blend into an "Asian" identity. KBS believes that all Christians should be united; however, they feel that unity does not mean uniformity. They feel that there is a special bond among Koreans that expresses itself corporately through their worship.

Among the fourteen Korean groups, the Korean InterVarsity Fellowship (KIVF) is the most "Koreanized." The group started in 1997, and all or most of its members immigrated recently from Korea. All of its services are conducted in Korean, and the subculture of the group closely mirrors the subculture of Korean Christian college students in Korea. The main vision of the group is to "bring inner healing and wholeness to Korean American students who are struggling to cope with their dual identities as American and Korean."[11] The group is completely independent from the InterVarsity Fellowship at UCLA. In fact, according to the president of KIVF, "I don't know if they [IV] even know that we exist. I don't know if they'd be too supportive of us. . . . I need to get into contact with them." In the early 1970s, a Korean exchange student at an Ivy League university joined InterVarsity ministries. Upon returning to Korea, he began the first chapter of Korean InterVarsity Fellowship (KIVF) at an elite South Korean university. Several students who were members of the KIVF in Korea immigrated to the United States and began KIVF chapters at American universities. Although the two groups may share the same name and a common historical tie, they are entirely distinct from each other and exist independently. The history of KIVF gives insights into the transnational aspects and complexities of religious organizations and how they reinvent themselves as they move from one country to another.

Stretching the Boundaries: From Ethnicity to Race

The newer groups are moving away from an exclusively Korean-American membership and becoming increasingly Asian American. The leaders of these new groups argue that cultural preservation should be second in importance to evangelizing the lost. In casting their nets of evangelism, the Korean ministries have largely attracted and pulled in other Asian-American students. This, according to many I interviewed, is due to the fact that students at UCLA identify themselves in racial as opposed to ethnic categories. Yen Le Espiritu (1992) argues that racialist constructions of Asians as homogenous contribute to the forging of alliances and affiliations among ethnic and immigrant groups of Asian origin. Her focus is on how Asian Americans have institutionalized pan-Asianism as their political instrument; but I have found that panethnicity is also playing a major role in the formation and growth of an

Asian-American religious movement on the UCLA campus. Several members and leaders of the campus ministries credit the high percentage of Christian Asian Americans at UCLA to the "divine hand of God" that is leading Asian Americans to elite universities, getting them "fired up for God" at these universities, in order to positively change the mainstream society. According to one leader, "American society needs to change. However, this change will not happen solely through politics. America needs a spiritual revival that will change people's hearts. Only God can change people's hearts. Laws and politics will not." As Max Weber noted (1992), ideal interests can often provide a powerful impetus for social action and social change. In the 1950s, UCLA was home to the student revivals spearheaded by Bill Bright and the Campus Crusade for Christ. Many ministry leaders I interviewed made references to the historical legacy of spirituality at UCLA and envisioned a new season of spiritual revival on the UCLA campus, which would spill over and affect mainstream American society.

Most ministries that began as Korean have modified and enlarged their vision to include the other Asian groups. At these campus ministries, the ethnic boundary of "Korean" has been widened to a racial boundary of "Asian." This shift is seen in the ways that some groups have changed their names by substituting "Asian" for "Korean." The newer groups that were established and run by Korean Americans are omitting Korean expressions and opting for more inclusive language. In addition, they are diversifying their leadership to include non-Korean voices in decision-making processes. The events sponsored by some of the groups reflect this trend toward an Asian-American leaning. I received a flyer during the first week of school inviting me to a Welcome Night, and on the flyer the words "Free Asian Food" was boldly printed. Curious to see what was considered Asian food, I attended the event and saw that it included samplings of different ethnic cuisines such as Korean bulgogi, Japanese California rolls, and Chinese potstickers. The ministries' shift from exclusively Korean to Asian American reflects the importance of race as a primary organizing principle for relationships in the United States.

The emphasis on ethnicity and ethnic group experiences in the United States has often confused the important distinctions between race and ethnicity. Unlike the immigrant generation, 1.5- and second-generation Korean Americans fundamentally identify themselves in racial categories because of their day-to-day experiences; they're treated as Asian Americans, as opposed to Korean Americans. According to one second-generation Korean-American woman, "Most people here on campus or anywhere else for that matter don't see me as a Korean but rather as an Asian. Because that's how people in this country classify people—by their race."

Michael Omi and Howard Winant (1986) argue that race has always played a central role in American politics and life. Race in the United States, they argue, should be treated as a fundamental and independent category through which relationships are ordered. They disagree with scholars who have interpreted the existence of ethnic voluntary institutions as evidence of an egalitarian society: "In America it was easy to establish the institutions that one desired . . . every variant of liberalism and orthodoxy could express itself freely in institutional form. It is American freedom that makes possible the maintenance and continuity and branching out of whatever part of their ethnic heritage immigrants and their children want to pursue" (Glazer 1975, 27). Omi and Winant point out that studies on ethnicity and ethnic experience dismiss or deemphasize the importance of race or racism.

Similarly, Mary Waters (1992) argues that ethnicity is largely symbolic, flexible, and harmless for white middle-class Americans who have a lot more choice and room to maneuver and that this is not the case for nonwhite Americans. The social and political consequences of being Asian or Hispanic or black are not symbolic for the most part, or voluntary. The lives of Korean Americans are strongly influenced by their race or national origin, regardless of how much they may choose not to identify themselves in ethnic or racial terms. Ethnic choices are not an option for all. Korean Americans of both the 1.5 and second generations experience racial marginalization regardless of their level of acculturation. This marginalization plays a significant part in the shaping of their identities, their primary encounters with the mainstream society, and their participation in ethnic ministries. The reality of an increased move toward panethnicity among Christian groups at UCLA demonstrates that religion does not necessarily transcend the boundaries of race.

According to one student whose Korean-American group is becoming increasingly Asian American, "Last year our group used to be practically all Korean. It's changed this year. About 20 percent now are from other Asian groups. Most of the non-Koreans came either through their friends or through street evangelism. Asians do have a lot in common, we've shared a similar set of life experiences because of the way we look. . . . I have more in common with a third-generation Japanese than a first-generation Korean or a foreign student from Korea." Although these ministries are bounded by race, race and racism form more of a subtext. It is rarely explicitly addressed either in teaching or in conversations among the members. Nonetheless, the individuals I interviewed were conscious of the influence that their race continues to assert in their daily lives. They could each give an account, often with vivid detail and intense emotions, of specific incidences in their past when they were discriminated against because of their race. Racial discrimination poses more of a threat to their individual life chances than does ethnic discrimination.

In fact, UCLA's entire Christian community is becoming increasingly Asian American. In addition to the numerous Korean groups, mainstream para-church organizations such as Navigators and InterVarsity are also experiencing an influx of Asian-American students. This trend is evident throughout the nation. *Christianity Today* has reported that InterVarsity's seventeenth triennial conference on missions, Urbana '93, "noticed a fundamental change in the makeup of the delegates," with two-fifths of the 17,000 attendees ethnic minorities (Kennedy 1994). Asian Americans represented over 20 percent of the conferees, and Korean Americans accounted for nearly 10 percent.

At UCLA the percentages of Asians in parachurch groups are even more dramatic. Every spring, all of UCLA's Christian groups come together to sponsor the Ask Me Week, a week specially designed to promote unity among the different ministries and to mobilize for campus outreach. Among the nearly one thousand students present at the Ask Me Revival Night in 1996, over 80 percent were Asian. I heard several people muttering to one another, "Gosh, look at all the Asians here," and "I didn't know there were so many Asian Christians." At UCLA, there are currently fourteen Korean-American ministries, six Asian-American ministries, and four Chinese ministries. There are a total of twelve multiethnic ministries, but even within them there is a high percentage of Asian Americans—60 percent of InterVarsity and 80 percent of Navigators is Asian American.

Conclusion

The study of UCLA's ethnic ministries is sociologically important because it helps us to better understand the role that religion and religious organizations plays in the adaptation process of second-generation Korean Americans. The social realities of Korean-American ministries cannot be understood in the framework of immigration and assimilation that is applied to European immigrant organizations. Unlike white ethnic groups, second-generation Korean Americans are not assimilating into mainstream organizations. The Korean Americans who join these ministries were raised in the United States, are fluent in English, and understand the "American" way of life. However, they tend to remain within their own ethnic group largely in campus ministries for most of their intimate, primary group relationships, interacting with other ethnic and racial groups largely in impersonal secondary group settings such as in the classrooms.

Past studies have pointed out that as individuals culturally and structurally assimilate into the mainstream society, ethnic institutions tend to gradually diminish, since social and religious needs can be met equally well within the organizations of the host society (Mullins 1987). However, in their study of second- and third-generation Japanese Americans, Stephen S. Fujita and David J. O'Brien (1991) found that, in comparison with white ethnic groups in the same stage of assimilation, Japanese Americans exhibit a higher degree of ethnic identification through attachments to and involvements with their ethnic community. Fujita and O'Brien argue that the orientations and characteristics of the ethnic groups themselves determine the long-term cohesiveness of a group. I have found that second-generation Korean Americans, like Japanese Americans, demonstrate a high level of acculturation in English mastery, educational achievements, and occupational mobility—yet they still exhibit a high level of ethnic and racial identification through their participation in campus evangelical ministries. Phenomena such as the Asian-American movement, anti-Asian discrimination, the racially diverse and divided landscape of UCLA, and continuing immigration from Asian countries reinforce ethnic and racial identity among college students at UCLA. Furthermore, the development and growth of Korean-American and Asian-American ministries act to strengthen ethnic identity.

Ethnic campus Christian organizations play a significant role in the lives of Korean-American students at UCLA. However, the interaction between individuals and religious organizations does not occur within a vacuum. Rather, the interaction is shaped and generated by various structural realities. The racially segregated landscape of UCLA, which encourages identification with one's particular ethnic group and involvement in ethnic institutions, encourages Korean-American students to seek out associations with coethnics. The pressure toward Anglo-conformity and assimilation at the university is not as strong as it has been for racial minorities in past decades, and the high level of momentum and marketing of campus ministries further encourages Korean-American student involvement. Finally, the campus ministries serve as sites where Korean Americans can express, experience, and explore their ethno-religious identities as Korean Christians in the context of affirming relationships with coethnics. At UCLA, Korean Americans are carving out a space where they can be Korean-American Christians, and this new culture and identity plays itself out in the ethnic ministries.

Notes

1. I went to the Office of Student Programming at UCLA and counted the number of Korean groups listed; there are probably several other groups that are not officially registered. The following were listed: California Bible Student Fellowship, Collegians in Action, Fellowship in Christ at Los Angeles, Graduate Fellowship at UCLA, Immanuel Chapel Campus Ministry, Klesis College Life, Korean American

Christian Fellowship, Korean Bible Study, Korean Campus Crusade for Christ, Korean InterVarsity Fellowship, Kyrie Catholic Fellowship, Little Spark Mission, Oikos Christian Fellowship, and Upper Room Bible Fellowship.

2. Of the 1,345 Korean undergraduates at UCLA, approximately 730 are involved in the fourteen groups—hence, 54 percent of the Korean undergraduate population.

3. Thirteen of the students I interviewed were women, and ten were men. Most of them were second-generation Korean Americans. The respondents represented the following groups: Agape, Korean American Christian Fellowship, Korean Bible Study, Korean InterVarsity Fellowship, Little Spark Mission, Navigators, Oikos Christian Fellowship, and Upper Room Ministries. I chose the respondents by attending the different groups and asking people that I met if they were willing to give me an interview. The interviews lasted from 45 to 90 minutes.

4. At UCLA, there has been an ongoing effort to unite the different Christian ministries. The students of the different groups formed an umbrella organization called the Inter-Christian Council (ICC). The ICC holds regular weekly prayer meetings and yearly rallies to promote Christian unity and momentum on the UCLA campus. I attended their spring rally in 1999; there were over 1,000 students in attendance, and nearly 85 percent of the attendees were Asian American.

5. These figures were calculated by contacting the leaders of the ministries, who informed me of the size of their group in 1990. They also told me the names of the other groups that existed in that year. I took the total number of Korean Americans that participated in these ministries and arrived at the percentage of Korean Americans who joined Korean Christian groups.

6. This quote was taken from the cover of the CD album *Revival Generation.* The artists throughout the album refer to Generation X as the Revival Generation.

7. Many scholars and pastors have argued that there has been an ongoing "silent exodus" of the second generation from immigrant churches. However, I have found that among UCLA students, the majority of them do not leave the church during their college years. Many attend the immigrant churches on Sundays and attend parachurch groups during the week.

8. The term *1.5 generation* refers to Korean Americans who were born in Korea but moved to the United States as infants; *second generation* are those who were born in the United States to immigrant parents.

9. See Breton 1964, on the influence of "institutional completeness" and the social integration of the immigrant.

10. *Sunbae* means upperclassman. *Hubae* means lowerclassman.

11. Interview with the president of Korean InterVarsity Fellowship.

References

Busto, Rudy. 1996. "The Gospel According to the Model Minority: Hazarding an Interpretation of Asian American Evangelical College Students." *Amerasia Journal* 22, no. 1: 140.

Cho, David. 1999. "Asians Embrace Campus Christian Groups." *San Jose Mercury News*, February 13, 3E.

D'Souza, Dinesh. 1991. *Illiberal Education: The Politics of Race and Sex on Campus*. New York: Free Press.

Finke, Roger, and Rodney Stark. 1992. *The Churching of America, 1776–1990: Winners and Losers in Our Religious Economy*. New Brunswick, N.J.: Rutgers University Press.

Fujita, Stephen S., and David J. O'Brien. 1991. *Japanese American Ethnicity: The Persistence of Community*. Seattle: University of Washington Press.

Gans, Herbert. 1979. "Symbolic Ethnicity: The Future of Ethnic Groups and Cultures in America." *Ethnic and Racial Studies* 2: 1–20.

Glazer, Nathan. 1975. *Ethnicity: Theory and Experience*, edited by Nathan Glazer and Daniel P. Moynihan. Cambridge, Mass.: Harvard University Press.

Hurh, Won Moo, and Kwang Chung Kim. 1990. "Religious Participation of Korean Immigrants in the United States." *Journal for the Scientific Study of Religion* 29, no. 1 (March): 19–34.

Kennedy, John W. 1994. "Urbana '93: Mission Force Looking More Asian in Future." *Christianity Today*, February 7, 48–49.

Kim, Ilsoo. 1981. *New Urban Immigrants: The Korean Community in New York*. Princeton, N.J.: Princeton University Press.

Kim, Kwang Chung, and Shin Kim. 1996. "Ethnic Meanings of Korean Immigrant Churches." Paper presented at the Sixth North Park College Korean Symposium, Chicago, October 12.

Lee, Helen. 1996. "Silent Exodus." *Christianity Today*, August 12, 51–52.

Le Espiritu, Yen. 1992. *Asian American Panethnicity: Bridging Institutions and Identities*. Philadelphia: Temple University Press.

Min, Pyong Gap. 1990. "The Structure and Social Functions of Korean Immigrant Churches in the United States." Paper presented at the Annual Meeting of the Association for Asian Studies, Washington, D.C.

Mullins, Mark. 1987. "Life Cycle in Ethnic Churches in Sociological Perspective." *Japanese Journal of Religious Studies* 14, no. 4: 321–34.

Omi, Michael, and Howard Winant. 1986. *Racial Formation in the United States: From the 1960s to the 1980s*. New York: Routledge and Kegan Paul.

Park, Sharon. 1996. *Generational Transition wthin Korean Churches in Los Angeles*. M.A. thesis, University of California, Los Angeles.

Portes, Alejandro, and Min Zhou. 1993. "The New Second Generation: Segmented Assimilation and Its Variants." *Annals of the American Academy of Political and Social Science* 530 (November): 74–97.

Simpson, George Eaton, and J. Milton Yinger. 1972. *Racial and Cultural Minorities: An Analysis of Prejudice and Discrimination*. New York: Harper and Row.

Waters, Mary. 1990. *Ethnic Options: Choosing Identities in America*. Berkeley: University of California Press.

Weber, Max. [1930] 1992. *The Protestant Ethic and the Spirit of Capitalism*. New York: Routledge.

6

The Traditional
as Alternative

The GenX Appeal of the
International Church of Christ

Gregory C. Stanczak

We've got to address the issue of what the 'X' is going to stand for in Generation X. Will they be exploited introverts, or exploring extroverts? Will they possess an exaggerated sense of self, or an exaltation of God? Will they have explosive tempers or be examples of control? Will they have expanding waistlines or will they be expanding the kingdom? Will they be exclusive in their race and culture, or exert influence against prejudice? Ultimately, the children of the church are either going to extinguish God's movement or exceed all expectations. The call of the hour to the church is to be excellent in everything. Let us pray together!

—Kip McKean

The words of Kip McKean, the founder of the International Church of Christ (ICC), reveal, with zeal and humor, the characteristics needed by Generation X for the success of the church. The ICC is an innovative, rapidly expanding restoration movement that has thrived amid allegations of mind control and excessive authority.[1] This success may seem difficult to accomplish when we are faced with a new generation characterized as alienated, apathetic, agnostic, and atomistic. Yet this conservative religious movement, based on commitment, conformity, and close community, is one of many securing a foothold in society and among this younger generation. While "too much religion" fuels the concerns of parents, friends, and academic institutions, that same degree of religion also provides the missing elements of a satisfying life to many new believers.

Over the past year, I have spent time attending services in the Los Angeles

113

region of the ICC (LACC)[2] as well as taking part in special events and interviewing members, known as disciples. The primary goal of this chapter is to describe this dynamic and complex new religious movement, which has previously eluded much academic analysis. To focus this description, I will detail several dominant themes that I see as pertinent to a better understanding of the group. These are the daily, lived experience of religious convictions and the ways in which these are constructed and maintained; the negotiations, acceptance, and utilization of the remarkable racial and ethnic integration among disciples; and finally, the appropriation of popular culture and technology. I will argue that through the religious authority of members' deep convictions, and the ways in which this is structured and maintained, a unique form of not only religious but also racial identification occurs. Throughout this process I argue that popular culture is an essential organizational tool, religious conduit, and lubricant for the smooth transition of identity, the construction of community, and the evangelization of others.

The ICC in Context

The origins of what is now known as the ICC date back to 1967, when radical commitment standards and recruitment practices were first developed and employed at a denominational Church of Christ in Florida. Though largely successful where implemented, these "discipling" principles caused splits with the denominational Churches of Christ over doctrine and practices, including the confession of sins, peer pressure, overriding authority, and the use of excessive control. Kip McKean, the group's founder and current world evangelist, was introduced to this recruitment style in 1976. For years, McKean revitalized struggling ministries in denominational Churches of Christ; however, older members of these churches were not as open to change and often rejected this new style of conviction and practice. This gulf between young and old members resulted in many divided churches. McKean eventually found a base from which to organize a movement in which all members were expected to commit to the strict ideals and lifestyle principles of this form of Christianity. Beginning on June 1, 1979, an initial group of thirty members gathered in a living room in the Boston suburb of Lexington, Massachusetts.

A worldwide ministry was envisioned and set in motion in 1981 through the deployment of mission teams across America and the world. This "pillar church plan for evangelizing the world" has planted ICC churches in strategic worldwide metropolitan areas, from which larger geographical areas are still being successfully evangelized. In 1992 the organizational center of the movement moved from Boston to Los Angeles, where it remains today. It was also at this time that the movement adopted its current name, the

International Church of Christ, to reflect its widening demographics and mission goals. By 1994 the ICC had become so successful in worldwide growth that it implemented the Evangelization Proclamation, which promises plantings for every country with a city population over 100,000 by the year 2000. Today, by most recent church accounts, the ICC is composed of 358 churches in 155 countries worldwide.[3]

The ICC is best characterized as a Christian restoration movement that is earnestly attempting to reapply the Christian standards of the first-century church to create the one and only true church in the contemporary world.[4] In doing so, it navigates the waters of contemporary culture and addresses the social concerns and stereotypes facing youth today, while at the same time maintaining strict biblical standards. McKean's statement at the beginning of this chapter captures the values and qualities the ICC sees as important for this new generation. These commitments are upheld through comprehensive interpersonal and organizational networks as well as through the cultivation of a lifestyle that attempts to relate to those in the secular world. The combination has worked.

A Church without a Church

Before, unless my mom woke me up, I wouldn't think about going [to church]. Just sit there for an hour listening to something I didn't understand. . . . You look around and every one is not into it. It looked like a funeral. People half singing. You could tell people were just there because they felt guilty that they had to be there. Then I went to our church and first of all I saw people that wanted to be there. Young people going!

—*James*

The LACC is definitely not a "funeral church." In fact, there is little that resembles the ideas conjured up by the word *church*. Physically speaking, the only time I attended an LACC function in a church building was for Friday-night campus devotionals, and even these were held in a large, all-purpose room in the church's basement. The majority of the time I found myself attending services in hotel conference rooms, elementary schools, and outdoor parks. When several regions of the LACC get together for services, they use the lavish, higher-capacity Wiltern or Shrine Theaters, the Los Angeles Convention Center, or most recently, the Rose Bowl in Pasadena. The LACC is less conventional in its venues for special events, renting out an ice hockey arena or an industrial park warehouse south of Los Angeles. Since many of these spaces are rented or donated, there is often no set or predictable pattern of where services will be held. This left me standing in front of a dark and empty building several times, but partly due to the church's extensive social networks, this does not seem to be a major problem for the LACC. One account of LACC lore recalls that one Saturday night around midnight, the Sunday service location had to be changed. The next morning, by the time service began, not a single disciple was missing.

Once inside the location, no other physical religious symbolism is used. A table by the door displays the ICC's books, study guides, and other publications. Inside the room where the service will be held, crosses, candles, or robes are replaced by only verbal cues about the "power of the cross." Disciples show up to midweek services in whatever they are wearing. Many come straight from work in polo shirts emblazoned with company names, while others arrive in shorts, T-shirts, and baseball caps. On Sundays, however, everyone is at their best in suits, ties, dresses, and pantsuits.

The interaction is electric before an LACC service. In all of my visits to services and events, there has been an overabundance of energy. People are casually walking around, giving hugs, shrieking at the sight of friends, and introducing visitors. Once the service begins, visitors are easy to pick out, since they are the only people not singing, clapping, and waving hellos from across the room. The singing is usually unaccompanied but very energetic and often includes clapping, finger snapping, and sometimes even gestures. During the announcements, there is often cheering, more clapping, and laughs. Even once the sermon, or "lesson," begins, the atmosphere is interactive. Disciples dig through backpacks for their Bibles, notepads, and pens. Notes are scribbled and scriptures jotted down for later reflection, as the evangelist begins to build the emotion and impact of his lesson.[5] Humor is almost always used at some point of the lesson, but the underlying tone is serious. Typically, by the end of a lesson, a challenge is made by the evangelist that lays out ways for disciples to improve their lives or be more productive. In driving the point home, the evangelist can verbally attack the congregation in calling them to higher commitment levels or increased participation and action in getting out their message. The evangelist at one of the first lessons I heard was chastising those who had lost their zeal and developed a "hard heart." His face reddened, veins popped in his neck, and he was waving his arms, yelling, "I'm looking at exit signs all around this room! If you don't want to be here, get up and leave now!" During all of this, I sat cowering in my seat as disciples called out their encouragement. "Tell it!" "C'mon!" "Amen!" These dramatic and volatile lessons always end with positive encouragement about the challenges posed and the ability of disciples to attain these goals. Discussing the lessons after service, disciples often comment about how "impacted" or "fired up" they got by the lesson.

Like James at the beginning of this section, many told me the contrast between an LACC service and the type of services with which they were familiar was striking. Not many mentioned the physical space, but most commented on the interaction and emotion. For some, this correlated directly with their spiritual understanding or sense of what religion had to offer. Brittany described her experience growing up by relating the actions of the congregation to her understanding of God. "When I would go to church I was like, God's not here. It was really weird. Even though I was a little girl I felt that. 'Cause I saw people not loving each other. I saw people gossiping, or things. I felt like, 'Well, God didn't do that.'" But after her first visit to the LACC, Brittany called her mom and said, "Mom, you'll never guess! . . . I went to church today and God was there!"

Disciples take this correlation between God "being there" and the fellowship of the community very seriously. At least among the disciples I spoke with, the focus on the ways in which religion is carried out in individual and community interaction indicates that disciples who shunned religion in their teen or adult life were not necessarily doing so because of a lack of faith. More commonly they expressed how they did not accept the institutions that embodied that faith. Repeatedly disciples complained about the perceived hypocrisy of their past church experiences. In contrast, they now interpret the way they live their lives to be examples of what true Christian lives should be. When effectively maintained, this dispels the feeling of hypocrisy many experienced in the past. Jesse remembers saying, "'Wow, here's a group of people who are really living this out.' 'Cause I already hung out with them, not just on Sunday and I know they're living this and I'm not." Living the life of a disciple is clearly more significant to members than the physical church or representations. In fact, these symbols often conjure up past connections to unfulfilling religious experiences. But living this every day does not come without significant time commitment, sacrifice, and effort.

Being a Disciple

Q: What's a typical day like for you?

James: I have quiet time every morning . . . like this morning I was up at 6:30. Read [the Bible] about an hour, that's kinda standard . . . and it gives me a lot more energy, I'm a lot more joyful . . . then I do other sorts of church things. I usually set up times with others to go out for what we call "sharing," inviting others to church. Then I'll have uh, Bible studies with students who are interested probably three times a week. . . . There's services on Sunday and then Wednesday. Sometimes we have other Friday devotionals. . . . I rarely watch TV or sit around the house, which is actually better. I keep myself busy.

"I keep myself busy" is an understatement when we start to unpack the integrated place of religion in the everyday lives of disciples. Most disciples are similar to James and keep busy with church commitments, but they also transfer these high levels of devotion to the secular tasks, jobs, or schoolwork they have.[6] Even social time is filled with fellowship between disciples, sharing their faith, and highly regulated dating of other disciples. While time management is often challenging, member support is constantly available to help maintain religious focus. For example, photocopied forms were distributed at one service as guidelines for structuring time during any given week. This guidance from the church and especially from others is seen as a core element of being a disciple. As Jesse told me, "You can't be a Lone Ranger Christian."

The high levels of involvement disciples have in each other's lives stems from their commitment to "discipling." Discipling is a one-to-one mentoring relationship found between all members. Every disciple has a discipler to whom he or she remains "accountable." A discipler knows the individual hurdles that each of his or her disciples faces daily. These can include actions like premarital sex, masturbation, drinking alcohol, smoking, and thoughts like lust, pride, and laziness. Being overweight even became an indiscretion seen as a lack of personal discipline.[7] It is the discipler's responsibility to find out how these hurdles are being overcome and if daily spiritual tools, like early-morning "quiet times," reading the Bible, prayer, and sharing the faith with others, are being practiced. While this personal authority over other disciples is a point often cited in much of the controversy surrounding the ICC, disciples see this practice as indispensable and not as authoritarian as critics depict.[8] Most describe it as an intense friendship that helps them stay true to their faith. Erica explained the extent to which not only her discipling relationship but the extended community of disciples helps her maintain her commitment:

> All of my friends were so superficial. Now that I'm part of this church, every single one of them I can call. Yeah, name it, hundreds. I like that family. I know somebody's got my back. Really, there's like no downfall to it at all. Plus they want to see me do good. They want to see me succeed.... [At other churches], if I show up on Sunday or if I don't show up on Sunday it doesn't matter. Nobody knows. Its just like a bland version of ours.... Over here, I miss like one Sunday and they're over. "How's everything going?" Like they care!

Tran described the relationship somewhat differently, acknowledging the daily challenges and struggles inherent in it. He compared discipling to training for a marathon.

Training is the thing that's going to save you. And to understand God you have to be trained. And how are you going to do that? Having a relationship with other disciples who will call you higher. The reason we have people in our lives who are older spiritually, and all these different qualities that people have, calls you higher. A lot of people might think, oh, well, it's chosen by the leadership who disciples you and that stuff. No. God puts these people for a reason. I've found that every relationship that I've had, I've learned from. I learned what I needed to learn.

From what other disciples have told me, Tran's description captures the experience well. Discipling is usually a relationship between people who are or become friends. But the challenges that the disciplers impose on their disciples adds a component of work or personal struggle. As with a trainer, one sometimes likes the growth or development more than the process it takes to get there. Disciples attribute this reluctance to their "prideful" natures that, when unchecked, are sinful. Marcia expressed this more directly: "It's funny because sometimes I'll fight it. Like, 'I'll tell this sister later.' And finally when I do it's like, 'Why didn't I do that earlier today?'"

These discipling relationships not only foster spiritual growth, they are also crucial in constructing community. Beyond the single unit of one discipling relationship are multiple layers that continue in a pyramidal network of checks and balances of personal action, belief, and struggle. Each discipler is also discipled by someone else. Part of the accountability in this second round of relationships is making sure that the original discipler is maintaining the spiritual needs of his or her disciples as well as his or her own. As such, a web of social cohesion and authority locates each disciple, regardless of time within the church, into a uniform standard of accountability.[9] This not only buffers against competing worldviews and apostasy, it also cultivates a community bond of mutual respect, strengthened interpersonal skills, and an understanding of shared responsibilities and expectations.[10]

Discipling, weekly services, midweek services, Bible talks, quiet times, fellowship, strict codes of personal behavior, and prayer all combine to form the necessary building blocks in helping shape and merge the wide array of religious, educational, socioeconomic, and ethnic backgrounds of disciples into a unified Christian community.[11] The common purpose becomes making new disciples and maintaining one's own personal relationship with God. Many explained that only through a close relationship with God could other problems be managed. Chad summed this up in terms many evangelical churches would echo. "The greatest commandment of all is to love God with all your heart, with all your soul, and the second is to love people and if you have those standards then everything else is easy to follow." Anna also discussed all else falling into place: "I never get confused because I know that I have the Bible and everything I do is according to the Bible."

Chad and Anna's freedom from confusion through reliance on faith and the community of disciples suggests a clarity that was not available to them through secular means. The LACC repeatedly reminds disciples of the immorality, violence, and divorce plaguing the secular world, and suggests resolution through the church. Research on new religious movements have discussed the effects of the dissolution of moral absolutism, social fragmentation, and the increase of pluralism, pointing to a cultural malaise that while empowering to some is confusing to others. Some are satisfied with a bricolage of diversely influenced and personally constructed belief systems, both secular and spiritual.[12] But many are unable to reconcile this with other aspects of their lives. Jesse recalled his life before becoming a disciple: "I didn't feel authentic. I'd feel like I had two different lives. One that my mom knows about where I always get straight As, respectful, go to church and the one that some of my friends saw, like I just mentioned [looking at pornography]." He saw this as the biggest change in his life since becoming a disciple. "You know for the first time in my life, since I'm a Christian, I don't feel like I have a dual, a divided life. You know, 'some people see this, some people see that,' you know. People get to see everything." Jesse was unable to pull together these conflicting identities on his own. But with the church, he was able to find a community of people with whom he could be open about his struggles and develop a unified sense of identity and purpose. Other disciples, like Jesse, have chosen this highly structured, demanding, committed community to make sense of pervasive ambiguity and a conflicted sense of self. This becomes clearer when we turn to the ways in which a strict Christian identity helps navigate one of the most ambiguous and contested areas in society, racial and ethnic identity.

Race and Ethnicity

All the other churches I had ever gone to, it was always . . . everybody was Latin or we were the only Latin family there. And I come here and I walk in and they're speaking English and I hear them translating, you know, they have little translations in Korean, Chinese, Spanish. So that right off the bat, it was a good thing.

—*Jesse*

The ICC is a pioneering movement with regards to pursuing and maintaining a racially representative congregation both in Los Angeles and around the

120

world. Religious communities today remain one of the few areas in which segregation (albeit self-segregation) continues unquestioned. While change is occurring, it is a slow process. Religion is embedded in and influenced by ethnic practices, cultural traditions, and common experience to the extent that some have argued religion and culture are synonymous.[13] To a certain extent, this may explain why ethnically homogenous religious communities persist; they retain and transmit a sense of an individual's cultural identity in an increasingly pluralistic society. Therefore, when we are faced with a multiracial or multiethnic community, complex questions arise. The integrated following of the LACC represents this change well. While this integration may be open to several interpretations, I will focus on the ways in which disciples express their experience of it. I will focus on the attraction to potential converts, the process of individual ethnic identity transformation, and the actively pursued manifestation of a biblical mandate.

A recent survey taken by the ICC indicates that in the greater Los Angeles Church, the racial breakdown was 19 percent African American, 10 percent Asian/Pacific Islander, 29 percent Latin, and 35 percent white (with 7 percent other). In the south region, where I conducted this research, the congregation was 19 percent African American, 11 percent Asian/Pacific Islander, 33 percent Latin, and 31 percent white (6 percent other). As if this were not physically noticeable or perceived, disciples were repeatedly reminded from the pulpit that this was a unique phenomenon. Most disciples I spoke with noticed the diverse congregation or had internalized these reminders. James said, "It's multiracial. It reflects the demographics of the city. Its not like it's a one race church and I think that blows people away."

Like Jesse, whose quote opened this section, many of the disciples who were surprised by the composition of the congregation had come from a church background that fit the more standard, homogeneous model. Michael said, "I came from an all-black church, you know. And that was just the way it was." This reality made sense growing up. But for some, this model did not correspond with either their secular life experiences or their conception of a Christian community. In contrast, the LACC was vastly different. Michelle noticed this as well at her first woman's Bible talk, but was more impressed with the way the women related to each other.

The one thing I noticed is that I walked into this woman's house and there were all these different nationalities. All different kinds of people and I remember there was a black woman, an Asian woman, a Latin woman, a tall, huge white woman, and I wasn't really too impressed. I thought it was kind of interesting. Like, wow, these are all different people and they live together. But one thing I still remember was that there was a plate that was covered in the kitchen and I said, "Oh, what's that?" And she said, "Oh that's just my meal for my roommate. She hasn't come home yet." And that blew me away.

For Michelle, while it was interesting that these women would live together, it was more remarkable that they actually looked out for each other. In today's society, where many of us work, shop, and take classes side by side with people from all backgrounds, physical integration may not appear to be an unusual occurrence. But keeping a meal for someone of a different background expresses a deeper relationship often not even found with those of our own race or ethnicity.[14]

The integrated following of the LACC was an initial attraction for some disciples, but not all disciples viewed this positively. Some expressed their prejudices and fears before converting. Chad, who emigrated from the Philippines at a young age, felt strong social bonds and ethnic allegiances toward Filipinos and Asians in general. He told me how a disciple at a video arcade at school met him: "If he wasn't Filipino, if he was white, black, Latino, any other racial background, I wouldn't be in the church. I was really more into Asian things, being involved with Asians, just a lot of partying with just Asians. And if he was black I wouldn't probably have gone to the church." Chad mentioned that he was impressed by how the disciple had walked and talked and presented a "sharp" image. This, coupled with a Filipino identity, made the disciple an influential role model. Chad's experience suggests that a profound transformation of ethnic identification occurs at some point in becoming a disciple. This process makes sense for those like Jesse, who felt out of place in a single race or ethnically homogeneous church. But religious ideals or a past faith community had not influenced Chad's sense of ethnic identity. Chad was agnostic before becoming a disciple. While he could not express exactly how this transformation occurred, he suggested it was the church. "I never felt this happy in my life before. And I never had any white best friends. I never had any black best friends. I mean it's just the church itself, the Kingdom. Just how you build your relationship with them."

This experience is more of a struggle for those who felt a great affinity for their ethnic identity and how that was expressed as part of their religious upbringing. Ismael, whose family is from El Salvador, felt the weight of his decision heavily. He told me that growing up, "I was Catholic before and uh, I felt pretty strongly about my religion too. And mostly because, mostly because of the ethnic part of it. I was Hispanic and when I went to church I usually went to a Spanish service sometimes and it was good for me to see a lot of Hispanics there, you know, it gave me a sense of identity." Ismael came from a background where ethnicity and religion were entwined in generations and even centuries of cultural tradition. For Ismael, this link between his religious upbringing and cultural identity could not survive when faced with the scriptural challenges that disciples posed. Ismael struggled with his ethnic ties to his faith. However, the biblical interpretations he learned through the ICC's study series solidified his decision to become a disciple. He then had to deal with the repercussions and the pain it caused his family: "My dad respected my decision. My mom did not accept the decision. She just thought that I had betrayed, not only the religion, but the family, culture, and I didn't want to do that! She was very disappointed and disagreed with the decision and I didn't want to do that. But I knew that deep down inside, this was the best thing for me. And so that's why I insisted that I do this, you know."

Naseen also struggled with letting down her parents' cultural and religious expectations. Naseen emigrated from West Asia to Los Angeles with her parents when she was seven. Becoming a Christian and renouncing her Muslim faith was not as difficult for her as it had been for Ismael to change his faith. She discussed the mosque much as other disciples had discussed bad prior church experiences: the people seemed fake, and the religion did not give her the structure she was searching for in her life. Beyond not having a strong connection to her faith, she had also distanced herself from her ethnic community in Los Angeles. She explained, "It's so funny because it's my culture, but I'm so Americanized that I just feel like an American, and I am!" Even though her parents knew about her assimilation away from Islam and her ethnic background, this decision still struck a blow. It has now been several years, but her mother still feels the burden of her daughter's choice. Naseen said, "Once in a while my mom's like, 'Oh my God! You've become a Christian! How am I going to live this down? And you're not going to go to heaven! And . . . ' Oh my gosh, I'm sorry Mom. Because she feels like, she's the mother and she's responsible for my soul and she needs to be the one to take me to heaven. So now she thinks that I'm not going to go to heaven [Naseen laughs]."

The strong reactions of parents suggest a generational difference in the internalization and importance of religious and ethnic identity. Through these painful transitions and years of rebuilding family ties and/or reconciling internal prejudices toward other ethnic groups, individual identities can dramatically shift. The religious identity becomes primary. Disciples discuss how their primary goal after being baptized often becomes baptizing their families. Through this process, ethnicity is not lost completely, however. The LACC expresses the ethnic trends in Los Angeles and acknowledges the diversity in the disciples' backgrounds. I attended a campus devotional in the foothills east of Los Angeles, where the church recently bought an old mission site. For dinner, we gathered around a picnic area where colored lights were strung from the trees over tables of *carne asada* and steaming tortillas. After dinner, a piñata was hoisted up into the trees while mariachi music blared from stereo speakers. On another occasion, a disciple told me the church had asked various members to volunteer to translate the Great Commission into their native or family language. At the service, a variety of translations were recited, including one in an Inuit dialect.

This retention of ethnicity is found at the individual level as well. Most disciples I spoke with seemed to retain aspects of their ethnic identity, but as a member of the church they perceived its importance differently. I asked Ismael, who had felt a strong sense of Latino identity in the Catholic church, if he felt he sacrificed part of that identity by becoming a disciple. He replied, "No. Honestly no. I still have that Latino identity. I mean, I just came back from a trip to El Salvador and you know for the last four years I haven't been in the Catholic church but I've been speaking Spanish here and there and I listen to the radio in Spanish once and a while, just so I won't forget it. And I was able to communicate still over there. And the funny thing is, it seems that most people there aren't even Catholic [smiling]. They're like Protestant or this or that." Ismael's Latino identity was not compromised, in his view. In fact, in a subtle way, he realized that in his home culture, the ties that used to bind Salvadorian identity with Catholicism were fraying.

Juan also struggled with his Latin identity as a source of personal and political pride. However, he struck a balance between this identity and the priorities of being a disciple. "For a while I would be going after the positive Latino role model. And I still want to be some positive role model, but that's not what it's all about. It's about more you're waging your spiritual battle. Heaven and eternity or hell, you know. Getting that bigger perspective. . . . You know if anything. I mean I have to watch it for myself. Not to be too Soul Latino. . . . So I gotta be like, yeah, I'm Latino. I'm a disciple first. . . . But I do want to say this is who I am. This is my background. This is what I eat, you know." Juan's statement addresses the priority that his religious identity now has, without diminishing his pride in his heritage. Subsuming one's ethnicity under a religious standard has consequences for the individual—for example, affecting perceived salvation—but also is interpreted by some to have a secular practicality as well. For example, Juan went on to say that a strong Christian identity is the only way he sees that will adequately provide solutions to the Latino community. From his experience, social and political organizations fracture the community more than they help it: "I think, if anything, I realize that as far as being a good model for Latinos, I'm like, man, the only way I'm gonna win them over is through Christianity and becoming a disciple because these political organizations, they're at each other, you know? They're not, they're either local power or you know, I mean causing divisions among

Americans and even causing divisions among themselves. It's not, that's not going to win them over."

Juan sees a greater social power on a community level for his new identity. Michael, however, takes advantage of the integrated following and utilizes it as a tool for evangelizing. Michael explained that being part of an integrated community provides an opportunity for him to improve his skills in reaching out to other racial and ethnic groups.

> We all have this foundation that if you love God you have to love one another. And I can ask one of the disciples anything about their past, or about their lives. You know, what's it like to be white? I don't know. I've never lived that kind of life. And I've done that, you know. I've asked them, so what's it like to be a white girl? Or what's it like to be an Asian guy? And they'll talk about it. Well, you know, it's like this and I grew up like that. Different ones of us came from different places.... Um, so I really try to take a hold of that and use that when I'm talking to other people who aren't in the church. And really understanding where they're coming from based on what I've heard from disciples.

The practicality in using ethnic experiences to make more Christians is found not only in the interpersonal experiences of individual disciples. It is a strategy realized at the most fundamental level of maintaining a blended congregation. ICC leaders have expressed that their intention is to have each church reflect the demographics of their community. They see this as inseparable from the biblical call to make disciples of all nations. For example, the community surrounding the sector that I studied has a large Asian population, but the congregation, as the statistics above show, does not have a proportionate amount of Asians. To rectify this, an Asian ministry was created to invigorate greater outreach to and successful retention of Asian visitors. Asians from other ministries in and around Los Angeles were recruited to move to this sector and start this ministry. I asked Derrick, an Asian involved in the ministry, why it is important to have an Asian ministry. He said,

> I mean, Koreans hang out with Koreans. Chinese hang out with Chinese. Very, very committed to their churches.... I'll say, do you know what the Bible says about that? Talks about how all nations gotta get together. Not just all Korean, not just all Chinese or Filipino. But whites, blacks, Latinos, all that stuff. You gotta come to the church here and see what I mean.... That's been a major challenge, is tradition. We still have faith that we're gonna baptize a lot of Asians. But you know, whoever we get, whether it's Asian or Latino—we've even been baptizing Latinos, man! And the Latinos have been baptizing Asians [laughs]!

Derrick's comments reveal the significance of race and ethnicity in reaching out to all nations. Since most sectors of the LACC cover several geographic communities, it is inevitable that, if the recruitment plan is truly implemented, a blended congregation will result. Pursuing and maintaining a multiracial following in Los Angeles carries with it the benefit of attracting others, as mentioned above. But the primary motivation disciples give for this is not the attractiveness of the community but a regulating apparatus derived from the Bible. Members have said that if one group is underrepresented, it may indicate that they are not reaching out to that group enough or in the right ways. Specific racially targeted ministries attempt to more effectively reach "all nations."

While I have focused on the importance of ethnicity and race in the LACC, Derrick's comment about "whoever we get" indicates the priority of religious conversion over racial or ethnic diversity. Fundamentally, this is the overriding common link between these different backgrounds. The disciple's newfound religious identity and aspirations subsume ethnicity or race. For some this process develops more smoothly than for others, but eventually and to varying degrees, all disciples have placed their religious identity first.[15] This may be obvious to any group intent upon evangelizing as many people as possible. But the role of race and religion is much more complex with regard to individual identity and requires future attention in increasing numbers of religious organizations.

The integrated following of the LACC emerges from organizational orchestration as well as individual introspection and acceptance. This difference is easily embraced by some, while for others it entails struggling with cultural, familial, social, and personal beliefs and traditions. Regardless of the process of coming to accept this integration, or perhaps because of this, racial and ethnic integration is acknowledged as an attribute that sets the LACC apart from other churches. This attribute in turn is seen as a byproduct of being a disciple. In other words, it is perceived that any socially or culturally constructed differences due to skin type or ethnicity can only be ameliorated and superceded through the strong commitment of being a disciple. The notion that all disciples are the same regardless of race or ethnicity, coupled with the distinction that as a church, it is different in accomplishing an integrated religious community, reinforces the LACC's perceived status of being the one true church.[16] However, this distinction, or being seen and labeled as different, also holds the potential threat of alienation and may result in barriers to evangelization, a central focus of being a disciple. In order to mediate the differences between being a disciple and relating to the society at large, the LACC and the ICC as a whole have turned to popular culture and technology.

Popular Culture

We teach a lifestyle—relating to people in all areas. Like in the Middle East they have to deal with hard-core persecution. But here we need to deal with TV and movies and Starbucks. Being a Christian is a lifestyle, and we have to be able to relate [raising his Starbucks paper cup for emphasis].

—Derrick

The ICC aggressively takes advantage of contemporary society's tools in getting out its message. This, along with its unique historical emergence, young following, and somewhat mythical notoriety, has garnered the ICC a spot in the ranks of late twentieth-century culture. In *Alt.culture: An A-to-Z Guide to the '90s—Underground, Online, and Over-the-counter,* Steven Daly and Nathaniel West (1995) list *Church of Christ* along with other *C*s like *CD-ROMs, crack,* and *cybercafés.* As I said above, there exists a delicate balance between contemporary culture and a restoration movement looking to the first century for codes and guidelines for religious beliefs and actions. But the ICC does not shrink from the challenge. The most striking example of this is the ICC's video news journal, the *Kingdom News Network,* or KNN. Utilizing superb graphics, contemporary music sound tracks, and seamless production quality, KNN is broadcast periodically on large screens at ICC services. The format is similar to many of the popular tabloid news programs in the secular media. Each program includes feature stories, a "Spotlight" segment that selects several disciples in the news, "Mission Minutes" that detail the work being done around the world, and the "Nations Countdown" of how many nations have churches and how many are still "waiting." The moderators—Anthony, an Asian-American man, and Sonia, a white South African woman—have even exchanged high fives after delivering the journal's sign-off line: "The best news you'll ever hear."[17]

KNN was created to fill a void after a difficult period in the ICC's history. One of the churches in Indianapolis split from the ICC, reportedly over issues of congregational autonomy. This was during a time when the church had begun to expand rapidly throughout the world, at times pulling resources and spiritual leaders from struggling domestic churches. One of the ways the ICC recovered from this church split and loss of disciples was to try to rectify the lacking sense of a common identity and a unified focus on the mission of the movement. KNN was created to fulfill that purpose and acknowledge the accomplishments of the disciples worldwide. As Justin, a university student in the LACC, explained,

I think the real intent of . . . KNN is to unify the church. It's to help [pause] because we are so scattered everywhere. And being in L.A. you get to see and hear a lot of things. But if you're in Tucson, Arizona, if you're in El Paso, Texas, if you're in Lincoln, Nebraska, if you're in Johannesburg, if you're in Kiev, if you're in some place and you're just a small church of thirty or a hundred, you may not be able to see the whole big picture of what's going on around the world or even some inspirational stories of the faith of some people in the church.

Justin sums up the primary function of KNN well. However, other functions are also at work. Disciples view these broadcasts with a lot of enthusiasm, often cheering, clapping, and calling out to the giant screens. Naseen told me how she felt when watching a KNN broadcast: "Oh my gosh, its so amazing! . . . It really moves me, like emotionally. And sometimes I just cry, I mean, wow. Look at all these people sacrificing. Like there are disciples in Bangladesh. And they get baptized in those, like do you know those gasoline cans? I mean I'm like look at that! People are everywhere around the world. What am I doing!" I heard this sentiment both from disciples and from the evangelists at services. They use the stories of personal sacrifice and commitment around the world to reanalyze the extent to which their commitment and actions show sacrifice in the daily lives at home. In this role, KNN can be a powerful conduit of religious motivation. Justin agreed, "Stuff like that makes you step back and think, okay, what am I doing? . . . Being in L.A., your heart sort of stray[s] because your life is so busy with things and you may forget your first purpose in life or your love or wanting to seek and save the lost like Jesus did." KNN's anchor, Anthony, saw the other side of the coin as well: "It really gets out to small churches where they don't have the fellowship to hear the good news from other places." By doing so, it draws these disciples into the ICC fold and encourages them to persevere.

Beyond motivation and information, others draw strength, reassurance, and a deepening sense of faith by seeing worldwide examples and the global growth of the movement. In this role, KNN was described by one disciple as replicating biblical examples of the timeless need for visual verification as the basis for faith. "'Show us something so that we may believe,'" Tom explained, quoting the Pharisees desire for visual proof. "I think KNN really does a good job of that." He recalled being impressed with a clip that showed an African witch doctor eventually succumbing to the disciples' preaching. Tom's wife, Kelly, went on to discuss the global scope portrayed on KNN and the reassurance she gains: "It's incredible. Seeing that really shows that this is something more than just man. It really must be God's movement to spread so quickly all over the world. And knowing that you can go anywhere in the world, Italy, Milan, Germany, and knock on any disciple's door and you could just walk in and stay with them. It's like a big family." In both cases, scenes from KNN strengthen faith through videotaped, virtual examples. It also fosters a sense of community, or "family," to the extent that Kelly felt she could knock on any disciple's door throughout the world and be welcome.

KNN has broader cultural functions as well. As I mentioned, most episodes resemble secular news journals. One special episode broke this mold to parody the formats of *Larry King Live* and a late-night talk show. These formats and the contemporary music sound tracks that accompany the broadcasts and special events of the church link the strict religious implications of the church's message to the cultural context that most disciples experience around them. For example, in the past year the LACC has used Green Day, Paula Cole, the Goo Goo Dolls, Sly and the Family Stone, Elastica, Alanis Morrisette, Bruce Springsteen, and Crystal Method as both background music and sermon topics.

Beyond video and music, more blatant forms of consumer culture have crept into the church's frame of reference. One lead-in to the Nations Countdown had Sonia proclaiming with a smile that "we're now in more nations than McDonald's." This trickles down to the individual ways the ICC is discussed. In one of my earliest interviews, James proudly informed me that "the church is in like 110 countries now. Almost 300 churches. That's in like fifteen years. And that's unprecedented. Like even Coca-Cola is only in like sixty countries." These consumer reference points indicate what disciples, as members of and reaching out to Generation X, see as sociocultural yardsticks of success. It is assumed, and most likely correctly assumed, that references to the success of Coca-Cola and McDonald's means something to the culturally aware listener.

This contextualization through consumer culture, music, video, and, as Derrick said, "lifestyle" integrates disciples on a cultural level, back into the world from which they came. More important, from what disciples have expressed, this pop-cultural ease extends as a tool in evangelizing or sharing. Monica said that this is important to make the church palatable, or as disciples say, "relatable," to visitors: "I think they do it to make people feel less scared. Like if I were to walk in and see a bunch of people that I had nothing in common with and nobody that I could relate to you know, I would really think I couldn't handle this. . . . We're not a bunch of weirdos. We're cool normal people too, we just have God in our lives." And as cool, normal people with God in their lives, disciples take the initiative of cultural appropriation and apply it daily. Secular music is not sacred only when played at a church-related function or service; disciples make the popular sacred every day. Karen said, "Even like secular songs, some of them are love songs, that you can see as a love song to God or from God."

KNN and Starbucks are not the only links to contemporary culture. The ICC went online with their official website in 1996 (www.icoc.org). Today the website provides general information about the church and its mission, charts on church growth, the Nations Countdown, and a directory of churches and contacts around the world, accessible through an interactive world map. Disciples may download texts for Bible studies or check out church news in their home countries. During a recent planting of a church in Peru, disciples sent and uploaded e-mails of each day's progress. Links, provided through the home page, will send you around the virtual Kingdom of up to fifty-five other church websites. The LACC site (losangeles.icoc.org) is impressive. The home page includes an animated picture of Los Angeles from the ocean to the Hollywood Hills to downtown. A surfer, the La Brea tar pits, and of course a freeway are just a few of the graphics on this site. Links to a Los Angeles directory provides contacts for any of forty-four sectors in the greater Los Angeles region. Disciples have told me that having a website indicates that the church is in touch with the advancements in the world and is able to keep up with necessary aspects of their social reality.

Tapping these ubiquitous sources of popular culture and secular lifestyles to attract people to a conservative, religious message may seem counterintuitive on the surface. Yet for the ICC this tactic works. Ernst Troelsch argued at the beginning of this century that religions must adapt to the surrounding culture in order to survive. Some current scholars at the end of this century argue the same.[18] But other contemporary scholars of religion argue that a delicate balance exists between the accommodation of cultural forms and the accommodation of cultural values, both of which have the tendency to lead to decline.[19] The full extension of this argument is that the stricter the church, the more it will grow. The ICC, however, has been innovative in its approach, maintaining strong doctrine while appropriating the forms, styles, and technology of secular culture, from its inception. Popular or secular culture has therefore acted as the church's mode of operation all along. Rather than the ICC relinquishing power to cultural cues, it is perceived as harnessing and transforming those cultural cues as its tool. For scholars of social movements and culture, the appropriation of secular cultural values, forms, and styles, such as mediated technology and music, is useful in "framing" a message and providing cultural continuity between the group and the larger worldview.[20] In fact, it has been argued that these links or frames to popular culture may actually strengthen the claims made by the group that uses them.[21]

Summary

Establishing a firm belief system and coupling that with an interpersonal, organizational structure of accountability and authority has been successful for the LACC in maintaining religious identity, at least over short periods of time.[22] Accepting that belief as a lifestyle allows the authority of that system to be transferred onto other socially constructed definitions of morality, values, behavior codes, and even ethnicity. Remarkably, the LACC has been very successful in constructing a community that can agree, more than many religious and even secular organizations, on not just the idea but the reality of an ethnically integrated community. The strict religious standards in everyday life coupled with the ethnic integration of the LACC combine to strengthen the disciples' overall perception of a unified community, upholding equal standards and expectations of accountability. Even the popular culture that lamentably plagues society's values and morals has been harnessed and appropriated as a tool to reinforce religious identity and help spread the LACC's message. KNN reveals the perceived similarity of religious identity among disciples throughout the Kingdom. But this entire process of identification refers to difference as much as it refers to similarity. Therefore, the same strict behavioral codes and constant reminders about the unique integration of the movement that establish the perception of similarity also reinforce the idea that disciples are different from other churches and the rest of the world. The reason for the similarities is the same as the reason for the differences. Disciples believe they comprise the one true church of God's modern-day movement.

The LACC raises complex questions about religious identity and community, race and ethnicity, and the trend toward adapting popular cultural forms for religious ends. This is especially pertinent for those of us trying to decipher the ways in which Generation X conceptualizes religion. My experience with disciples suggests that the wholesale apathy and skepticism often seen as characteristic of this generation are actually more tactically directed at specific forms of failed social organization than at overarching religious or moral principles. The strict organizational style and accountability in the LACC has satisfied many converts' expectations that what is preached is what is practiced. This correlation between ideals and action is important to satisfy many GenX disciples' suspicions regarding religion—but the divide between religion and daily living is often erased. At least for many disciples, any overarching belief system that intends to religiously or morally shape their daily lives must challenge, incorporate, or relate to all aspects of these lives, from the songs they hear to the ethnically diverse streets they walk and even to the coffeeshops where they buy their lattes. As disciples of the LACC show, some members of Generation X have not turned away from the most basic principles of religious faith. However, their devotion comes only after a skeptical study of the ways in which religion is organized and implemented to satisfy their doubts, relate to their experiences, and ensure their perceived salvation.

Notes

1. For example, the ICC still does not have permission to organize as a student group on my campus, and yearly university sponsored programs, with titles such as "Cults on Campus," almost exclusively single out ICC recruitment and practices. Much of the criticism of the ICC can be found on the Internet, including past members' accounts of their experiences as well as reports by so-called cult networks. Rick Bauer (1994), a past disciple and leader in the ICC, has also compiled a thorough overview of articles on the ICC.

2. Uniformity across churches is fairly strictly maintained. However, my research has focused exclusively on two "sectors," similar to parishes, in Los Angeles. I will use the LACC shorthand when discussing the findings of my ethnographic research in these sectors, but I do not mean to generalize to the entire Los Angeles church in doing so. When I use the ICC shorthand I will be referring to church literature, video data, or interviews with ICC leaders that refer to the movement as a totality.

3. www.icoc.org, July 1999.

4. Based on this belief, members interchangeably use the terms *Christian* and *disciple* to delineate their exclusive status. Followers of other Christian faiths are often referred to as either "so-called Christians" or "quote, unquote Christians."

5. Only men can preach lessons (in service or Bible studies) to male and female congregations. Women have parallel roles and give lessons only when the church splits by gender for a specific service or event.

6. James, by the way, completed his bachelor's degree from a prestigious school in southern California and went on to complete a master's degree while in the church.

7. This especially became popular in the sector I was studying after one of the World Sector Leaders emotionally confessed to personally being at fault for his weight problem. Members told me that one of the female song leaders was asked to step down a couple of months after this until she could bring her weight under control.

8. See note 1 for a discussion of the controversy around the ICC.

9. Local role differentiation, regional organization, and ultimately, the global geographical breakdowns of the ICC emerge out of these one-to-one discipling rela-

tionships. For example, the region of the LACC that I studied looked over the Middle East geographical region of the world church. The leaders of the Middle East region remain accountable to the leaders of the southern region of the Los Angeles church.

10. Peter L. Berger and Thomas Luckmann (1967) discuss how shifting subjective realities involves an alternation of plausibility structures, or in other words, changing the people and things around you that make the world meaningful. The church and the awareness of shared beliefs and expectations construct a larger framework or legitimating apparatus that makes the disciple's decision appear normal or real. Much of this depends upon the significant others in one's life (138–73).

11. It has been argued that "strict" religions (those that impose substantial time commitments, stigmatization, and restricted boundaries of social interaction and personal behavior) do "more to explain individual rates of religious participation than does any standard individual-level characteristic, such as age, sex, race, religion, income, education, or marital status" (Iannaccome 1994, 1200). See also Finke and Stark 1992; Kelley 1972.

12. See Bellah et al. 1985.

13. See Toulis 1997 for an excellent discussion of religion, ethnicity, and culture. See also Lincoln and Mamiya 1990.

14. Ellis Cose (1993) has argued that in spite of the economic and social achievements and mobility of many African Americans in the middle class, they continue to experience subtle and at times overt acts of discrimination. Michelle's experience illustrates that the integration of the LACC is not purely legalistic or nominal but experienced in the relationships of all disciples.

15. Of course this doesn't account for the individuals or potential converts who did not join because of their ethnic identity or culture.

16. The elements that make the LACC different from the world are as important to defining their identity as the elements that make them similar to each other. See Jenkins 1997.

17. Sonia has been the female anchor for the majority of KNN episodes. However, more recently, Anthony's wife, Song, has returned to fill the female anchor role that she established in the first few episodes.

18. See Miller 1998 and Shibley's (1996) discussion on the "Californianization" of evangelicalism.

19. James Davison Hunter (1987) does an excellent job of teasing out the subtle forms of this among young evangelicals. Hunter, however, sees this process as gradual and not inevitable. See also Kelley 1972 and Roof 1993.

20. Ann Swidler, in her well-known "tool kit" model of culture (1986) has said that "even the most fanatical ideological movement, which seeks to remake completely

the cultural capacities of its members, will inevitably draw many tacit assumptions from the existing culture" (278). For the use of frames see Snow et al. 1986 and 1988 and Wuthnow 1994.

21. See Binder 1993 and Gitlin 1980.

22. Currently, only 32 percent of the southern region sectors where I conducted this study have been in the LACC for over five years. Twenty-four percent have been in for three to five years, 21 percent, one to two years, and 21 percent have been disciples for less than a year.

References

Bauer, Rick. 1994. *Toxic Christianity: The International Churches of Christ/Boston Movement Cult.* Bowie, Md.: Freedom House Ministries.

Bellah, Robert, et al. 1985. *Habits of the Heart: Individualism and Commitment in American Life.* Berkeley and Los Angeles: University of California Press.

Berger, Peter L., and Thomas Luckmann. 1967. *The Social Construction of Reality: A Treatise in the Sociology of Knowledge.* New York: Doubleday.

Binder, Amy. 1993. "Constructing Racial Rhetoric—Media Depictions of Harm in Heavy-Metal and Rap Music." *American Sociological Review* 58, no. 6: 753–67.

Cose, Ellis. 1993. *The Rage of a Privileged Class.* New York: HarperCollins.

Daly, Steven, and Nathaniel West. 1995. *Alt.culture: An A-to-Z Guide to the '90s—Underground, Online, and Over-the-counter.* New York: HarperCollins.

Finke, Roger, and Rodney Stark. 1992. *The Churching of America, 1776–1990: Winners and Losers in Our Religious Economy.* New Brunswick, N.J.: Rutgers University Press.

Gitlin, Todd. 1980. *The Whole World Is Watching: Mass Media in the Making and Unmaking of the New Left.* Berkeley and Los Angeles: University of California Press.

Hunter, James Davison. 1987. *Evangelicalism: The Coming Generation.* Chicago: University of Chicago Press.

Iannaccone, Laurence R. 1994. "Why Strict Churches Are Strong." *American Journal of Sociology* 99, no. 5: 1180–1204.

Jenkins, Richard. 1997. *Rethinking Ethnicity: Arguments and Explorations.* Thousand Oaks, Calif.: Sage.

Kelley, Dean. 1972. *Why Conservative Churches Are Growing.* New York: Harper and Row.

Lincoln, Eric C., and Lawrence H. Mamiya. 1990. *The Black Church in the African American Experience.* Durham, N.C.: Duke University Press.

Miller, Donald E. 1997. *Reinventing American Protestantism: Christianity in the New Millennium.* Berkeley and Los Angeles: University of California Press.

Roof, Wade Clark. 1993. *A Generation of Seekers: The Spiritual Journey of the Baby Boom Generation*. New York: HarperCollins.

Shibly, Mark A. 1996. *Resurgent Evangelicalism in the United States: Mapping Cultural Change since 1970*. Columbia: University of South Carolina Press.

Snow, David A., E. Burke Rochford Jr., Steven K. Worden, and Robert D. Benford. 1986. "Frame Alignment Processes, Micromobilization, and Movement Participation." *American Sociological Review* 51: 464–81.

Snow, David A., and Robert D. Benford. 1988. "Ideology, Frame Resonance, and Participant Mobilization." *International Social Movement Research* 1: 197–217.

Swidler, Ann. 1986. "Culture in Action: Symbols and Strategies." *American Sociological Review* 51: 273–86.

Toulis, Nicole Rodriguez. 1997. *Believing Identity: Pentecostalism and the Mediation of Jamaican Ethnicity and Gender in England*. New York: Berg.

Wuthnow, Robert. 1994. *Producing the Sacred: An Essay on Public Religion*. Urbana: University of Illinois.

Part 3

Community and Congregation

7

When Two Worlds Collide

Generation X Culture and Conservative Evangelicalism

Lori Jensen

It gave me a new view of God. . . . Everyone was just like this neo-postmodern Christian punk rock. I was like, are these people for real, or what? I don't know. It was just different. It kinda gave me a new outlook on [Christianity]. And like, 'cause all the kids would be like, oh, this is cool. They're all positive, they have this great attitude, and yet they looked totally dysfunctional! I thought that was great. Yeah, I thought that was great. I don't know. It just, it gave—it's like you think one way about something, and then someone comes around and like, they'll show you another way to look at it. It's refreshing. That's what it was for me.

—*Paige, on her first time attending Committed Christian Fellowship*

From where I sit in the large sanctuary that holds about six hundred, I see quite a motley bunch of young people. The back two rows on the right side are filled with punk rockers, complete with combat boots, piercings, chains, and spiked hair. Toward the front there is a row of skinheads, with their shaved heads, cuffed jeans, suspenders, and flight jackets. Sitting over on the left is a tattooist and his wife, along with some of their rockabilly friends. Numerous surfers are here, as well as some hippies and generically "alternative" styles. Of course, there are "normal" young people here as well (that is, without an obvious subcultural affiliation). They all are intently listening to the pastor teach about love out of the Gospel of John. The pastor, himself a surfer, is casually dressed in corduroy shorts and a short-sleeved plaid shirt. He elaborates about how love is supposed to be unconditional, expressing joy and grace, and not dependent upon how the other person responds. He says that love is ultimately embodied in the servanthood and sacrifice of Jesus.

Suddenly a whistle shrilly announces the impending roar of an approaching train, but no one seems to notice. The pastor continues preaching, the congregation continues listening. Housed next to the railroad tracks in an industrial complex in the business district of Santa Fe Springs, California, Committed Christian Fellowship appears oblivious to its unconventional surroundings. The youth instead seem to welcome the cement floors, the unplastered ceilings, and the lack of customary church trappings such as pews or stained glass. After the service, many will gather next door at the combination coffeehouse and bookstore to experience what they call "koinonia"—the Greek word for fellowship. Coffee will be poured, and alternative music will be played. People will discuss the pastor's message, the hottest surf spots, or their latest tattoos. As I listen and look around, I ask myself this question: If Jesus were on earth today, would he be dressed in a suit and tie, or would he instead be like any one of these young people?

Committed Christian Fellowship is indeed an unconventional congregation, not just in surroundings but in makeup as well. Committed is an affiliate church of the Calvary Chapel movement, and thus shares many aspects of other Calvary Chapels. The Calvary Chapel movement presently consists of over seven hundred loosely affiliated congregations that are marked by a conservative strand of evangelical Protestant Christianity, a contemporary worship style, a loose organizational structure, and a unique acceptance of popular culture. Coming out of the baby-boomer Jesus movement in the late 1960s, the original Calvary Chapel in Costa Mesa, California, under the guidance of Pastor Chuck Smith, stirred up controversy by allowing hippies into their pews—long hair, dirty jeans, bare feet, and all. Over the past thirty years, numerous churches have either spun off from or adopted themselves into Calvary Chapel. Committed Christian Fellowship might be called a grandchild of the original Costa Mesa church, in that Committed's pastor and founder, Lance Cook, is the "disciple" of Raul Ries (of Calvary Chapel Golden Springs in Diamond Bar, California), who in turn was originally converted and trained by Chuck Smith.

As the children of the baby boomers, what we would now call Generation X, have come of age in their own rebellious ways, the next generation of Calvary Chapels is continuing to meet their religious needs in a new manner. This research was originally conducted as a congregational case study in the fall of 1995. At that time I utilized participant observation, observing services, baptisms, potlucks, and other such events. I also conducted in-depth interviews, talking with both laypeople and those in leadership. In the spring of 1997, I conducted more personal interviews, in order to supplement the original research. And so, as we take a closer look at Committed Christian

Fellowship—its history, people, beliefs, rituals, and organization—we will see how and why this new generation of the Calvary Chapel movement is drawing Generation X youth through an alternative take on Christianity.

I. Portrait of Committed Christian Fellowship

Alternative History: From Surf Shop to Warehouse

Committed Christian Fellowship began as a small Bible study group over fifteen years ago at a surfboard shop owned and operated by a young businessman and surfer, Lance Cook. Although Lance had been raised as a Christian and regularly practiced his faith, he was at that time "by no means a spiritual giant." Nevertheless, he did have a desire to minister to the many young people who came in and out of his shop, and beginning in 1982, Lance started a weekly Bible study that met in the shop. According to Chris, one of the early attendees at the study, "Your typical study would be [that] everyone would get together and they would just go through a passage [of the Bible] or watch a surf movie and pray a little bit. . . . It was really comical the people who showed up. You know, half the people there had no idea what Christianity was, and were sleeping with their girlfriends or smoking pot. A lot of people came and smoked pot or took drugs and then came to the study. . . . It never really went anywhere. It got bigger and smaller, and kinda flowed with the seasons. In the summertime it got big, and in the wintertime nobody came." The original Bible study continued like this for several years. However, around late 1988 and early 1989, things began to change. Chris continues: "Everybody got serious around the same time. . . . Something happened with Lance. He got serious with God, and there was a trickle-down effect. . . . I saw him change, and that's really when the Bible study started getting more people. That's when everybody started getting more serious."

Around this time Lance became acquainted with Raul Ries, pastor of the mega-church Calvary Chapel Golden Springs in Diamond Bar, California, as Ries's son was a customer of Lance's at the surf shop. The members of Lance's Bible study began attending Ries's church on Sunday evenings, and they also went to a youth camp with the church's youth group. From here, the Bible study added more elements to its meetings, increasingly becoming like a regular church. According to Chris, "At the camp, I remember a guy named Terry was leading the kids and he played guitar, and up until this time we never had music before our service because nobody knew how to play guitar. It turns out later a bunch of people knew how to play guitar, but no one would admit, 'cause everyone was too cool. They were afraid that they'd get rubbed into it, and we never had any music. So I said, 'Well, I'll learn how to play the guitar,' so I learned how to play the guitar. We started having singing before our services." Soon after, they began renting a room from Granada Heights Friends Church in La Mirada, California, and meeting on Tuesday nights. Ronnee first visited Committed at this time, and later went on to become Committed's worship leader. He recalls, "As soon as I went in, everybody there was pretty friendly. . . . I remember Lance had long hair in back, and Chris was leading worship. . . . It looked to me like the majority of the people there were surfers. . . . The one thing I didn't understand was the surfer lingo that Lance would use a lot. . . . There was somewhere between maybe fifty and seventy-five people—there wasn't like a lot. It was pretty small, real intimate."

After about another year of renting a hall for a short time, as well as meeting in a nearby park, Committed finally came into its own building—a warehouse in an industrial park in Santa Fe Springs, California. It was also during this time that Lance sold his surf shop so that he could go into full-time ministry and receive a salary from the church, obtaining his pastoral training at Calvary Chapel Bible College.

April first came to Committed in 1992, soon after they moved into the new building. She describes it as such: "They didn't even have carpet, and they didn't have a stage. Everyone there was barefoot, and you know, like it was really cool. I was so stoked on that, because coming from a high school environment, it's so important how you look and how you are and how you act. . . . There were only like a hundred people there, and like it was all like cement everywhere. . . . It didn't have air conditioning, and like people sat on the floor. It was cool."

Although they eventually got carpet, air conditioning, chairs, and a stage, Committed continued to utilize the warehouse feel of their building, holding numerous concerts and events there to attract young people. Abe, a former skinhead, first visited Committed in late 1994 to see a concert, and similarly enjoyed the different, accepting atmosphere.

> I had gone with some friends from school to Committed to see a band, and I was like in full Nazi uniform. I had like the swastikas on my jacket, the boots with red laces. I was sitting out front smoking a cigarette, and this guy comes up with red hair and glasses. He's all, "How's it going?" I'm like, "All right." I'm all, "You go here?" And he's all, "Yeah, you could say that." I was like, "Oh, that's cool." I'm all, "Doesn't it bother you I'm smoking?" I was like worried I was going to offend someone. He's all, "Nah, you can do whatever you want. That's your own deal." He's all, "When you're finished, though, just don't throw it on the ground; put it out and throw it away." I was like, "Oh, that's cool—this church is pretty cool." So I went into the service. . . . All of a sudden, the pastor comes up to speak, and I look up, and there's the guy with red hair and glasses. It's Lance.

By September 1995, when I first visited Committed, the growing church had over six hundred regular attendees in two Sunday-morning services, as well as the Tuesday-evening study. They also had a bookstore and coffeehouse located next to the main sanctuary, as well as numerous Sunday school rooms for the growing number of young children. By the fall of 1996, due both to growth and increased zoning difficulties with the owners of the property, Committed was forced to find another location. In one weekend, the church completely packed up and moved, leaving the former sanctuary an empty warehouse once again. After temporarily meeting on Tuesday nights in a park and Sunday mornings in a hotel banquet room, Committed eventually moved into a larger facility in the neighboring city of La Habra, California. They bought a vacant supermarket building, as well as part of the adjoining strip mall, and by spring of 1997 they were holding services in their newly converted facility. Attendance dropped significantly during this transition, but began to pick up as they settled down once again.

Thus, Committed has come a long way from a group of stoned teenagers meeting in a surf shop to study the Bible. Yet the continued appeal to young people, no matter what they look like or what they are doing, has remained consistent. Despite the downturn in attendance during the transition, Committed remains active. Besides the Tuesday-evening and Sunday-morning services, the church has many other ministries. They operate a bookstore and coffeehouse adjacent to their new church, which although open to the public is primarily used by the people in the congregation. They also have a house for young men to live in, called the Discipleship House, or "D-House," and for those who are in leadership positions in the church, they run a "Shepherd's School" for further training. Committed also has weekly prayer meetings, as well as a weekly high school group. There are regular Bible studies for men, and for women, and home fellowships for singles, couples, and families. Returning to their surfer roots, they have started a sister Committed church in the surf mecca of Huntington Beach. They also have a "Surfers for Christ" ministry, which periodically goes to the beaches to surf and to evangelize. Committed also continues to send missionaries to Japan, which they have done for several years, and they have had enough converts to start a Committed congregation there as well.

Alternative People: Punks, Skinheads, and Tattoos

Individual Portrait. Sitting in front of a crowded Starbucks coffeehouse on Main Street in Huntington Beach on a chilly evening, Paige had a story to tell. A twenty-one-year-old Caucasian college student, she works as a cocktail waitress at a Black Angus steakhouse. With her Dickies work pants and a black velvet jacket with fur collar, she comes across as feminine yet tough, defiant yet vulnerable. Holding a cigarette in one hand and a coffee in the other, Paige began to reminisce about her experiences: "Oh, I went to Catholic school, but that was against my will. . . . They used to yank me out of class, like even before school started, in homeroom, and they'd bring me into the office. She'd make me take off my red lipstick, and anything I was wearing was unsuitable, because I was all punk rock." This was her freshman year of high school only, as she was unable to return the next year. She "kinda blamed" the events of her next years on that sour experience with religion and religious people, because "they threw me out there, into the world without knowledge": "And so I was kinda thrown out into the public school and never heard about God. And I started getting in the full on—I was raped when I was fifteen, and I got in the whole club scene and everything, and it was just downhill from that point on, into the drugs and everything. I was a mess."

She began to practice paganism as a witch with her boyfriend and fellow drug addict. Eventually she sobered up on her own and left him. However, a short time after that, he took his own life—something that affected her tremendously and for which she blamed herself: "I was very angry. Oh man, I was dark. Everyone used to say I was dark. But I was very angry and bitter, and I didn't want to believe, and I didn't want to let go. . . . That really changed me. That made me question a lot; that made me see the world in a different way." Around that time, a good friend of hers invited her to Committed Christian Fellowship. Paige had been asking her friend questions about her beliefs, and finally she agreed to attend church.

> I went there, and it was so beautiful. Like the worship was very pretty and everyone there was so young and it's like they had an understanding of God and of love and of the way things should be. . . . But there's a reason for everything happening. And I remember I was asking so many questions. That night it was Lance speaking. He was talking about like when people don't come to him [God] and when you die, what happens. . . . It really struck me, it really struck me. . . . At that moment I knew I should [accept Jesus]. It was like, it was somebody who was in much pain, and somebody who was like, who hadn't really seen anyone that was very accepting, and coming from the background that I came from. . . . I caused a lot of pain to myself. That was what I needed. It was very comforting. . . . I was like crying, because he had talked about death—it was like he was speaking to me.

It was at this point, in February 1996, that Paige became a born-again Christian. She readily received the comforting message presented to her of a God who loved and accepted her, despite her turbulent past. She describes her faith in this way: "I guess it's like that comfort when you know that you live in total hell and chaos . . . and your world is crumbling right down before your eyes. . . . He's there. He's like, 'It's okay—I'll be here when the smoke clears.' He's all, 'I'm already here, but you'll just be able to see me, like when you get your head clear.' That's all. It's just like a constant hope, a constant something to look forward to, something to believe in. Just knowing that someday, everything's going to be better."

Group Snapshot. Paige is typical of many of the people at Committed, both in her background history and in her conversion account. Many of the people I met had had dramatic transformations when they became Christians, including instantaneous "deliverances" from drugs, alcohol, occult practices, and racism.

Let's take a closer look at the makeup of the people at Committed. The vast majority of the six hundred or so regular attenders are young adults, primarily between the ages of fifteen and twenty-five. Most are in school, be it high school or college. Many attend local evangelical Christian schools, such as Whittier Christian High School, Biola University, or Calvary Chapel Bible College. There are also many young children, as more people are getting married and starting families. Besides the youth, there are many people in their thirties, forties, and fifties—often parents or other family members related to the young people. Even a sprinkling of seniors attends, their gray or white hair noticeably standing out in the crowd.

As for race and ethnicity, the majority is Caucasian. However, there is a large representation of Hispanics, probably reflecting the large Latino population of Santa Fe Springs and the surrounding communities of southern California. There is a small number of African Americans, as well as a handful of Asian Americans.[1] Although the pastor is Caucasian, the worship team, as well as the ushers and greeters, are quite mixed in ethnic background.

The socioeconomic status of the majority of the members is somewhere between working class and middle class. Many of the young people have graduated from college, or are anticipating the pursuit of higher education, reflecting their middle-class background. However, many of the men in leadership hold jobs as electricians, construction workers, mechanics, and so on—from a working-class background. On the other end of the spectrum, the upper classes are represented, such as the young lawyer who handles many of the legal matters concerning the church. Thus, the vast majority appears to be of sufficient means.

As for the actual dress of the congregation, it is primarily informal. For the men, most wear shorts or jeans with T-shirts or other casual tops. Many wear tennis shoes, others wear thongs, and still others have on Doc Martens boots. Some have hats on. Obviously, there are no ties, blazers, or suits to be found. Women dress in a similarly casual style, although some wear skirts or dresses. However, there are no high heels, fancy hairdos, or long and flowery dresses.

As the congregation is diverse, anyone from any background is made to feel welcome there. This is even true for "deviant" youth whose subcultures are often stigmatized by the larger society. For example, there is a small group of "straight-edge"[2] skinheads who attend, always sitting near the front. The young women have the characteristic short hair with long "fringe," and the young men have shaved heads or closely cropped cuts. All dress in the typical skinhead style, wearing steel-toed boots, thin suspenders called braces, flight jackets, and rolled-up jeans. Some in the group are in a Christian ska band called the Israelites, which plays locally with both Christian and secular bands.

There is also a fairly large group of punks, perhaps twenty or twenty-five, who always sit in the first two to three rows during the service. These are not "gutter" or "ghetto" punks, with their Mohawks, ripped T-shirts, safety pins, and bondage pants. Rather, these are the more clean-cut surfer punk style, with spiked hair, Vans shoes, and Black Fly sunglasses. Most have body piercings, tattoos, and dyed hair. They shop at thrift stores for their clothing and have a certain neatness to their otherwise mismatched attire. Many are members of various Christian punk or alternative bands, such as Spud Puddle, Holy Cow, Rich Young Ruler, or Plankeye, and some have even recorded albums for the evangelical Christian record label Tooth and Nail.

A prominent local tattooist and his wife attend Committed as well, sometimes bringing clients from his shop or other tattooists. Ace is "fully sleeved" on both arms with tattoos, as well as covered with tattoos on his legs, chest, and back. He wears long-sleeved shirts to church, though, and dresses in the typical rockabilly style of most traditional-style tattooists. His wife, Ruth, dresses in vintage clothing, wearing little that is not from the 1940s or 1950s. Ace first heard about Committed while tattooing an ichthus (Christian fish symbol) on Abe, one of the young skinheads who attends Committed. He recalls, "So Abe gave me a card for Committed, and he started telling me about it. He was with his buddy, you know—he's this quasi-skinhead-looking guy, and then with this other pierced guy. And they're like, 'Yeah, it's cool, it's all younger.' And so I said, 'Listen, no offense, but this isn't like a freak thing, right? Like where "everything's okay," right? Because I'm not into that. I may be a tattooist, but I'm not like, "everything's okay."' He wasn't offended at all, and he said it was all straight from the book."

Thus, Committed has an attraction for many who are uncomfortable or unwelcome in more traditional church settings. But more than finding company with one's peers who are similar in unconventional style and appearance, all of these people share the common bond of their faith. For Ruth,

Ace's wife, Committed provides a safe haven for her to be a "freak"—in this case, a Christian—and to still be accepted by others. She remarks,

> Some people are like, "Wow, that's good, you're trying to do something good." But then they're like, "Oh yeah, Born-agains. . . ." and they think you're a freak! They really do. They pride themselves on being freaks, mind you. But they're freaks in the *acceptable* way: "Look, did you see my piercings?" or "I tied this girl up this way," or whatever. And we're supposed to be, "Wow, that's cool . . . but did I tell you that I love Jesus?" Ugh, you know?! And you're [considered] a weirdo. "I can't hang out with *you*. . . . Don't invite *them* to our party. . . . Don't say *that* around *them*." . . . It's just nice that at Committed you have a common goal, a common ground with these people. They're your same age group. They understand where you're coming from, and they believe the same thing you believe. It's nice to come there and be like, "There's hope! Lookit—there's young people here, and there's lots of them!"

Alternative Beliefs: Good News for the Lost

The set of beliefs that Committed offers its members may best be summarized as a theologically conservative strand of evangelical Protestant Christianity. The church's Statement of Faith consists of ten core doctrines revolving around the deity of Jesus Christ, the Trinity, the infallibility of the Bible, and indwelling of the Holy Spirit, and the fulfillment of End Times prophecy. The Statement of Faith reads,

1. Committed is a fellowship founded on the lordship of Jesus Christ—that He is living and powerful and wholly capable of changing the lives and eternal destiny of those who will deny themselves, take up their cross and follow Him.

2. Our supreme desire is to know Jesus Christ and to be conformed into His image. Proverbs 16:3

3. We believe that the Scriptures are the inspired, infallible, inerrant authoritative Word of God. Therefore, we place a great emphasis on the teaching of the Word.

4. We believe in the preexistence and full deity of the Lord Jesus Christ, who through the incarnation became man without ceasing to be God— fully human and fully divine, in one person.

5. We believe there is one God, eternally existent in three co-equal, co-eternal, co-substantial Persons—the trinity: Father, Son and Holy Spirit.

6. We believe in the absolute necessity of regeneration by the Holy Spirit for salvation because of the exceeding sinfulness of human nature; that men are justified only by God's grace received by faith through the shed blood of Jesus Christ.

7. We believe in the present indwelling ministry of the Holy Spirit, enabling the Christian to live a godly life. We believe that the gifts of the Holy Spirit are valid for today's church.

8. We believe in the rapture of the church, where Jesus Himself will descend from Heaven with a shout, the trumpet of God will sound, and the dead in Christ will be taken up first, then we (His Church) that are alive in Christ will be caught up in the clouds to meet the Lord in the air.

9. We believe in the Second Coming of Jesus Christ, in which He will return with His bride (the Church) to destroy all those who oppose His right to rule as Messiah over the earth.

10. We believe in a final judgment by Jesus Christ, where those who have received Him as their personal Lord and Savior will inherit eternal life with God, and those who rejected Jesus Christ will face an eternal, righteous punishment in Hell.

Thus, Committed's beliefs are typical of most any evangelical Protestant church. The deity of Jesus is upheld, as well as the authority of the Bible. And perhaps most important, there is the emphasis on an individual's decision to accept or reject these beliefs, with the resulting consequences. In other words, one is not born a Christian here; one must make the choice to become Christian.

There is a strong emphasis at Committed upon the Holy Spirit. Lance often urges his congregation to respond to the "moving" of the Holy Spirit, and reminds the church that the Spirit is not just needed for Sundays, but for every day.[3] Gifts of the Spirit are encouraged, including speaking in tongues, so long as it is in an orderly manner. From the pulpit, Lance has condemned what he considers misused spiritual gifts, such as the "Toronto Blessing," "holy laughter," and other extreme displays in worship services like barking and other animal noises, shaking uncontrollably, rolling around on the floor, and hysterical laughter. He has likened the actions of such participants to the inhabitants of ancient Babylon as described in Jeremiah 51:37–40, who howled and hissed and acted as if they were intoxicated. Lance further called this "blessing" at best extreme emotionalism, and at worst a heresy that directly contradicts the Bible.[4]

Evangelism and a strong focus on "reaching out" to others are also of great importance. Each service includes some sort of an altar call, and almost every prayer Lance utters concerns those who are "lost." For example, during one Sunday-morning service, Lance prayed, "Lord, you're a gracious God, long-suffering, not willing that any should perish, but that all would come to repentance. And so you allow us to share that love, to share that good news with the lost. And Lord, you give those people a chance to congregate with us as well, that they might be able to see the truth, to be set free from the grip of Satan, to be grafted into your family. . . . For anybody here who doesn't know you personally, they're not born again, they're not a Christian, we ask that they would make a decision before they would leave this place."[5] Usually at least two or three people per service respond to Lance's invitation to "receive Christ." The "Great Commission" of Matthew 28 is taken very seriously here, and missions are now becoming of greater importance for this growing and expanding congregation, such as with their missionaries in Japan.[6]

Although the published Statement of Faith contains three articles referring to eschatology, or "end times" beliefs, Lance has stated that there is no way of determining which particular position is the correct one. It seems that he personally holds to a pretribulation viewpoint as outlined in the Statement of Faith, but he has made references to a posttribulation position as well.[7] Ultimately, he seems to leave it up to individual interpretation. Even though he recognizes the importance of the impending "last days," Lance has said that he would rather not get bogged down in theological debates over what the Bible says about the rapture, tribulation, and the millennium. Rather, he focuses on what one can know: who Jesus Christ is, and what he has done for those who believe in him.[8]

This conservative evangelical theology has implications for a conservative social stance. Lance will not preach about social or political issues from the pulpit, since he says he is "a sojourner, a pilgrim" in this world and does not want to endorse any other ideology besides Christianity.[9] However, he does every now and then mention a social issue when it is relevant to the passage of the Bible that he is teaching. For example, television has been decried as the "idiot box," as it has "the habit of making idiots."[10] However, Lance has praised The Cosby Show and its portrayal of family values. When compared with the Bundy family of Married with Children, the Huxtables are "God's ideal for the family."[11]

Lance has further claimed in his preaching that the rebellious teens of today are looking for consistency in those they see around them, and that whoever they see continuity and stability of words and actions in is who the teens will listen to. Authority and legitimacy thus come from consistency, Lance claims, with the ultimate example being Jesus Christ. Similarly, he says the social problems of today are the result of people being distant from God. Lance exhorts his congregation to pray for their leaders and for American society in general, so that they might "return to God." Positive social change would then be the result.[12]

Alternative Rituals: Worship and Water

Participating in corporate rituals reinforces this common set of beliefs that the people at Committed hold to. It is this agreed-upon behavior that is entered into at certain occasions that cements group beliefs, solidifies group identity, and compounds group solidarity.

The most basic ritual for Committed is the worship service/Bible study held on Sunday mornings and Tuesday evenings. All services follow the same basic structure, with the only difference being the book of the Bible out of which Lance teaches. Each service begins with the worship team leading the congregation in two or three upbeat songs. The worship team varies from service to service, but usually consists of the leader playing keyboards, two guitars, a drummer, and three backup vocalists. Sometimes there are more instruments, like an added cello or bongo drums, and sometimes there are fewer, as with only guitars. There are no hymnals or song sheets for the congregation, so the songs are sung from memory. During this first set of upbeat songs, everybody stands. Most everyone claps along, although some are more reserved and simply tap their feet. Many have their eyes closed and sway to the rhythm of the music. Others are more animated, dancing to the music.

An announcer comes up onstage during the last song of this faster set, and once the singing is finished, he has everyone turn and greet each other and then take a seat. He then proceeds to update the church with the latest announcements, the majority of which are not mentioned in the bulletin. When finished, he leaves the stage, the lights are dimmed, and the worship team leads a set of four or five slower, more subdued songs. Now many heads are bowed and eyes are closed. Some sway slightly in their seats. Others lift their hands, some half way, some straight up. A few even stand, with hands lifted or folded, as in prayer.

The worship leader has everyone stand toward the end of the last song, as Lance comes to the front and leads the congregation in prayer. When he is finished, he has everyone greet each other again as they sit down. The lights come up again, and Lance begins teaching, going through a chapter of a book of the Bible, verse by verse, in a typical Calvary Chapel style. When he has finished teaching, he again prays. The lights dim once more, the worship team comes up onstage again and begins playing softly, and Lance in effect makes an "altar call," although there is no actual altar in the room. He asks if there is anyone present who desires to "make a commitment" to Jesus Christ, and has those who wish to do so raise their hands while everyone has their eyes closed and heads bowed. Sometimes Lance asks them to come up to the front of the room, physically "taking that step of faith." He then leads the respondents in a prayer for salvation, having them ask forgiveness for their sins and then asking Jesus to "come into their heart." After the prayer, everyone stands, sings one last song, and is then dismissed.

Thus, Committed's worship service is quite similar to many other "contemporary" church services. There is a casual, open, youthful, and worshipful feel to it—perhaps even more so than many other contemporary worship services. But construction or design does not necessarily achieve this climate. Although it is structured and in many ways seems to follow a formula of what is most conducive to a "successful" worship experience, there is still an acknowledged willingness by the leadership to set no expectations upon the congregation other than that of "responding" to the Holy Spirit. Thus, "if the Spirit leads," they may spend extra time singing, or in prayer, or conduct different types of altar calls at the end of the service to better meet the perceived spiritual needs of the congregation. Nevertheless, the emphasis is on the individual "meeting God" during this time. There is no conspicuous reference to the act or ritual that one is doing (perhaps the most blatant is the lack of a "program" or "schedule" printed in the bulletin); rather all actions are designed to naturally lead to an encounter with God.

Of course, there are the traditional Christian rituals that Committed participates in as well, often giving new twists to the standard acts. For example, communion is practiced regularly, held the second Tuesday of every month during the evening service. A table is set up in the front of the sanctuary, with four or so baskets containing small loaves of bread and three or four silver holders that hold small plastic cups of grape juice. Lance prays over the elements, and each row of worshipers then proceeds to file by the table. Individuals tear off a piece of bread and take a cup of juice back to their seats. Everyone partakes whenever they feel ready to do so—not together as a corporate act. The worship team plays music during this whole time, creating a calm, worshipful environment for a spiritual communion with God. Although this is a group ritual, there are strong individualistic overtones to it, which set it apart from most other celebrations of the Eucharist.

Committed then usually follows the communion service with a potluck dinner, based on the New Testament church's "love-feasts" as recorded in the Book of Acts. The potluck is held outside, behind the church building, lit by the parking lot lights. Chairs are set up in circles, and the garage door in the back of the warehouse sanctuary is rolled up for easy access into and out of the building. The homemade food dishes are served on paper plates, giving a picnic atmosphere to the occasion. Because of the simplicity of the setup, it is very conducive to interaction and fellowship among the members in a comfortable, laid-back atmosphere.

Another ritual that Committed regularly conducts is that of public baptism. Baptisms are held every few months, as weather permits. These baptisms strongly reflect the surfer beginnings of the church, as they take place at the beach. Those being baptized, as well as family and friends, gather at Bolsa Chica State Beach, in the city of Huntington Beach. They have a cookout and spend time eating, talking, and relaxing. After a while, Lance gets up and gives a brief evangelistic talk on the subject of baptism. This message is aimed not only at those who are there from the church but also any passersby who might overhear and inquire as to what is going on. After the talk, Lance and three other men, usually elders in the church, put on their wet suits and go out in pairs in the Pacific Ocean, about waist deep. Those wishing to be baptized (usually around thirty to forty people) line up in two lines and file out one at a time to the pairs of "dunkers." The person makes a public proclamation of his or her faith, and is then immersed. This ritual thus identifies the individual as a convert to Christianity in that it not only symbolizes one's sins being washed away but also represents the person as becoming a new member of the Committed family.

Alternative Organization: Programless Prosperity

Although all the people at Committed are taught that they are considered equal before God and that no person is to be treated as better, more spiritual, or more holy than another, there is a definite hierarchical structure in place for governing the church. This structure is based on the design set forth by the founder of the Calvary Chapel movement, Chuck Smith.[13]

Committed, using Smith's guidelines, is modeled after the New Testament church as described in the Book of Acts, which in turn reflects the Old Testament model of Judaic theocracy exemplified under Moses. In the New Testament model, Jesus Christ is seen as the head of the church, and the pastor is subordinate to him. Lance has been "called" to this position of "shepherding" the church, and recognizes his subservience to the leadership of the "Great Shepherd." A council of five men, who could be likened to assistant pastors, aids Lance in spiritual decisions affecting Committed. There is also a board, which governs business and financial matters concerning the church. And finally, there are leaders of various ministries (such as ushering, counseling, missions, and so on), which are synonymous with the elders of the New Testament church. The vast majority of this leadership is under thirty, although there are a few older persons on the board as well.

Thus, everyone at Committed knows where in the hierarchy they belong, although the configurations are loose and emphasis is not placed upon titles or positions. There is much flexibility and mobility within the framework, and each individual is invited to participate in some sort of church involvement, from being head of a ministry to volunteering at the bookstore or in the nursery.

This sort of structure echoes Max Weber's description (1946) of the group directly under the influence of the charismatic leader, which Lance surely is. Weber writes, "The administrative staff of a charismatic leader does not consist of 'officials'; at least its members are not technically trained.... There is only a 'call' at the instance of the leader on the basis of the charismatic qualification of those he summons. There is no hierarchy.... There is no such thing as a definite sphere of authority.... There is no such thing as a salary or benefice" (50). Indeed, Lance is a charismatic leader to this group, and as such exercises charismatic authority. Charisma, according to Weber, is that quality, seen as divine in origin, by which the leader is "set apart" and treated as "endowed with supernatural, superhuman, or at least specifically exceptional powers or qualities" (1968, 48). The members of Committed do not see Lance as a charismatic leader in the most extreme sense, as they do not believe he is divine or that he possesses supernatural powers. However, they do recognize him as "called by God" to teach the Bible and to lead this group as its "Shepherd."

Moreover, although there is a recognized need for some degree of order and establishment, there is plenty of room left for spontaneity and freedom under this type of charismatic leadership. Indeed, organization is not a priority for Committed; in fact, in some instances it is even looked down upon. For instance, Lance once mentioned in a sermon that Committed is not based on any sort of "programs," "methods," or "strategies," as they are seen as ineffective and stifling to the work of the Holy Spirit. He gave the example of one time early in Committed's history when he thought they should have a specific program for the high school group, to minister to the many youth there. That didn't go over so well—in the initial stages of the program development, a fistfight actually broke out between two of the leaders who couldn't agree upon the right way to plan it! So then Lance claims that Committed, rather than being founded upon structures and strategies, is instead based upon the principles of worship, Bible study, and evangelism. All the rest, says Lance, then follows through accordingly.[14]

II. Analysis of Committed Christian Fellowship

The Backdrop: Anomic Contemporary Society

To begin with, we need to locate Committed within its larger context; that is, contemporary American society. For over a century sociologists have maintained that the modern, industrial, capitalist society is one marked by drastic social changes—changes that, more than just affecting modes of production and widespread urbanization, focus rather on the actual structure of society itself. These writers theorize that because of the rapid modernization and industrialization of the nineteenth century, societies consequently have been held together no longer by the similarities of their members, but rather by their differences. This second type of society has been viewed as less stable than the first, in that social ties are weakened, and society, because it is so large and consists of so many competing ideas, loses its ability to constrain and regulate the behavior of the individuals within it.

Modern societies are further marked by another disturbing characteristic—anomie. This "state of deregulation" results from swift social changes, when an already weakly integrated society is further thrown out of equilibrium and can no longer regulate the norms of behavior. In the past, this anomie was absent, as strong social subgroups within the larger society provided the necessary integration and regulation for its members, especially through strong institutions such as religion, the family, and the political system. But as these forces were debilitated by the social changes accompanying modernity, the overall integration of society was weakened, thus allowing for anomie to run unchecked. Expressed in various forms, anomie ranges from a general agitation and sense of discontentment to the worst-case scenario, suicide.[15]

One solution offered by classical theorists for strengthening modern society and hence controlling the ill effects of anomie has been for the formation of new subsocieties, typified by the "occupational group or corporation," since it already "consists of individuals devoted to the same tasks, with solidary or even combined interests" (Durkheim [1897] 1951, 378). Although this is one possible type of solution, certainly it is not the only one. It would seem that any integrated group, be it occupational, religious, familial, or peer group, can provide the regulation necessary to combat anomie.

More contemporary sociologists have posited that modernity seemingly culminated in the 1960s, as increased technology, production, bureaucracy, and rationalization reached never-before-seen extents. This modern society is marked by various characteristics: rationality, componentiality, multirelationality, plurality, and progressivity.[16] These attributes have a combined ultimate effect of dividing the public and private spheres within the individual, causing an inherent identity crisis and creating a sense of anomie, or "homelessness" (Berger et al. 1973).

As acute as such "homelessness" was some thirty years ago, how much more has it deepened as modern American society has moved to the end of the twentieth century? The question of postmodernity has only heightened the confusion and compounded the already fractured notions of self and community. Thus the anomie, loss of identity, and indeed "homelessness" of the individual are all the more accentuated in contemporary society. However, it would seem that the solutions offered over a century ago by Durkheim would still hold true—a thoroughly integrated group that is able to enforce regulation upon its individual members. And although Committed seems to be a viable example of this, how is it that a group such as Committed could emerge within this context?

The Foreground: Youth and Subcultures

Out of this backdrop colored by anomie arises the specific context from which Committed emerges—the various subcultural groupings of Generation X. Our analytical picture of Committed comes more sharply into focus here as we look at the young people in their contemporary context, as well as the subcultures they form in reaction to their social location.

Talcott Parsons, a sociologist writing in the 1960s, analyzed what he saw as the unique situation of that generation of youth in anomic American society. He thought that the essential problem youth were facing was a "relatively stable" value system that was in conflict with the "complex" changes that the societal structure has undergone (1963, 113). He saw this discrepancy between values and norms (resulting from structural changes) resulting in a sense of "indeterminacy" or anomie, in which "the individual is subject to conflicting expectations that are impossible to fulfill all at once" (127–28).

Parsons further claimed that this anomie is especially pressing upon youth, as most young people are not directly involved with the "major agents for initiating processes of change," such as government, science and technology, and other "higher" areas of society (128). The primary associations that adolescents have—families and schools—are not as far-reaching or impacting as other institutions. Thus youth (both the previous and the current generation) are at a disadvantage when combating the trend toward anomie through traditional means.

Subcultures, then, provide an innovative way for this generation of youth to counter the ill effects of anomie. By adopting a new set of values, an unconventional set of behavioral standards, and a distinctive identity, groups of young people create their own regulating norms and provide for themselves integrative, adaptive mechanisms within the larger society. The outwardly visible evidence is the unique dress, speech, and attitudes of the hippie, the surfer, the punk, or any other distinct group. The more latent results are acceptance, community, self-esteem, and replacement ideologies that the youth experience and adhere to.

Although it is certain that much of these Xers' need for new norms, values, and a sense of direction are met through these various subcultures, something still remains missing for many. Surely these "scenes" are effective to some degree, but just because these groups are different does not necessarily guarantee their success in combating anomie. Some of the subcultures prove harmless, many prove helpful, but some prove dangerous and even destructive.

It seems to me that that is why many in Generation X, who although on the outside are still attracted to the trappings of various subcultures, are on the inside looking for more fulfillment and a sense of ultimate meaning. For some this means turning, or returning, to religion, and a conservative strain of religion at that. This seems to be the case with Committed, as numerous Generation X youth involved in various subcultures are "finding God" and gathering several times a week for worship, fellowship, and Bible teaching.

Yet does Committed actually behave like a subculture? Is it successful in warding off anomie? Its subcultural effectiveness may be shown in how it has successfully replaced the larger culture for the individual. According to sociologist Hans Sebald (1968), a group must meet certain prerequisites to successfully usurp the dominant society. First and most obvious, new values and norms must be established and agreed upon. Next, a specific lingo, mode of behavior, and standards of appearance need to be established. Inclusion within a peer group and a "we" mentality are also necessary. The successful subculture must also institute status relations between different positions within the group. Last, there must be a gratification of specific needs that the larger culture does not meet (Sebald 1968, 206). Thus, for Committed to be a viable subcultural alternative for young people, both as a youth culture and as a religious culture, it must—and does—fulfill the above prerequisites. By offering a Bible-based conservative theology, a unique set of ritual actions, acceptance and reinvention of popular culture, a sense of belonging within a structured "body," and the meeting of spiritual and emotional needs, Committed indeed acts as a replacement subculture for many of these youth.

A Closer Look: Individual Conversion and Identity

Having established the theoretical background and the specific context out of which Committed has emerged, let us now turn to the individuals who make up this congregation and the personal meaning that they find in the church. These individuals, now converted and with a holistic Christian identity, are joined together to comprise Committed.

As mentioned before, a fundamental effect of modernity is the division of the public and private within the individual, which leads to a "permanent identity crisis" (Berger et al. 1973, 78). Such a "divided self" was similarly described by psychologist William James (1958) as having "a certain discordancy or heterogeneity in the native temperament of the subject, an incompletely unified moral and intellectual constitution" (153). Conversion then, for James, was the unification of the self. He writes, "To be converted, to be regenerated, to receive grace, to experience religion, to gain an assurance, are so many phrases which denote the process, gradual or sudden, by which a self hitherto divided, and consciously wrong, inferior and unhappy, becomes unified and unconsciously right, superior and happy, in consequence of its firmer hold upon religious realities" (171). The result of such an experience is, according to James, "a characteristic sort of relief . . . Happiness! happiness!" (159). Thus for Paige, who, as we saw earlier, was converted at Committed, the people there were "all positive, they have this great attitude. . . . It's refreshing." For April, a twenty-year-old singer involved with the worship team, her conversion resulted in her experience of "the most peaceful feeling. . . . I remember I felt really peaceful."

Furthermore, this self-unification accomplished at conversion brings about a coherent identity. According to sociologist Craig Calhoun (1994), this identity hinges on a subjective self-recognition and recognition by others that is constantly being re-created: "Recognition is at the heart of the matter. No matter when and where one looks, subjectivity is perhaps best understood as a project, as something always under construction, never perfect. In varying degrees for different people and in different circumstance it may be more or less challenging, but it is never automatic. . . . This component of recognition may be the aspect of identity made most problematic by the social changes of modernity" (20). The construction of a Christian identity as facilitated through Committed depends upon recognition from the initial moment of conversion. For example, when an individual prays the prayer for salvation at the close of a service (self-recognition), they are often asked to make a public proclamation of their new faith by walking up to the front of the sanctuary (recognition by others). Later, the new convert is encouraged to solidify his or her Christian identity through the ritual of baptism, which signifies both an inner transformation and an outward identification with the church.

Furthermore, as far as the individuals are Christians "not just on Sunday morning," but throughout the rest of their time and activities, it can be said that Committed has successfully converted these young people and given them a new, encompassing identity. For instance, when trying to describe himself, Abe says, "All I think of myself now is like someone who's seeking and wanting a relationship with God, you know? That's my concern—learning more about God." Abe goes on to describe his concept of a Christian: "They're putting all of their faith, their trust in what Jesus Christ did on the cross. . . . They're looking unto Him for their salvation—for eternity, and day by day. . . . A Christian is governed by God's word daily. . . . That's evident throughout their life and the way they live." April similarly describes what it means to her to be a Christian in this way: "I think to be a Christian, it means like that everything you do would bring glory to God, you know? Every little thing, and like just waking up in the morning. . . . Hopefully in my life I would want every little thing, you know, even just like talking to like that checker at the supermarket, you know. . . . It really comes down to abandoning yourself to God, and to his, you know, divine plan." Thus, Christianity, as practiced by these individuals at Committed, is a round-the-clock job, at least in the abstract. And it does seem that their actual practices approach this ideal to some degree, indicating a more full Christian identity.

So then their conversion experiences, more than giving them hope at times when they seemingly had none, have also given these individuals a new identity, that of a Christian, and as a part of Committed Christian Fellowship. Recalls Paige, "Yeah, it was great. It was like so many new people I met, so many new people. It was like a new start. You were reborn, because you commit yourself to something so wonderful, and so naturally a lot of wonderful things will happen." Ronnee, the worship leader at Committed, had this to say on conversion and identity: "What I know is, is in the Scriptures how God says that we're a new creation, and in that basically we're being made, we're being made holy. We're being made perfect. We're being made to be all the things he needs us to be."

Ultimately, then, we have at Committed a group of young people who, regardless of their past experiences (both with religion and with life in general), have "started over" and embraced an all-encompassing religious identity.

The Final Details: High-Cost Christianity

So what then is the ultimate motivation or driving force for why these young individuals are coming to and staying at Committed? Following a "rational choice" approach to religious behavior, high-cost religious organizations are described as being stronger "to the degree that they impose significant costs in terms of sacrifices and even stigma upon their members" (Finke and Stark 1992, 238). As such, their ability to reward their adherents increases proportionately, while low-cost religious groups are only able to offer lesser rewards.

This is certainly played out at Committed, which while demanding strict attitude and behavior guidelines based on the Bible in return offers the promise of salvation from one's sins here on earth and eternal life in heaven after death. For Chris, turning to this type of Christianity was a calculated choice, whereby he suffered certain costs in order to gain certain benefits: "I think it's done purely for selfish reasons, 'cause you want peace. So in order to have peace, you give up these things [partying, premarital sex, 'just doing whatever you felt like doing']. . . . I gradually started giving up all these things and said, 'Okay God, if you're real, you know, I'm giving up all these things—make yourself real to me.' And he did." Abe reflects this notion of benefits outweighing costs, in which abstinence from certain activities is transformed into more spiritual terms, with definite spiritual rewards of fulfillment and satisfaction: "You know, it's not so much like, Oh, I just stopped drinking or I just stopped doing drugs, or I just stopped doing this. But rather, it's I don't need to do it anymore, you know? To solve my problems, I don't have to escape from it. I can, you know, I can talk to the Lord and give it to him, and ask for strength where I'm weak. . . . There's not that need anymore. Before it was, Man, my life sucks—I've gotta get away from this, you know? And now, now I give it to God, and I trust in him to help me deal with and work things out, you know?" These statements affirm what has been termed the "nonrefundable registration fees" for entrance into the high-cost religion—that is, "conversion," "being born again," or "submitting their lives to the Lord" (Finke and Stark 1992, 254).

One area of high-cost religion peculiar to Committed is that of Christian tattooing.[17] Although by no means a requirement for group membership, it is quite popular among a large segment of the youth there. For instance, Abe has an ichthus (Christian fish) on his upper back, April has Praying Hands on her lower back, and Paige has an angel and a Bible verse written around one of her ankles—not to mention Ace, the tattoo artist, and his number of tattoos, both religious and secular. This permanent—and often stigmatized—way of marking one's body with religious symbols certainly would be considered a "high-cost" religious act. But perhaps more important, the tattoos are indicative of the strength of conviction that these young people hold, as well as their belief in the high rewards that, to them, such markings represent.

Thus, the overarching motivation for why these young people are at Committed is the prospect of a high-reward religious faith, making it possible to endure the high costs that such rewards demand.

Putting It All Together

Ultimately, then, how is Committed to be explained? It is evident that this church is a unique product of contemporary society, and that it caters to another product of such a society—Generation X youth and their various subcultures. These Xers are increasingly anomic, floating about "homeless" and in need of regulatory and integrative forces to act upon their lives to provide them structure and meaning. Many turn to various subcultures and "scenes" but do not find transcendent or ultimate meaning, purpose, and identity therein. Thus there develops a need and desire for religion as the one force in society that has always served this function. However, given their often unconventional or even offensive appearances, many young people are not accepted at more traditional churches. Such a backdrop is ready and waiting for charismatic leaders and innovative religious groups to step in and provide new answers for a searching group.

Committed Christian Fellowship, from its inception at the surf shop, has offered its congregants a straightforward, uncompromising set of beliefs based on a literal interpretation of the Bible, as well as an emotionally transcendent form of worship that raises the participants beyond the mundane. This, coupled with an acceptance of subcultures, makes Committed a logical choice for many Xers. There they are offered clear-cut prescriptions for correct belief and correct practice, and black-and-white answers in an otherwise gray-toned world. And they are able to receive these answers without having to conform to the larger culture; they are able to "come just as you are."[18]

Once they come as they are, their religious commitment is solidified as an encompassing Christian identity is created, which is recognized not just by the individual but by others as well. This identity begins at conversion and is reinforced as the public and private selves are ultimately united. This results in the "staying power" of the Committed, as it has continued in spite of many ups and downs.

The ultimate motivation for the young people, then, is that of a high-cost belief system with high rewards for its adherents. By demanding sacrifices in lifestyle and even promoting stigmatized behavior, Committed imposes high costs. However, it is able to balance this with high rewards, from a more immediate peace, happiness, and belonging, to eternal life in heaven.

In conclusion, perhaps the essence of Committed—the "Spirit" of what ultimately goes on there—may best be described by April:

> I remember at the old building, like before they got carpeting, and we used to have shows there and stuff. I used to get really excited about that, because I thought that, that's such a big void as far as genuine young people reaching out to youth, like other people, their peers and whatever. . . . I remember being there, and that band Mortal played . . . and I was kinda bummed because I don't like them. But then there was this part in the middle where they just sang this praise song. And I remember looking around and seeing all these freaky people, with tattoos and bad haircuts, and like green hair and whatever. And everyone was just raising up their hands and singing and these people were just standing there, and you could feel the Spirit in the room. And it was so intense, and people were really worshiping God . . . it was *so cool* for me, because it was really neat to look around and see all these people that I didn't even know, but I could relate to . . . to see that we have this bond that is so much bigger than, you know, [that] we both have tattoos. You know, it was so much more.

This bond, which transcends subcultural backgrounds, is that which allows an otherwise unruly generation of young people to reach out to others and to worship God in one accord. And as long as Committed continues to offer these youth a sense of openness, acceptance, and the opportunity to express themselves, the congregation will remain an appealing, innovative, and viable religious alternative for an ever-increasing number of this generation.

Notes

All names of Committed members have been changed to protect their identity. All quotes are from personal interviews, unless otherwise noted. The name of the church pastor is public record; therefore it has not been changed here. His congregation calls him "Lance," and I will do so here as well.

1. Interestingly, since Committed conducts missions trips to Japan, the congregation has on occasion sung well-known worship songs in Japanese.

2. "Straight-edge" refers to the fact that they do not hold to the racist ideology put forth by neo-Nazi skinheads. It can also refer to a "clean" lifestyle, but does not always mean this. Straight-edge skinheads may also be called "Sharps": Skinheads Against Racial Prejudice.

3. Sermon, November 5, 1995.

4. Sermon, October 22, 1995.

5. Sermon, October 8, 1995.

6. The Great Commission is one of the final commands Jesus gives to his disciples, as recorded in Matthew 28:18–20. Jesus says, "Therefore, go and make disciples of all nations, baptizing them in the name of the Father and of the Son and of the Holy Spirit, and teaching them to obey everything I have commanded you. And surely I am with you always, to the very end of the age."

7. A pretribulation position states that Christians will be "raptured," or taken up into heaven, before a period of seven years of God's judgment of the world, and at the end of which Jesus will return to the earth. Posttribulationists believe that Christians will be present during the tribulation time, and will leave earth when Jesus Christ returns at the end of the seven years. In both positions, Jesus will return to establish his kingdom on earth for one thousand years, or the millennium.

8. Sermon, November 7, 1995.

9. Sermon, September 26, 1995.

10. Sermon, October 29, 1995.

11. Sermon, September 26, 1995.

12. Sermon, October 24, 1995.

13. These guidelines are explained in Smith's booklet, *The Philosophy of Ministry of Calvary Chapel* (1992), as well as in *Harvest*, a book by Chuck Smith and Tal Brooke

(1993) that details the history of the Calvary Chapel movement and the principles on which the churches are built.

14. Sermon, October 15, 1995.

15. See Durkheim, *Suicide* ([1897] 1951) and *The Division of Labor in Society* ([1893] 1933).

16. In componentiality, "the components of reality are self-contained units which can be brought into relation with other such units—that is, reality is *not* conceived as an ongoing flux of juncture and disjuncture of unique entities" (Berger et al. 1973, 27); in multirelationality, the individual's "relations both with material objects and other persons become very complex. To keep up with this complexity necessitates a particular tension of consciousness characterized by a quick alertness to ever-changing constellations of phenomena" (37).

17. For a full treatment of this development, see chapter 1 in this volume, "Marked for Jesus"; see also chapter 2 on Gothics for a non-Christian comparison case.

18. This is the opening line to a common Calvary Chapel worship song.

References

Berger, Peter L., Brigette Berger, and Hansford Kellner. 1973. *The Homeless Mind*. New York: Random House.

Calhoun, Craig, ed. 1994. *Social Theory and the Politics of Identity*. Cambridge: Blackwell.

Durkheim, Emile. [1897] 1951. *Suicide*. Glencoe, Ill.: Free Press.

———. [1893] 1933. *The Division of Labor in Society.* New York: Macmillan.

Finke, Roger, and Rodney Stark. 1992. *The Churching of America, 1776–1990: Winners and Losers in Our Religious Economy*. New Brunswick, N.J.: Rutgers University Press.

James, William. 1958. *The Varieties of Religious Experience*. New York: Mentor Books.

Parsons, Talcott. 1965. "Youth in the Context of American Society." In *The Challenge of Youth,* ed. Erik H. Erikson, 110–41. Garden City, N.Y.: Anchor Books.

Sebald, Hans. 1968. *Adolescence: A Sociological Analysis*. New York: Appleton-Century-Crofts.

Smith, Chuck. 1992. *The Philosophy of Ministry of Calvary Chapel*. Diamond Bar, Calif.: Logos Media Group.

Smith, Chuck, and Tal Brooke. 1993. *Harvest*. Costa Mesa, Calif.: Word for Today Publishing.

Weber, Max. 1968. *Max Weber: On Charisma and Institution Building*, ed. S. N. Eisenstadt. Chicago: University of Chicago Press.

———. 1946. *From Max Weber: Essays in Sociology*, ed. H. H. Gerth. and C. Wright Mills. New York: Oxford University Press.

8

Saturday Night in Pasadena

Wholeness, Healing, and Holiness at Harvest Rock Church

Douglas Hayward

It is Saturday night in Los Angeles, and south of the city a lively crowd of GenXers have gathered to dance and stomp to the beat of a live band at the Cowboy Boogie Dance Hall. North of the city another crowd of GenXers, much smaller in number, is dancing and singing to a different kind of music, responding to a different generational need, at a gathering in the Mott Auditorium on the aging campus of William Carey University in Pasadena. While the Saturday-night crowd in Pasadena is small (eight to a hundred people), on Sunday at a more traditional hour the crowd here will swell to ten times this number. This is the meeting place for Harvest Rock Church, and on Saturday evening people have come to worship at an alternative service for those who cannot make it, or who choose not to attend the traditional Sunday-morning service when this same meeting will be replicated.

The meeting starts under the leadership of the music worship team, consisting of three guitarists, a drummer, a keyboardist, and two vocalists, who announce the first song and begin to play. There are no hymnbooks in this church, but the words of the choruses are prominently displayed on a large screen projected behind the band so that everyone can join in. Indeed, all the songs are a part of the new praise choruses of today's Christian community, and few of them are more than a few years old. These praise choruses focus upon worship and praise, and are replete with the use of personal pronouns allowing worshipers to express their adoration directly to God.

The first several choruses have a lively beat, and members of the audience join in with the singing—mostly with hand clapping, but several start to jump up and down in place or raise their hands in praise and begin to sway. A few move out of their seats and proceed toward an open area located on each side of the platform, where they begin to dance with joy. Some of these dancers have even brought banners or flags to wave as they dance out their worship.

After a while the pace of the music slows down somewhat as the mood of the worship service shifts from a high-energy phase into a reflective one. During this portion of the service worshipers are invited to engage in deep reflection on the glory, majesty, and work of God. While most of the audience responds by lifting their hands in a gesture of praise and worship, a few folk choose to bow down on their knees, or even move out into the aisles to lie prostrate before the Lord. It seems apparent that most everyone is caught up in his own personal world of worship and adoration, facilitated by the leadership of the music worship team.

After an hour, more or less, depending upon the nature of this evening's service, the worship portion of the service concludes with a prayer or a special word to encourage or exhort the congregation, given as a prophecy by an acknowledged prophet or prophetess of the church. This is followed by some announcements about upcoming events, a time of friendly greeting with other members of the congregation, and usually the offering. A musical number accompanies the offering, which may involve passing buckets down each aisle, or the buckets may be placed on the edge of the platform at the front, with people invited to come forward to place their contributions into them.

The service now enters its second phase, the instructional period when one of the eight pastors, or a designated guest speaker, gives an address. The pastor is dressed casually in a pair of shorts and a sport shirt. His casual manner is typical of everyone in attendance, and virtually no one is wearing a suit or tie; indeed, there is an almost palpable atmosphere of disdain for fashion consciousness or social pretensions in dress.

The message is not some well-exegeted portion of Scripture, nor is it a well-crafted lecture on some aspect of Christian doctrine. It is not even a call for social action. Rather it is a message on wholeness, healing, and holiness, three themes that recur often in the messages given at Harvest Rock Church. The form of the preaching, in keeping with the casual nature of the entire service, is not didactic, exhortative, or grandly eloquent. Rather it is personal and narrative in format. It is a message that tells a story, or several stories that illustrate a point. These stories may be from the Bible, from the speaker's own life, or from the experiences of individuals in the church, their point of commonality being that in Christ there are solutions to life's situations, and no matter how bad things have been, there is hope, healing, and the prospects of a better future.

After speaking for about an hour, the pastor brings his reflections to a close, and the service enters its third phase, the ministry period. The pastor invites all those in attendance to come forward if they want to be prayed for, if they want to make a special commitment to God, or if they simply want to experience a greater fullness of the Holy Spirit in their lives. It is the kind of invitation that members of the church can respond to many times if they wish, and indeed only reprobates, people in deep malaise, or the rebellious could justify not coming forward at least once in a while if they attended services very often.

On this particular evening approximately forty people go forward, carefully lining up in two lines waiting to be ministered to. As the worship team begins again to play worshipful and reverent music in the background, the pastor moves down the first line of people, joined by a small group of people who have been appointed to serve on the ministry teams. As the pastor approaches each of those who have gathered at the front, he gently lays his hand upon his forehead or shoulder and prays for him in words appropriate to the invitation. In the meantime, a member of the ministry team stands behind the person in the event he is "slain in the spirit." This happens when the presence of the Holy Spirit becomes so overpowering that the individual is unable to stand anymore and swoons backwards, when the ministry team is there to catch him and to ease him down onto the floor. The pastor then moves on to the next person to pray for her, and his ministry team follows him. Not everyone falls down in a swoon, so if the pastor completes his prayer and the person is still standing, he moves on to the next individual. Some people may respond to the pastor's prayer by falling to their knees in prayer, others may begin to convulse or jerk and perhaps start to cry out or speak in tongues. There is no predetermined pattern of responses to this time of ministry; as with the worship portion of the service, there is a highly individualized response to the prayer ministry.

By the time the pastor has prayed for the last individuals, many of those who have been prayed for earlier have recovered from their swoon and have gotten up and left to go home. If they have come with friends or family, these have waited for them, or in some cases have come to the front to sit with them while they complete their "business" with God. Some two and a half or three hours after the service started, all but a few people have gone home. It will be just twelve short hours before this entire service will be repeated for a Sunday-morning crowd of from eight hundred to one thousand more people, likewise attracted to the music, the form of worship, the message, and the time of ministry that are the unique features of this church.

A Deeper Look at Harvest Rock Church

As I survey the audience in attendance at Harvest Rock Church, it is interesting to note that approximately 80 percent of the adults in attendance are members of the so-called Generation X. Quite obviously, understanding how Harvest Rock Church appeals to GenXers will require a deeper-level analysis than simply observing one service, especially since the church has not intentionally set about to attract a GenX audience. The question before me, then, was, What is it that Harvest Rock Church is doing that appeals to GenX? The answer to that question, I believe, will be found by looking deeply into the origins of the church and its growth into a movement, followed up by an examination of the philosophy of ministry of the church, particularly as these impact what social science researchers such as Tom Beaudoin (1998), Geoffrey Holtz (1995), and Neil Howe and Bill Strauss (1993) have described as characteristic traits of Generation X.

The Start of a Church and a Movement

Harvest Rock Church officially began to hold meetings early in 1994, starting with prayer meetings that evolved into regularly scheduled church meetings. The nature of these services and the models from which they drew their inspiration were quite distinct, as Pastor Che Ahn, the founder and chief architect of the movement, describes in his book *Into the Fire* (1998). Prior to starting his present church, Pastor Ahn, who is Korean American, was a pastor for nineteen years serving under the direction of People of Destiny, a network of charismatic churches. The lack of a global vision and a commitment to world missions prompted Ahn to withdraw from this group, and through an experience of personal renewal at the nearby Anaheim Vineyard fellowship, which is another network of charismatic churches, set about to build his new church in association with the Vineyard churches.

The spiritual renewal that Ahn experienced was what has come to be known as the "laughing revival," which began at the Toronto Vineyard and subsequently spread to other areas. Pastor Ahn and some of his staff visited the Toronto Vineyard church and were themselves "blessed" by their time there and became convinced the revival was a genuine outpouring of the Spirit of God. Not everyone has been so convinced, and a number of criticisms and critiques of the movement have been published in books and Christian journals (especially Thomas 1995; Hanegraaf 1997; and Beverley 1995). The controversy surrounding this movement ultimately prompted the main body of the Vineyard movement to dissociate themselves from the Toronto church, creating a crisis of conscience for Pastor Che.

Wanting very much to be open to the work of the Spirit of God, and believing in the legitimacy of what was happening in Toronto, Pastor Che withdrew his association from the Vineyard network, but instead of forming an alliance with the Toronto church, he decided to establish his own network of churches, which he decided to name Harvest Rock Church (HRC), and later its affiliates, Harvest International Ministries (HIM), and Harvest International School (HIS).

This spiritual legacy is important because, for anyone familiar with the history of revivalism or of the evangelical awakenings, the development of the Harvest Rock movement follows a familiar pattern. Virtually every evangelical awakening in America, from the time of the Puritans to the present, has resulted in the formation of a new denomination or set of denominations. This accounts for the emergence of the Puritans themselves, then the Methodists, the Baptists, the holiness movement, the Pentecostals, and more recently the charismatics. The charismatic movement, dating back to the 1960s, has itself experienced three distinct phases: the "Jesus People" stage that prompted the formation of the Calvary Chapel movement and other charismatic churches; the "third wave" movement (see esp. Wagner 1988) out of which the Vineyard Fellowship was established; and now the "renewal" movement, of which the Toronto church and HRC are representative.

The reason for these new denominations is that every evangelical awakening prompts new theological debates, challenges existing ecclesiastical traditions and authority, and seeks to address the spiritual needs of the day in an unorthodox manner. Inevitably, such movements strain the organizational constraints of traditional churches, and their leaders are forced, or feel they are forced, to form their own more "seeker-sensitive" and "Spirit-friendly" organizations.

For HRC the theological tension arises from the church's willingness to embrace the so-called signs and wonders manifestations of the presence of the Holy Spirit, including prophecies and the not so traditional manifestation of uncontrollable laughing. The challenge to ecclesiastical authority comes in the church's desire to be free to follow the Spirit of God wherever, whenever, and however it is manifest, even in the face of controversy. And in its desire to meet the spiritual needs of this generation, it has committed not only to following the free-form worship styles of charismatics, but also to taking its message worldwide.

An important correlation to this study is the intimate association of HRC with the "laughing revival." I would prefer to call this renewal movement, as it is being designated, the Joyful Revival, inasmuch as it is more than just laughter but the return of a spirit of joy and hope. This has a particular appeal for GenXers, who seem to stand in need of a special message of joy and hope. According to an early cover story in *Time* magazine on Generation X (July 16, 1990), this age group has been described as a generation that "grew up in a time of drugs, divorce and economic strain." Their desire, we were told, was "to avoid risk, pain and rapid change." They were described as "paralyzed" and "passive." Picking up on this theme, GenXers, we were told, face diminishing job prospects, lower salaries, deteriorating schools, fracturing families, endemic cynicism, and low self-esteem (Holtz 1995). If any generation needs some joy and hope, then it is Generation X; this is exactly what the Joyful

Revival has brought them, and it is in turn a prominent feature at HRC. Interestingly, though, the uncontrolled gales of laughter that marked the start of this revival seem to have passed; at least at HRC, they have moved into a more subdued experience of joy and exhilaration.

Philosophy of the Ministry at Harvest Rock Church

The pastoral staff at Harvest Rock Church has sought to combine a mission statement and their philosophy of ministry through twelve finely focused value statements. These statements set the character and tone of HRC and establish their unique identity among many churches. A close examination of these twelve statements reveals why HRC appeals to Generation X.

1. *WORSHIP: As we worship, we seek to passionately love and glorify Jesus and to celebrate the presence of the Holy Spirit.*

Two traits stand out as appropriate expressions of the worship behaviors at HRC. The first is what I would call "multi-individual" worship behaviors. That is, every individual is engaged in his or her own individual acts of worship while at the same time sharing in this experience with others who are under the direction of the worship team. The second trait is perhaps best described as "participatory worship," or worship in which every individual has an active role. Such worship stands in contrast to what some people refer to as "dead orthodoxy," in which the priest and his helpers carry out the acts of worship while the congregation is relegated to passive participation, with only occasional singing, kneeling, or reading from a prearranged script chosen by the leaders of the church. In participatory worship, when it comes to singing, members of the congregation are encouraged to sing their praises directly to God, which, as Michael Hamilton argues in his article "The Triumph of the Praise Songs" (1999), intensifies an individual's experience of God. For this reason "first person pronouns tend to eclipse every other subject" (34). In further describing the musical quality of praise songs, Hamilton writes: "The starting place for the revolutionaries was secular rock'n roll, so they eagerly used guitars and drums, simple accessible lyrics, and the conventions of popular music—simple harmonies, steady rhythm, frequent repetition" (34). An example of this style is seen in the following praise song popular at HRC:

> This is the air I breathe
> This is the air I breathe
> Your holy presence living in me.
> *Chorus:*
> And I am desperate for you
> And I am lost without you

(repeat)
This is my daily bread
This is my daily bread
Your very word spoken to me.

In participatory worship, movement is another important component: people are both allowed and encouraged to dance, jump, wave banners, raise their hands, or fall down on their knees or faces as legitimate expressions of their faith. The potential for pandemonium in such an environment is a danger, though, so the church has set controls on personal behaviors during this time. Dancers, with one or two exceptions, are restricted to the side of the auditorium, and anyone who becomes disruptive of the service, or a distraction to other members of the audience, will be restrained. The term "free-spirited orderliness" might be appropriate to describe the boundaries for worshipful expressions at HRC.

2. *PRAYER: Because God's house is a house of prayer for all nations, we are committed to pray and fast that His Kingdom will come and His will be done on earth as it is in heaven.*

Prayer and fasting have long been favored religious exercises for saints and mystics. This is relevant for GenXers inasmuch as Beaudoin, in his book *Virtual Faith: The Irreverent Spiritual Quest of Generation X* (1998), has concluded that GenXers are dissatisfied with rationalism and have responded with "a growing enchantment with mysticism" (25). In their own search for spiritual solutions, they have been drawn to mysticism and any other related dynamics and experiences that will allow the human spirit to transcend the bounds of the body and even the physical universe in order to make contact with the supernatural other. For non-Christian GenXers this has led to a fascination with neopaganism, shamanism, and Eastern mysticism. For GenXers within the Christian tradition, this fascination has led them to experiment with those Christian spiritual disciplines that encourage a denial of the self in search of direct communion with God. These include extended periods of prayer, times of meditation, fasting, and the existential experience of God's presence (see also Crouch 1996).

In putting this value statement into practice, therefore, HRC has instituted a twenty-four-hour prayer ministry in which individuals are encouraged to sign up for prayer at allocated times so that every minute of every day is covered by someone engaging in prayer on behalf of HRC and the advancement of the Kingdom of God. It is also common to hear members of the HRC staff and some of its members talking about engaging in prolonged fasting, including forty-day liquid diets, particularly at the start of new endeavors or times of special need.

This focus on prayer has also taken on a new dimension in recent days as an evangelism and mission strategy for proclaiming the Gospel of Jesus Christ to various communities. This strategy is known as "Warfare Praying" and involves targeting a particular community, region, or area resistant to Christian influence and then "praying against the ruling spirits" of that area whereby their unseen influence in support of evil or resistance to the Gospel will be held in restraint, allowing the Gospel to be proclaimed "with power and clarity" throughout the community. This is a theology that takes seriously the Christian belief in Satan and demonic beings, and holds that these beings actively encourage resistance to Christian influence and confusion about the Christian message.

3. *PROPHETIC: Because the church is founded on Apostles and Prophets, we welcome and honor the prophetic ministry. We are called to be a prophetic people and are committed to do only what we see our Father say and do.*

The prophetic ministry that HRC acknowledges and encourages is one of the most controversial aspects of the entire charismatic movement. Virtually all of the charismatic churches, as well as the Pentecostal churches, acknowledge the legitimacy of what are known as the "sign gifts" of the Holy Spirit. That is, they believe that when a person becomes a Christian and/or receives the Holy Spirit, certain outward signs of the Holy Spirit's presence will become manifest. These "sign gifts" include, among others, speaking in tongues (i.e., glossolalia, which may or may not be actual languages), miracles, convulsing, swooning or being slain in the spirit, trances, and speaking prophetically (i.e., speaking a special message from God for that time and place). The different emphases, interpretations, and uses of these sign gifts that a church or movement endorses often determine their denominational affiliation. For instance, many Pentecostal churches believe that anyone who becomes a Christian must speak in tongues or their conversion is not genuine, whereas most charismatic churches (including HRC) hold that speaking in tongues is a gift for certain people but not all. Likewise, the Calvary Chapel movement has rejected the gift of prophecy, which in part led to the formation of the Vineyard movement, where this gift is accepted, as it is accepted in the Harvest Rock movement.

The prophetic ministry concept is based upon the belief that God still speaks to his people as individuals, and not just through the Bible. Such messages are words of encouragement and hope, messages of instruction or guidance for future activity, or personal messages in a time of need. These messages may come through individuals intimately associated with HRC, or they may come through "spirit filled prophets or prophetesses" who are somewhat distant from the movement but part of the wider charismatic/renewal movement. The role of the prophetic ministry at HRC is evidenced both by the place of prophecy in the services and by its prominence in decision making. In Pastor Che's book about the church, he records that virtually every major decision affecting the work of HRC has been launched and confirmed on the basis of prophetic words understood to be God's signal that the church was engaging in doing "only what we see our Father say and do."

Churches that encourage the prophetic ministry, though, face a special danger, since prophecy can be used as a mechanism for individuals to claim spiritual authority for their own purposes; therefore, not just anyone is allowed to speak for God in HRC. Only those individuals who have a proven record of prophetic messages are allowed to speak out in the public meetings, and even these during specific times in the services. All others who feel they have something to say from God are encouraged to speak their mind in private, or during the "cell meetings" (small groups), where they can be subjected to testing and review for authentication.

For GenXers this particular emphasis is important inasmuch as they might be described as skeptical of political processes and promises, public figures, and most of the cultural institutions in American society (see esp. Giles 1994). They are also painfully aware of the fallibility of church leaders, having seen the downfall of prominent television evangelists including Jim Bakker, Jimmy Swaggart, and several local personalities who never made the national news. The result, as described in this *Newsweek* article, is that Generation X has developed an alarm system far more sensitive than a seismograph for sensing hype, insincerity, and deception.

With authenticity and authority being such important issues for GenXers, hearing about a prophetic word from God—that a particular course of action has been directed by God himself, especially if that word can be confirmed in some credible manner—can be marvelously encouraging to GenXers. Here is a program to which GenXers can commit themselves. It has the mark of being God's work, not that of egomaniacs or an irrelevant institution touting hopeless middle-class values and objectives. It is personal, powerful, apparently authentic, and relevant to their lives. By the same token, God help those who seek to manipulate this prophetic ministry for their own goals and glory. If GenXers sense fakery, they will be the first to call upon the biblical injunction to "stone the false prophets"—perhaps not literally, but just as effectively. So far HRC has not had to face this problem, but other prophetic ministries in the charismatic movement have not been as fortunate and have suffered severe criticism and decline as a result.

4. *FAMILY: We believe strongly in the family and are committed to its strength as a building block of our church and society.*

Christianity has long emphasized the family. This is evident in metaphors for relationships used to describe a believer's relationship to God: "God our

Father," "children of God," "firstborn Son." In addition there are those terms that describe the relationship of believers to other believers, such as "family of God" and "brothers (and sisters) in Christ." Thus the emphasis on family at HRC is not unique to this church, but nevertheless it is an important focus for any ministry that hopes to draw membership from the GenX age group.

GenXers are the product of an incredible social upheaval in respect to the nature and function of the family in America. While GenX was growing up, the divorce rate in America more than doubled, as did births to unwed mothers, resulting in GenXers having at least a fifty-fifty chance of spending some portion of their youth growing up in a single-parent home, with all the emotional, financial, and social insecurities that go with this kind of parenting (see Holtz 1995; and Smith and Clurman 1996). Furthermore, this is the generation that grew up during a period when two-income families became the rule rather than the exception. Two-career families have become a common sociological reality in America, and for GenXers this has meant less parenting, at least by biological parents, and less time spent with parents. Chicago's Leo Burnett ad agency "discovered that [GenXers] had a surprising amount of anger and resentment about their absentee parents" (Gross and Scott, 1990).

The impact of all of these developments on GenX is perhaps best described by a twenty-year-old woman who stated in this same *Time* article that she believed her generation would become known as the "family generation." The reason for this, she said, personalizing her generation's experience: "I don't want my kids to go through what my parents put me through" (58). As this generation searches for models, for help in parenting, and for support in the task of raising children at a time when many of the social support systems that were once widely available are themselves in serious jeopardy, they are finding that the church is offering an answer. HRC, in particular, is saying, "We have a message for you"—one of the reasons, I believe, why the message and the emphasis on the family at HRC have a particular appeal for GenXers.

5.   *UNITY: Jesus gave us a commandment to love one another. Therefore we are committed to walk in love and unity in our home, our church, among the different ethnic groups, and among the churches in our city.*

The civil rights movement came into full bloom during the early years of the first GenXers, and the fruit of its success was made public policy during the early years of succeeding GenXers. GenXers, as a result, are the first generation of Americans for whom racial equality has been both an ideal and a requirement of law. While there continues to be evidence of racism right up to the present, nevertheless, for GenXers, racial equality is not a contested option; rather, it is a way of life that they are expected to live out. The task that has fallen upon GenX, therefore, has been to implement racial equality, and perhaps more importantly to facilitate reconciliation between the races over the abuses of the past (see esp. Giles 1994, 66). The experiment in which racial equality is being lived out during their generation has been variously labeled as pluralism or multiculturalism and extends beyond racial equality to tolerance on many levels—racial, religious, gender, and sexual orientation. One very concrete result in this new attitude of acceptance toward others is the 300 percent rise in interracial marriages among GenXers (Holtz 1995, 207).

The realities, though, are that the churches of America continue to be enclaves of racial segregation, fortresses in defense of their brand of Christianity, and belligerent toward any deviations in their traditional way of life. GenXers have also become dismayed by the discordance they see in attempts by traditional churches to preserve denominational segregation and isolation with what they perceive to be false boundaries and outdated identities. Baptists aren't the only ones going to heaven, and the Pentecostals don't have a lock on the generosity of the Spirit of God. Unity and tolerance are important values to GenXers.

The stated goal of the HRC, therefore, "to build a growing, multiethnic, cell-based church that is passionately in love with Jesus and others," has a wholesome ring to it. While the congregation continues to be predominantly white, nevertheless, with a Korean head pastor, a good many Asians feel comfortable in the church, as do a sprinkling of African Americans. Indeed, a look around the congregation during a worship service reveals a significant number of interracial couples sitting together.

To more fully meet the needs of these various communities, HRC has encouraged home fellowship groups (or cell groups) to form around ethnicity, and has encouraged public meetings and Bible study groups to be carried out in the language of minorities (i.e., Korean, Spanish, and so on). The church also holds regular services for Christians from Jewish backgrounds, who now identify themselves as Messianic Jews, and for Native Americans. During the time I was visiting the church, an entire Sunday-evening service was devoted to worshiping under the direction of a Native American pastor who introduced Native American–style hymns, spoke on the needs of Native Americans, and prompted a moving ceremony of repentance, reconciliation, and healing from the entire church and staff.

6. *EVANGELISM: We seek to demonstrate and declare the Good News, heal the sick and incorporate people into our church through personal and corporate evangelism.*

In its emphasis on evangelism, HRC identifies with the historical Christian church and the proclamation nature of its message, as recorded in the New

Testament by the apostles. By embracing the task of proclamation, the HRC movement disidentifies itself from secret societies, exclusivistic associations, or communes and opens up its teachings and practices to public scrutiny. This is not a movement that has anything to hide, and indeed it has already been examined and criticized from several quarters.

Nevertheless, the people and staff at HRC believe they have a message that deserves to be heard, and they are enthusiastic about spreading it. One of the emerging strategies to this end has been to engage in what they call "power evangelism." They do not simply share their beliefs and doctrines with others by trying to prove their truth through rational logic. Rather, their goal is to demonstrate this truth through a manifestation of how it works in personal experience, most notably through answered prayers and the healing of the sick. This remarkably personal ministry accords well with the trend reported in *Time* magazine: "Today's young adults want to stay in their own backyard and do their work in modest ways" (Gross and Scott 1990, 57). These people, having accepted the miraculous as an everyday occurrence, easily pray for healing, for God's miraculous intervention in people's lives, and readily accept the testimony and evidences of people who are healed or transformed following a time of prayer and ministry.

Such "miraculous" manifestations are of course filled with a high degree of ambiguity and are difficult to validate with scientific evidence, but for Generation X, according to Beaudoin, life itself is full of ambiguities, and they have learned to live with them, and even respond with their own ambiguities. As a consequence, validating—whether or not miracles are true—is not as important as the fact that lives have been changed and problems have been resolved. If, in addition, there is evidence of a scientific transformation, that is all the more reason to rejoice in what God has done.

7. *MISSIONS: Through missions, we seek to plant churches, especially among unreached people groups and the 10/40 window. This will be done through Harvest International Ministry, the missions arm of Harvest Rock Church.*

At a time when some Christians in the West, along with a significant number of non-Christians, are challenging the legitimacy of the entire missionary effort of the church, especially its claims that salvation is available only through profession of faith in Jesus Christ, HRC has affirmed its conviction in pursuing this historical goal.

The strategy HRC has chosen to follow in this endeavor is that of planting culturally appropriate churches in the least churched areas of the world, particularly those bounded by the so-called 10/40 window—that part of the world that lies between 10 degrees and 40 degrees latitude north. They have also chosen to welcome into their movement other national church groups who share a kindred spirit with HRC, and one of the outstanding developments of Pastor Che's international speaking engagements has been that of incorporating several hundred national churches into the HRC network from countries in Europe, Africa, and Asia.

The church, likewise, is committed to training and sending out church planters and missionaries to engage in such ministries. To this end they have established their own one-year training institute called Harvest International School (HIS). The purpose of this school is to instruct students in the teachings and emphasis of the HRC movement, and to equip them to take this message cross-culturally. They have chosen to start their own school rather than utilize one of the many other cross-cultural training programs available in the southern California area to conserve money (most academically credentialed schools are extremely expensive), to ensure the teaching of their own approach to Spirit-sensitive ministry, and to provide a venue for students to put into practice what they are learning through ministry within their own church.

This particular approach to ministry has a particular appeal to GenXers, who are often strapped for cash and unable or unwilling to spend several more years going to school to prepare for a career they are not certain they will want to commit to. With minimum financial commitment, and in a relatively brief period of time, students can attend HIS, test what they are learning in actual ministry settings, and in the process discover whether this is a way of life or a career option (calling?) that they feel comfortable pursuing.

8. *CELLS: Through small home groups, we seek to edify the body and reach the lost by creating loving, accepting, and nurturing "cells" where broken hearts can be healed, future leaders can be trained, and the body can be strengthened. We desire to identify specific needs in our church and community and act to meet those needs, as the Holy Spirit leads us, to become faithful stewards of God's blessings through cell groups. Cells can provide an evangelistic opportunity where every believer can experience the excitement of fulfilling the Great Commission.*

With the emergence of the so-called mega-churches during the last half of the twentieth century, the Christian church has struggled with how to maintain a focus on the needs of individuals. Large churches have the advantage of being able to offer specialized programs to their members that would not be possible in smaller churches, including support groups for individuals with addictions, the emotionally wounded, people recovering from broken marriages, single parents, and other special-interest groups with a wide variety of needs within their community. Many such churches also rely on a charismatic pastor to attract and hold the attention of large audiences. But one of the main complaints directed at such churches is that many people feel lost in the crowd. One common attempt to solve this problem has been to encourage smaller networks of believers to form into what are variously called "shepherd groups," "home fellowships," or "cell groups."

The attempt by HRC to implement such an approach, therefore, is not unique to this church, but it is significant in that it has such a prominent emphasis in the ministry of the church. While the pulpit ministry or the speaking ability of the pastors is an important function in HRC, I was impressed during my visits that most of the messages were not given with great erudition. There was no attempt to be particularly scholarly in exegeting a passage of Scripture; there was no attempt to display charisma, charm, or polish; rather the messages were given as simple sharing of thoughts in a narrative discourse, and most important, with intense sincerity. In fact, on several occasions the speaker would have difficulty in finding the right words, and would call upon the audience for their help and blessing, to which they would respond by raising their hands toward him to send blessing and power to continue. Altogether, these traits convey a message of authenticity and reliability that appeals to the highly skeptical nature of GenXers.

Returning, though, to the cell-based nature of the work of the church, it is in the cell groups that individuals are identified, instructed in the Word of God, encouraged in godly living, and given help for their personal needs, and where they form deep friendships with other like-minded people. The formation of numerous such cells also encourages greater participation of church members in the work of the church and effectively extends the ability of the church's staff to minister to such a large membership.

All of this is particularly important for GenXers, inasmuch as they are already cynical about public institutions and prominent leaders and largely unwilling to commit to them. At HRC, though, the pastoral staff are open and honest about their own shortcomings and struggles, and by thus identifying with the people in the pews, they become even more trustworthy. Furthermore, while GenXers have difficulty giving loyalty to an institution, in the cell groups they interact and encounter other individuals to whom they are willing to commit, so that while they may still struggle with long-term commitments, the cell-based approach provides them with the best opportunity to begin to build trusting relationships in their lives.

9. *DISCIPLESHIP: In our discipleship and training, we seek to call people to Jesus, to grow in Him, to radically live out His Word, and to release people and leaders to ministry.*

Since the very birth of Christianity in the first century, the church has functioned to fulfill five primary tasks: facilitate worship of God, instruct its followers in the Word of God, foster a community of believers, promote spiritual growth and godly living among its members, and propagate the faith to all nations and peoples of the world. The discipleship focus of HRC incorporates a number of these goals but gives them a special twist to meet the needs of today's Christians. Growth in godly living today also often means facilitating healing of emotional and spiritual traumas. As Beaudoin (1998) has pointed out, GenXers are acquainted with suffering; they identify with it, and seek answers and resolutions to their own experiences of suffering.

To this end HRC focuses many of the pulpit messages on pain, suffering, and its consequences; sponsors special conferences to promote healing; and has trained counselors available to minister to special needs. During my own visits to HRC I heard messages in which the theme was directed at inspiring hope, assuring individuals of God's control and purposes in their lives, and the promise of a bright future. In every instance, the emphasis was on achieving the promises of God by surrendering to the purposes of God and through personal commitment to godly living. Tom Beaudoin (1998) makes a pertinent observation on this point:

> GenX pop culture suggests that it is not wise for religious institutions to dwell heavily on GenX's suffering, but neither should they ignore or dismiss it. Institutions learning from GenX pop culture can relate suffering to the sacred, connecting it to God's presence and mercy, not to God's absence and judgment. I have witnessed many churches that try to lead Xers from situations of suffering to wholeness, but that are in too much of a rush to wipe away the suffering. If the pop culture is any evidence of a lived theology, a generation's suffering will not be easily or quickly dismissed. (170)

The emphasis I noted at HRC was not some rehash of the tired old "I'm O.K., you're O.K." message of the 1960s, but rather affirmed the suffering of the past and the effects of the past on the present, but always with the prospect of healing and with a message of hope that the Holy Spirit is this healing's source. Further, the messages emphasize what individuals can become, not how they have failed. These messages inspired the congregation to experience the Spirit of God and his work in their lives, rather than calling for a response that is primarily cognitive and based upon new facts and information, or some self-help formula.

To facilitate appropriate responses to these messages, it appeared that the staff intentionally sought to foster a nurturing environment throughout the various ministries of the church, and indeed even during the ministry sessions at the end of each service. Inevitably the invitations to come forward for ministry were a variation of the call to people to come forward to discover fresh resources from God to accomplish more of what they want to become, and what God wants to do in and through them. This emphasis on healing, building community, and preparing for service is further reinforced through special focus workshops and seminars. While I was visiting HRC a church newsletter was circulated to everyone in attendance with a message from the pastor emphasizing the importance of healthy relationships, in preparation for a coming seminar on sexual healing.

Whoever was speaking their message was abundantly clear that no matter what has happened to you, no matter how badly you have been treated, no matter what a mess things have become, Jesus Christ can overcome all and set you on the path toward wholeness, healing, and productive living. This, then, is the goal of the discipleship emphasis at HRC.

10. *YOUTH: Because the harvest is the greatest among the young and because we sense a responsibility to reach the next generation, we place a high priority to reach and minister to the youth in our church and city.*

Generation X has been heavily maligned in the press and in recent literature, prompting in turn a more sympathetic analysis by sociologists such as Geoffrey Holtz (1995), Neil Howe and Bill Strauss (1993), and others who describe them as largely unwanted, unwelcome, and disadvantaged. However one analyzes and interprets the data about this generation, one point that consistently emerges from the interviews with GenXers is their desire to see their own children have it better than themselves.

It is no surprise, therefore, to see that one of the attractive features of the values statement at HRC, at least for GenXers, is their focus upon working with children and youth. Indeed, the theme of the children's ministries director during the time that I was visiting HRC was, "The future generation is now." Building upon this theme, HRC seeks to emphasize the present needs of children as well as their future potential. In seeking volunteers to work with the children's ministries, the congregation was informed several times that this was considered a possible starting point for future ministries in the church.

As has already been noted, the failures of their own childhood homes has left an indelible impression upon GenXers; thus the emphasis on children and youth at HRC strikes a responsive chord with them. As *Time* magazine postulates, "The only solid commitment [GenXers] are willing to make is to their own children—someday" (Gross and Scott 1990, 58). That someday is becoming more apparent now as increasing numbers of GenXers are becoming parents and finding in churches such as HRC a source of help and a model much more akin to the generation of their grandparents, which has a strong appeal to them.

11. *GIVING: Because a sovereign God uses finances to expand His Kingdom, we believe that God wants us to give joyfully and sacrificially with our tithes and offerings, as a means to fulfill the Great Commission and compassionately give to the poor.*

Finances and pleas for funds have always been a touchy issue in American churches. Unlike to the state-supported churches of Europe, American churches have been forced to rely primarily upon the free-will giving of its members. How to solicit these funds is a delicate issue; there has seldom been enough, and the temptation to exert pressure through guilt, shame, or outright manipulation has always been present. Widespread abuses in the raising of funds have also been documented in the media, even becoming the theme of some popular movies.

At HRC, then, finding an appropriate balance has prompted a focus upon the fact that the only appropriate giving is joyful giving, arising from pure motivations and a genuine desire to support the ministries of the church. Not once while I was there did I hear a plea for funds based upon some ministry need, no promises were made that spiritual blessings were conditioned upon giving, and no appeals were made following some emotionally wrenching story. People were encouraged, on the other hand, to participate in the work of the church and in reaching out to meet the needs of less fortunate people. In fact, in his book, Pastor Che shares the story of HRC's generosity toward other churches in the area as they distributed some of their own finances to the ministries of churches in the nearby region.

This low-key approach to fund-raising makes it possible for GenXers, who from all accounts are already struggling financially to support themselves, to worship at HRC without feeling guilty or less than supportive of their church simply because they are unable to give. It does mean, though, that HRC must keep its priorities focused upon ministry needs rather than on building a more aesthetically refined worship auditorium, or some state-of-the-art instructional center. This in turn continues to appeal to GenXers and their own value system, which disdains materialism in favor of richness of experience.

12. RENEWAL: Recognizing that none of the above can be accomplished in our strength, we seek to be perpetually renewed and empowered by the Holy Spirit.

Having emerged as a product of the Joyful Revival, HRC is committed to perpetuating the renewal experience and work of the Holy Spirit associated with that revival. The problem that now confronts HRC is both a sociological concern and a theological issue. Every church and denomination born out of a revival experience has had to answer the theological question, Does the Holy Spirit continue to perform extraordinary manifestations on a regular basis, or are they, indeed, reserved for extraordinary times and places? They also struggle to answer the cultural question, How do you transform and routinize the extraordinary manifestations of the Holy Spirit into normative behavior for everyday living?

While these questions continue to hover in the background, one obvious answer already apparent to the HRC leaders is that the Holy Spirit cannot be regulated, so no program, no practice, no tradition can ever be allowed to substitute for what the Spirit of God intends to do. This means that a conscious strategy at HRC is that of continual flexibility and openness to that which is new and perhaps even revolutionary. Ascertaining whether such new developments are indeed from God or somewhere else requires constant vigilance by the staff as they continually exercise the gift of discernment and seek confirmation through the gift of prophecy. This openness to whatever new work the Holy Spirit seeks to do may mean that some mistakes are made, but this is the risk that such a strategy requires, and for the church and its staff the risk of temporarily embracing something less than genuine is preferable to the risk of missing out on a genuine moving of the Spirit of God and the work of God for today.

As I attended services at HRC, I found it significant that there were few of the manifestations of uncontrolled laughter common when Pastor Che was drawn into the movement. There were only limited instances of speaking in tongues, and these were always restricted to individuals speaking their own worship languages, and yet when one of the pastors concluded his message with an impassioned plea, accompanied by a loud wail for humility of spirit on the part of God's people, his wail was picked up by many members of the congregation. It seemed apparent, then, that members of the church tend to model the spiritual behaviors of their leaders. Thus if a new movement of the Spirit of God does take place and if certain fresh behaviors become associated with such a movement, the leaders at HRC will have to be at the forefront of those engaging in these behaviors for the rest of the church to join in.

I return, once again, to my original question: What is it about HRC that makes it so appealing to Generation X? In support of all that I have already said, I turn to Beaudoin (1998), who comments on the spirituality of Generation X: "Recovering a renewed sense of religious tradition will provide Xers with the resources to continue to do the following: reintegrate the spiritual and sensual; unite religion and politics; critique the Church's Jesus; emphasize a return to community; utter prophetic and apocalyptic words: and bring theological values of anti-institutionalism, personal experience, suffering, and ambiguity to bear on religion beyond this ephemeral moment in our culture" (151). In its own way HRC addresses most of these issues, and perhaps this accounts for its popularity with GenXers. Through the dancing and participatory worship services GenXers can worship kinesthetically, even sensually, without introducing sexuality into their worship. They are able to critique the domesticated Jesus and culturally captivated church by their emphasis on openness to the Spirit of God and the new work he is doing in their midst.

They are focused upon building community through their cell groups and youth ministries. They embrace the prophetic, and eschew dead traditions and institutionalism. They preach using a narrative format that transmits information in the context of personal significance by sharing stories, and this in turn prompts the hearers to reflect on how they too can appropriate and apply what they have heard to their own lives. And if all of this is too strange to fully comprehend, then this is the nature of the human-divine encounter: simply discover its power and get beyond making Christianity just a "head trip." The one area that Beaudoin addresses that I did not see at HRC was the area of uniting religion and politics. There was virtually no discussion regarding political issues or political action to be taken.

A few pages later, Beaudoin makes the following statement, which I find significant for HRC: "GenX's suspicion of institutions implies a threefold emphasis for ministry to Xers: a return to humility in ministry, a willingness to 'go virtual,' and a renewal of mystical practices or spiritual disciplines" (161). Again, HRC addresses each of these emphases in its own unique way. It demonstrates humility in ministry through the highly personalized narrative preaching of its staff. It addresses a willingness to "go virtual" by shrugging off all that is traditional and by embracing any relevant form of spirituality that promotes authentic communion with God, his Spirit, and the Lord Jesus Christ. And it has reintroduced mystical practices and spiritual disciplines by promoting individualized experiences of worship and direct communion with God through trancing (being slain in the Spirit), speaking in tongues, and words of prophecy.

In sum, the success of HRC in attracting substantial numbers of GenXers into their worship services is indicative of a deep level of spirituality among GenXers, even if they express this differently than did previous generations and are critical and cynical of that which they do not perceive to be real. Their participation in worship services and church activities such as those described here are indicative of the great potential that awaits those who are willing to direct their ministries toward the special requirements of GenX. As Holtz (1995) declares, "While this generation has sometimes seemed paralyzed with indifference or apathy, recent years have seen an increasing willingness to speak out, and, as if a sleeping giant has been woken, [its] influence in society has begun to accelerate. . . . And, given the strengths, flexibilities, and diversity of experiences of [GenX], anything can happen" (208).

Postscript: Methodology and Praxis

I come to this particular study as an anthropologist whose area of specialization is that of the anthropological study of religion, and more specifically the mutual influences of culture and Christianity upon each other. I have purposely elected to follow the approach of Clifford Geertz in conducting a "thick description" ethnography, whereby I attempt to assign meaning to behavioral patterns as the participants ascribe those meanings. This creates a stylistic problem: in writing about a people's beliefs and practices, should I write in a manner that reflects their own beliefs, or should I attempt to write as an outside neutral observer? With the latter approach, it appeared to me, my language would become distractingly repetitive, dominated by such phrases as "from their perspective," "in their view," and so forth. I have elected instead to write from an emic perspective, and yet in the restrained terminology of a social scientist. In most cases I also used the standard practice of writing in the present tense, effectively freezing for all time what was happening during my visit to HRC.

In interpreting the developments and behaviors that I observed at HRC, I draw upon a wide-ranging background of study in new religious movements, American evangelicalism, and the study of church growth patterns both in the United States and internationally.

I chose to rely on the standard participant observation techniques that are the mainstay of anthropological field methods, and I added to these a number of personal discussions with various members of the congregation, as well as a formal interview with the executive pastor of HRC. The participant observations were conducted while I attended eleven of their regularly scheduled services. The personal discussions were conducted with church members who greeted me, offered to answer any questions I had about their church, or were anxious to share their own knowledge of the church. The formal interview with the executive pastor was cordial and lasted for some two and a half hours. He was open and candid in all of his answers, and our time was mutually enjoyable. I had two pages of questions to ask him, most of which had to do with staff understandings about their own ministry, and the intentionality in what they were seeking to accomplish. Prior to the interview I had already read Che Ahn's book *Into the Fire* (1998), in which he describes the formative years of the church, and a recent article in *Charisma* magazine about Rev. Che Ahn's vision for an international ministry (Kilpatrick 1999), so I was already familiar with the basic history and philosophy of the church.

One final strategy that I utilized was the controversial new "experiential participation" that has been suggested as a corollary for people engaging in the study of religious behavior (see Young and Goulet 1994). In experiential participation the social scientist is encouraged, more than simply recording information while remaining intellectually and emotionally neutral, to both feel and experience what the people being observed are feeling.

While there are certain limitations to how much an outsider can experience what insiders are feeling, I nevertheless determined that I could genuinely respond and participate in at least one of the altar calls to go forward. On this particular Saturday evening the speaker invited all those who wanted to experience more of God's power and presence in their lives to come forward. This seemed a reasonable request and one that I could embrace without undue skepticism or mockery, so I went forward along with about forty other people. As the pastor moved down the rows of people lined up at the front of the auditorium, I was struck by the realization that all but one fell backward in the classic "slaying in the Spirit." My first thought was, Oh boy, this is going to be interesting. At last the pastor arrived at where I was standing. He placed his hand gently on my forehead and spoke a simple prayer, asking that I might receive the Holy Spirit. As he did so, though, he began to gently push my head farther and farther back, causing me to arch my head upward, and in this position, with my eyes closed, it became apparent that either I had to resist his gentle pressure, step backward to catch my balance, or allow myself to fall over into the waiting arms of the two men behind me. I elected to fall over and was gently allowed to settle down on the floor as the pastor moved on to the next person.

As I lay on the floor, I realized that I had just done what Pastor Ahn himself describes in his book as "the courtesy fall." This is not to say that some people are not genuinely overcome by the power of God's presence and that their swoon is not real and involuntary, nor does it discount that some people may "genuinely" fall as they are overcome by emotion and desire for a spiritual experience, but at least in my case the "slaying in the Spirit" was not a spiritual experience. As I lay on the floor, I realized that if any spiritual benefit was to come out of my going forward that evening, it would have to be in the old-fashioned manner that transpires in any other church—namely, that through an act of will and my own mental choice I would have to enter into my own personal covenant and decision-making time with God, even if on this particular occasion it was done lying on my back at the front of HRC.

I hasten to add that not everyone on staff at HRC uses this particular method of praying for people, for I did observe some of the other staff members gently laying their hands on people's shoulders or on the tops of their head, where they could not or did not engage in the gentle pushing technique I had experienced. These same individuals did not have as many people swoon during the ministry time, but swooning was nevertheless commonplace during all the ministry sessions.

As a spiritual experience, then, my attempt at experiential participation was somewhat disappointing, and as a research technique it proved to be no more illuminating than what I might have otherwise been able to conclude. My experience did confirm in a rather powerful way, though, not to be naive in uncritically accepting other people's interpretations of what is taking place, nor to confuse routinized manifestations of the presence of the Spirit of God for real ones.

References

Ahn, Che. 1998. *Into the Fire*. Ventura, Calif.: Gospel Light.

Beaudoin, Tom. 1998. *Virtual Faith: The Irreverent Spiritual Quest of Generation X*. San Francisco: Jossey-Bass.

Beverley, James. 1995. "Toronto's Mixed Blessing." *Christianity Today*, September 11, 22–27.

Crouch, Andy. "A Generation of Debtors." *Christianity Today*, November 11, 31–33.

Giles, Jeff. 1994. "The Myth of Generation X." *Newsweek*, June 6, 63–72.

Gross, David, and S. Scott. 1990. "Proceeding with Caution." *Time*, July 16, 56–62.

Hamilton, Michael. 1999. "The Triumph of the Praise Songs." *Christianity Today*, July 12, 29–35.

Hanegraaf, Hank. 1997. *Counterfeit Revival*. Waco, Tex.: Word Publishing.

Holtz, Geoffrey. 1995. *Welcome to the Jungle: The Why behind "Generation X."* New York: St. Martin's Griffin.

Hornblower, Margot. 1997. "Great Xpectations." *Time*, June 9.

Howe, Neil, and Bill Strauss. 1993. *Thirteenth Gen: Abort, Retry, Ignore, Fail?* New York: Vintage.

Kilpatrick, Joel. 1999. "Breaking through America's Bamboo Curtain." *Charisma and Christian Life*, June, 47–54.

Smith, J. Walker, and Ann Clurman. 1996. *Rocking the Ages: The Yankelovich Report on Generational Marketing*. New York: Harper Business.

Thomas, Larry. 1995. *No Laughing Matter*. Excelsior Springs, Mo.: Double Crown.

Wagner, C. Peter. 1988. *The Third Wave of the Holy Spirit*. Ann Arbor, Mich.: Servant Publications.

Young, David, and Jean-Guy Goulet. 1994. *Being Changed by Cross-Cultural Encounters: The Anthropology of Extraordinary Experience*. Broadview Press.

9

Spirit Made Flesh

The Tangible Spirituality of "LL Prime Time"

Kimberly Leaman Algallar
and Richard W. Flory

Xers ... know that if religion doesn't go into the streets, the streets will overtake religion. Religious institutions that heed this challenge from Generation X may find their comfortable positions destabilized, which means they will only be more authentic in Xers' eyes.

—*Tom Beaudoin*, Virtual Faith

I'm excited about LL Prime Time. We're planning on taking it on the road. I felt happiness. Now our generation can finally express ourselves.

—*Chuck Singleton Jr., Prime Time minister*

God is doing a new thing. Too many people [are] locked in a time zone. They only receive through traditional methods.

—*Kyle, Prime Time member*

Experiencing Prime Time

Fall 1998: LL Prime Time at Etiwanda High School. As I pass through the throngs of people who have just left the previous service and are now meandering, chatting, and generally enjoying one another in the sunny courtyard, I am very aware of the pale color of my skin, as nearly everyone around me is a beautiful, deep shade of brown. I make my way into the "sanctuary"—a high school gym. As soon as I walk through the doors, I am inundated with blaring rap music, pouring out of several large speakers. Facing me are hundreds of white stackable chairs, only sparsely filled, lined in dozens of neat rows and facing a portable stage. Behind the stage drop royal blue curtains that match the tarpaulin that covers the stage and the gym floor.

Shortly after I choose my seat, the countdown begins. A hip-hop beat blasts while the main players—the ministry staff—are introduced as they half walk, half dance onto the stage. Person by person is added to the small crowd of dance ministers onstage, who are executing the latest in hip-hop dance. Yelling into the microphone, one of them aptly announces, "You may be thinking, 'This ain't church!'" But, as anyone who has ever been to Prime Time will tell you, it is.

LL Prime Time is one of several different services held by Loveland, a non-denominational Protestant church in southern California's Inland Empire. Pronounced "double 'L' Prime Time," this service is geared for youth and young adults, from their late teens to their late twenties. Although a significant number of those who attend and run the service are GenXers, there are no overstuffed couches, no eclectic decor or dim lighting, and no coffeehouse atmosphere. The band does not even play alternative music. The "typical" Generation X paraphernalia seems to be altogether missing from this group. The popular portrayal of the member of Generation X is most often white, but what of the African-American segment of Generation X?

LL Prime Time demonstrates some of the unique ways in which the generational and cultural identities of African-American members of Generation X blend, within a religious setting. In this chapter, I will describe the unique worship service and atmosphere that has been created by Prime Time, the organization of the group, and its relation to its parent church and its members, and provide some observations about Prime Time as a distinctive Generation X religious group.

During the fall of 1998 and the summer and fall of 1999 I attended the Prime Time services many times, participating in the singing and worship and interacting with members of the congregation. I conducted formal interviews with Chuck Singleton Jr., the son of the senior pastor and, at the time, a minister in the Prime Time group, and with Rhoda Linton, the wife of one of the other Prime Time pastors and a member of the leadership team.[1]

Summer–Fall 1999: Prime Time at the Youth Center. By the summer of 1999, several changes had taken place at Prime Time. The service once held in a high school gym had, over the past year, changed in name, location, and content.[2] These significant changes in the service demonstrate its organic, responsive nature. Changes that might occur over a period of years at most churches happened within months with this group. As Prime Time is attempting to remain current with the quickly changing African-American GenX scene, keeping track of the constantly evolving service is difficult. Its constant growth, improvement, customizing, and planning for future change shows its fluid, quasi-institutional state.

These changes also demonstrate the service's coming of age. Beginning in the summer of 1999, its location at a new youth center placed it some distance away from the high school in which Loveland's main services meet. This new storefront venue has facilitated the development of its own character as a Generation X church. And while it retains strong ties to African-American religious traditions and with Loveland—of which it is still considered to be a service—the subtle but mounting changes confirm that at Prime Time, in the words of one member, "God is doing a new thing."

Arrival

Breathing a sigh of relief, I took a seat in the back row of Prime Time's new location just as the service was beginning. I had been told that the service began at eleven, and although it was nearly eleven-thirty, the service had just barely begun. I had been driving around the parking lot of the new shopping center location for some time before I finally found the unmarked storefront location. In later weeks, a large vinyl banner would indicate the presence of the "Loveland Youth Center," where the Prime Time services were held, as well as the "steppers" that could sometimes be seen practicing on the sidewalk just outside of the new location.

Setting

From the outside, the Youth Center is just one storefront among many in this large strip mall. Several of the stores are empty—including what appears to have been a large supermarket—but many businesses remain as well. There are several fast-food outlets, such as Taco Bell and Wienerschnitzel, a Wherehouse music store, and a large movie theater complex. In addition, there are several smaller businesses, such as the beauty supply store.

As I walked through the double glass doors so typical of modern strip-mall storefronts, I was greeted by a tall, friendly man with a wisp of a goatee. He wore a nice vest and pants, displaying developed arms that must have been the result of disciplined training. He shook my hand, gave me a program, and welcomed me. I was then met with another set of double doors—these of nicely finished wood—which opened into the main meeting room of the youth center. The front area where the worship leaders stood looked more like a miniature concert venue than a church stage, complete with speakers, microphone stands, drum set, electric guitars, and a stage lighting structure. A few trees and plants comprised most of the sparse yet cleanly attractive decor. Nothing appeared to be particularly sacred about this place, yet during the services, the leadership often spoke of the presence of the Holy Spirit dwelling there.

It was immediately evident that the Youth Center was a much more appropriate location for this service than the huge gym in which it was formerly held. The smaller location fostered greater interaction among those in attendance, evidenced by the fact that I was given warmer greetings than ever before by the people there, both from members of the "greeting team" positioned inside both sets of doors and from others in the church. Such warm greetings are common among those who attend Prime Time, offered in the form of smiles, handshakes, hugs, and even kisses to regulars and visitors alike.

People in attendance at Prime Time dress casually and are typically outfitted in contemporary urban fashion, including designer sports clothing such as FUBU and Nike, but also knit caps and Dodger hats. Skin-tight clothes, short shorts, and bare shoulders are commonplace among the young women; young men often wear oversize shirts and baggy, sagging pants. Some of the more physically fit young men wear fitted shirts or vests without a shirt underneath, leaving muscular arms exposed; at least one active member had visible tattoos. Sean Dade, the lead Prime Time pastor, can often be seen wearing nice athletic jerseys and long, baggy shorts or pants.

The Service

Music. While on my initial visits, Prime Time's music was primarily gospel and rap, by the summer it had changed to have more of an R&B flavor. A few of the same songs—and many new—blared out of the imposing speakers on either side of the stage, with no shortage of bass. The high level of musical excellence had not changed since my previous visits. At times I found myself engulfed in the deep, soulful rhythms performed by the talented young worshipers. The frequent repetition within the songs had a very soothing effect that was conducive to prayer and meditation within the congregation. At other times the music had the group on its feet, singing, stomping, and clapping, with an occasional shout. Spontaneous voice, both onstage and among those in attendance, punctuated the songs. The worship leaders sometimes shouted, "Feel free to party!" because the worship is often framed as "a Holy Ghost party."

According to Rhoda Linton, who, in her late twenties, is one of the older members of the leadership team, Prime Time tends to "gravitate toward youth-oriented music." Some music comes from Christian artists like Kirk Franklin, while other songs performed at Prime Time are written by their own members. Some of these creations include clips of reworded rap songs, even though rap music, due to some of its lyrics, has often been seen as a sure sign of the decline of American society in most churches. At Prime Time, however, these young lyricists are encouraged to "feel free" in their exploration of the rap form in the Christian context. This can lead to some very unique lyrics ("Lord, you knock me out"), which are often performed in the same set with songs with much more traditional lyrics, such as "Psalm 61," which is taken directly from the Bible.

During a frequently played song called "Jesus in Me," people leave their seats to join hands, move, and sing with others. The lyrics are simple: "Jesus in me, loves Jesus in you . . . It's so easy . . . " and repeats. At the end of each verse the pairs or small groups that have joined hands to sing hug one another and then leave to form new groups and repeat the same process. Often, the acting worship leader will direct—over the microphone—someone to approach, for example, "that girl over there." These directions are always followed. This song and others, like one that lyrically directs people to "get on up and hug somebody / grab a neck and love somebody," illustrates that at Prime Time, praising God moves beyond song—it includes loving each other. Clapping, raising hands, stomping, and dancing are also viewed as forms of worship. Up front, singers often have their eyes closed and hands raised. Some point upward, or reach toward the sky. It is evident that their focus is not on those who sit before them, but on the unseen above.

Having never before participated in such an interactive song as "Jesus in Me" during a church service, on the first Sunday that I experienced this song, I casually asked the young woman who had joined me in singing if it was a tradition at the service. Looking at me strangely, she answered, "This is praise!" At Prime Time, this simple demonstration of love for others is considered a means of praising God. In this service, praise is not narrowly confined to singing but demonstrated in a wide variety of means, many of which take on a more tangible, bodily form.

Worship. After a brief interlude, which includes announcements, greetings to members and visitors, and an offering—during which the music emanating from the stage continues and provides a musical backdrop to all the action taking place—the service becomes less predictable. Drama, dance, step, poetry, or a soloist may follow. One or more of these components will occur on any given Sunday, with a particular theme, such as "forgiveness," or "faith," uniting the components.

Some weeks, a drama team presents a short performance related to the theme of the day. One Sunday, for example, they performed a realistic situation about a young worker desiring promotion and the role of faith in the lives of believers. The situation was practical, demonstrative, and showed a concrete way in which the principles set forth in the Bible could be applied to daily life, so that spiritual concepts inform physical life.

At other times, a dance or step team performs. While hip-hop dance has been sprinkled throughout the worship segments in the past, at times a dance team, called the "Sanctified Steppers," performs choreographed routines. One Sunday they went up front to do "a little rendition" dressed identically in white T-shirts and loose-fitting, flax-colored pants. In perfect unison they executed step dancing, mixed with some hip-hop-inspired moves. Chants of Bible verses and declarations of faith were interspersed in the routine, which was met with shouts of encouragement from the onlookers, such as, "Come on, y'all!" and, "Let's go!" At the conclusion of this performance, amid the applause and yells, one young man literally jumped out of his seat as a show of appreciation. Rhoda Linton believes that step is another form of expression that the Holy Spirit has been leading churches to include as worship. It is relatively new in the spiritual realm, she says, as the Holy Spirit "dropped the same seed" in different churches about three years ago, which ultimately led to this year's formation of Christian step teams all over the country.

In addition to the more formalized dance onstage, some dance occurs in the congregation as well. Most movement is limited, such as people swaying or "grooving" while they stand up in their rows of seats. Actual dance does occur, albeit on a more limited basis, with the occasional worshipers getting out of their rows and dancing in the aisle. This has always been quite orderly and kept within the context of the worship service. Each form of dancing is condoned by the leadership of both Prime Time and Loveland; as Senior Pastor Chuck Singleton Sr. suggests, "People might think that dancing is wrong or strange in church as praise. But David danced before the Lord with all his might."

Another feature that may be included at this point in the service is poetry reading. One Sunday a young man announced that he would be doing a reading, and that it would be his first public performance. He was encouraged by the audience with comforting yells in response to his apparent nervousness, and read a poem on the topic of forgiveness. It sounded very sincere, was recited in plain, everyday language, and read from a paper that he clutched in his hand, while smooth R&B-style music accompanied his reading. Next a young woman—a more experienced poetess—took the microphone. She began her performance with the statement "He got verbal skills!" which inspired even more applause from the crowd for the young man who had preceded her. This young woman, Kadesha, performed a poem entitled "Forgiven, Not Forgotten," which she spoke with great emotion, and from memory. It was obvious that it was spoken out of personal experience, and that many in the audience could relate to the topics it addressed. At key moments of truth the church let out simultaneous hums of "Mmmm!" so as to indicate their strong agreement with her words. At other times they encouraged her with responses like "Go on!" and "Woo, hoo!"

Poetry is growing in popularity within hip-hop culture. Rhoda Linton stated that many young people involved at Prime Time had been "writing on the down-low, not letting other kids know." She spoke of simply listening to one of the young men speak, and telling him that it sounded like poetry. She soon discovered that he and many other young men had a gift and desire to write poetry. Now several of the members, both men and women, have come forward and recited their original poems during the Prime Time service. Rhoda stated that she was "very happy the young men have stepped forward" because reciting poetry "gives them the opportunity to worship in their own way." Further, she views this as a "move of the Holy Spirit," who has chosen this form as a way of reaching the young people who write it and hear it. The poetry they are writing, she says, is "full of the Word."

Sermon. After one or two of these kinds of presentations, and possibly some additional music, one of the several pastors associated with Prime Time comes forward to speak. As a structured part of the service, this portion has changed since the beginnings of the group—and will change again in the future. When Prime Time first started, three of the four ministers would speak in ten-minute slots of time. This gradually gave way to a more traditional twenty-to-thirty-minute time period for a sermon or lesson, but there are now plans to return to several seven-to-ten-minute blocks of time for a particular lesson, each interspersed around the music, step, drama, and poetry.

Call and response, characteristic of traditional African-American churches, runs throughout the service. Yet the exchange taking place at Prime Time is inspired not so much by tradition as by African-American popular culture. When the pastor called, "Y'all ready for the Word?" the people responded with a phrase more commonly spoken by rappers than church congregations—"Word up!" The ministers are charismatic and expressive without being overbearing, and the sermon is delivered without notes. The pastor walks around rather than standing behind a pulpit. He may point, jump, or make other kinds of motions while he is speaking, while always presenting himself in a very dignified manner.

The Bible—the Word. The Bible is believed to be the true word of God at Prime Time, which though progressive in its format has not abandoned historical Christian theology. There is a firm belief in the Bible as the inspired word of God, which continues to be applicable in today's world. "The Word" is read in poetry, sung in worship, and chanted in step performances. It is presented in the sermon and in drama, in a way that is made relevant to youth and young adults. Typical life situations that a young person could face in school, at home, or on the job are used in illustrations and skits, and enlightened by the perspective and wisdom offered in the Word. The emphasis is not heavy on theology; rather, stories are taken from the Bible, and their wisdom and lessons extracted and applied to life situations. Loveland and Prime Time might be called "fundamentalist" in the sense that they claim to know the truth, and are not open to the possibility of other truth claims, yet the approach is less in the form of the "proper" interpretation of the text in search of objective truth than it is a gleaning of the truth from the various stories found in "the Word."

Altar Call. Following the sermon—however brief or extended it may be—the service ends with a time in which the people in attendance are encouraged to "come forward" for more personalized prayer or ministry with lay leaders and members of the pastoral staff. At the beginning of this segment of the service, the congregation is instructed to stand and bow their heads, while the pastor calls for those who are unsaved and wish to become saved to come forward. Others who are encouraged to come forward are those who are already saved but in need of the "anointing of the Holy Spirit," as well as those Christians who might feel "out of gas" spiritually, or who otherwise feel that they are in need of special prayer.

The intent and results of the altar call can vary considerably. One Sunday, fully two-thirds of the approximately seventy-five people in attendance went forward, heeding the pastor's call. On another Sunday, the pastor not only directed the invitation to the group in general but went a step further by directly confronting three older teenagers, asking them some form of the question, "If you died tonight and stood before God, why should He let you into his heaven?" The first young man was silent (as was the rest of the room), then proceeded to look at the two other young men that stood at his left and right, searching for some way to respond. The pastor, directing the young man not to look there for the answer, interpreted his silence as a sign that he needed to come forward. The young man compliantly arose and approached the stage. The pastor then went through the same line of questioning with one of the young men who had flanked the first young man, which brought identical results in him. To the third young man, the pastor simply said, "Either I can go through all of that again, or you can just come up here," to which the young man responded by following his friends' examples.

Origins and Context of Prime Time

Prime Time is the third of three Sunday-morning services at Loveland Church. The first two services are more traditional in form, and each average over one thousand people in attendance, the majority of whom are African American. According to the church website, Loveland has been named one of the one hundred best-attended, and one of the fifteen fastest-growing, churches in the nation.

Loveland's Vision Statement, often referred to by the acronym WEDS, is printed in each week's church bulletin and gives insight into the organizational goals and religious commitments of the church:

Because Jesus is Lord, the vision of Loveland Church is to create an environment of cross-cultural people who:

Worship God in spirit and in truth,

Evangelize across the street and across the world,

Disciple champions through small group fellowship, and

Serve to heal hurts and build dreams, maximizing lives for triumphant living unto the glory of God.

Loveland views this mission statement as central to understanding the purpose and mission of the church, and it "serves as a filter to help determine the things we choose to do, or not to do." Thus the wide variety of programs and services that the church offers take place within the context of utilizing its resources to meet the needs, whether "spiritual, emotional, physical, social, or communal," that it feels "called" to meet, whether in its own community, the nation, or the world. As such, Loveland offers traditional church programs such as small groups and Bible studies meeting in members' homes, as well as other programs and services such as health care seminars, free dental checkups, and literacy classes. Indeed, the church states that it has "over 50 [different] ministries."

Leadership. The senior pastor of Loveland is Chuck Singleton, who in 1981, as pastor of the First Baptist Church of Fontana (California), announced to his congregation that he believed "God has called us to become Loveland." Loveland was established with a core of the Baptist congregation following Singleton and his vision, and by 1984 the church was holding six services each Sunday in order to accommodate all the attendees. The church currently claims eleven thousand members.

In February 1997, following the precedent set when Loveland was first established, Singleton again announced a vision from God that a new service should be established where "youth could express themselves in worship." Within a few months, LL Prime Time had held its first service, having been organized by a group of GenX youth ministers and lay leaders from within the church, chosen by Singleton specifically for that task.

Although Prime Time was organized, and is run, by this younger group, it is not completely free of Loveland influence; there are some elements of external church oversight. Singleton himself attends Prime Time every few weeks or so, speaks in the service on an occasional basis, and always appears to be very positive and supportive of the things going on at Prime Time. In addition, Loveland has mandated the presence of deacons and ushers, who are generally older adults, at every Prime Time service as well. These older adult leaders take special care to respect the form of worship practiced at Prime Time, and they try to ensure that the "young people are not feeling like their toes are being stepped on."

Disorganized Organization. While Chuck Singleton is seen as Prime Time's "official" pastor, functionally he acts more as an overseer than in a daily authority role, and he has placed Pastor Shawn Dade in charge of the Prime Time service. According to Rhoda, Pastor Shawn follows the vision of Singleton, although "in his own style," as he organizes the various elements of Prime Time. Although the leadership team is quite young—none of them are over thirty years of age—this is by design; the intent is to have "youth minister to youth" in the Prime Time congregation.

In practice, however, the organization of Prime Time appears to be very loose. No individual within the leadership seems to perform the same part of the service from week to week. Instead, duties are more often designated at the last minute. For example, during one week the speaker asked, over the microphone, who among the leaders was scheduled to close in prayer. When a member of the leadership team answered him with a name, the speaker overruled his answer and designated another person to pray. This is not uncommon. Other aspects that seem somewhat disorganized are the number of people moving about the room, some entering and leaving the room, all throughout the service, with no apparent regard for what is going on in the service at the time. Although such apparent disorganization often seems to slow the fast pace of the service, it is not overly disruptive and might be entirely appropriate for the type of group that Prime Time organizers have developed. What appears to be disorganization may just be a function of a more loosely structured organization, attempting to meet the needs of its members as best it can.[3]

African-American Culture Predominant. Although Loveland's Vision Statement speaks of a church of "cross-cultural people," and its literature states that "throughout the week people of all cultures and generations are helping and blessing one another," the church is in truth predominantly African American. This is true both of Prime Time and of Loveland as a whole. Being one of the few non-African-American people in attendance at the Prime Time service, I was often stared at not by African Americans but by the very sparsely represented Caucasians, Latinos, or Asians in attendance. It seems that those of us in the minority took special notice of one another. However, the church is correct in characterizing itself as a place of "open doors and a heartfelt welcome," as I was always warmly and sincerely greeted by people at the church.

African-American culture is infused in multiple facets of the life of the church, both at Prime Time and Loveland. At Prime Time, the hip-hop, R&B, gospel, and rap worship music performances are largely dominated by African-American talent. Speech patterns and terminology unique to African Americans—and some GenX segments (see Wesson 1997 on GenX terminology)—are frequently used in the service. Even the list of suggested food items for donation to the Loveland's "Jubilee Pantry" food distribution ministry reflects that heritage in requesting foods like grits, corn meal, black-eyed peas, and yams.

Age. The age of those in attendance at Prime Time services tends to skew to the younger end of the GenX continuum, due in part to an intention of including some older and mid-range teens, but also a result of Xer parents attending the service with their children in tow. This makes for an eclectic age grouping but ultimately adds to the family and community atmosphere of Prime Time. One such couple, Vanessa and Greg Sanders, recently switched from Loveland's main service to Prime Time because of their children. Although they still attend the main service from time to time, their eleven-year-old son prefers Prime Time.

LL Prime Time and GenX Culture

Invoking the term *Generation X* usually brings to mind such media stereotypes as disaffected, white middle-class eighteen-to-thirty-year-olds, complete with the requisite tattoos and piercings, hanging out in the local coffeehouse listening to the latest in alternative rock music. Or perhaps the image of the new breed of Internet start-up entrepreneurs more readily comes to mind. Neither of these, however, is very representative of the members of LL Prime Time. Instead, Prime Timers are predominantly black; they listen—and perform—hip-hop and R&B music and don't spend too much, if any, time in coffeehouses. Yet they do share generational characteristics with the rest of the Xer generation. They have had the same family upheavals, face the same uncertainties in the job market, and are fully immersed in their own GenX segment of the culture. How then do these characteristics play out among this predominantly African-American group, particularly as regards their religious experiences?

Tom Beaudoin, in his provocative book on GenX religion (1998), suggests several areas in which Xers are unique in their spiritual and religious pursuits. In particular, he notes the importance of pop-cultural references in the lives of Xers, such as music—including music videos—and movies, their "deep suspicion of religious institutions" (41), and their emphasis on religious experience and authenticity (74, 93). A brief discussion of Prime Time in light of Beaudoin's claims will help to determine the extent to which Prime Time shares the characteristics of other GenX religious groups.

Pop-Cultural References. Prime Time's entire existence is largely predicated upon its ability to adapt pop-cultural references to its Christian context. This is seen most obviously in its use of popular musical forms and dance—both as a formal part of the service, and more informally by those in attendance. With the exception of the time during which the pastor is giving his message, music is constantly being played during the service, either as accompaniment to the songs that are being performed or as background for the announcements and prayer. Similarly, lyrics of secular songs are changed and adapted to include words infused with Christian (or at least generally religious) symbolism, as is street slang. Thus, as the service is about ready to begin, the emcee may announce, "Let's get ready to rumble!" Or as the service is in progress, in order to encourage those in attendance that the service is indeed continuing on, "This is a Holy Ghost party. The party ain't over yet!" Or finally, the call prior to the minister giving "the Word," "Y'all ready for the Word?" Response: "Word up!"

Suspicion of Religious Institutions. Suspicion among GenXers about the authenticity and sincerity of religious institutions, largely due to the fall from grace of such public figures as Jimmy Swaggart and Jim Bakker, and the apparently meaningless religious pronouncements by different members of the political elite, leaves Xers searching for authentic religious leaders. Yet in comparing characteristics of Prime Time with what is known about typical Generation X religious settings, one particularly interesting contrast arises: Prime Time evidences strong support and respect for the church as an institution, and for its leadership.

For example, when Pastor Singleton speaks at Prime Time, he is received with high fives, warm greetings, and much verbal agreement with his preaching (lots of *amen*s and *go on*s). Even statements from Singleton that require adherence, or perhaps touch on delicate subjects, are met with such agreement by the Prime Time congregation. When interviewed, members of Prime Time indicated that they had begun their involvement as a direct result of the pastor placing them there to serve, indicating respect for the pastor, the highest authority figure within the institution, and a willingness to follow his institutional direction in helping to develop a religious program suited to the needs of primarily black Xers. Thus, as far as attitudes toward their own church and its leadership go, values perhaps more typical of the African-American church appear to override generational tendencies.

Nevertheless, evidence of suspicion of organized religion in general can be found at Prime Time, although this tends to be directed away from criticism of specific institutions and toward the tendencies of people to appear perhaps more religious than they really are. For example, the pastoral staff has encouraged the group to "serve the widow and the orphan," as a way to deepen one's relationship with God, rather than putting on a religious front, or that they "can be real with God," since "God is not impressed with religion." Thus authentic spirituality and religious identity are encouraged—anything other than that is indeed suspect at Prime Time.

Religious Experience and Authenticity. Beaudoin suggests that for Xers, religious truth is not simply accepted from a religious authority but must "meet the ultimate test: Xers' own personal experience," effectively taking religion to the streets (74). While Prime Time does not literally go to the streets, it has certainly escaped the bonds of the traditional church. The location in which the service is held, its format, and the vocabulary used in speech and worship throughout the service all reflect this. To some degree, the language of the streets is used in the services. This is done not for shock value but to relate the religious message to the life experiences of its members. While it may not be shocking to hear these words thrown about quite casually in daily conversation, it can become shocking when one considers the religious context in which they are being used. Nonetheless, these words aptly illustrate the real world in which the Prime Time members live.

A few examples: One Sunday, one of the pastors was speaking of the way that the Holy Spirit refines the lives of Christians, and specifically listed "fifths" (of alcohol), cigarettes, "daisy dukes," and marijuana as distractions from God, and "Studs" and pregnancy the results of another kind of distraction. In another message, the pastor referred to people who made them angry as "people who piss you off." His recommendation? "Love the hell out of them!" And in a kind of verbal caricature of the prayer of a sexually promiscuous young man during another sermon, the minister said, "I promise you [God], next time I'll wear a condom. Please don't let me catch no diseases." Prime Time, through the messages of its ministers and its ability to relate life's everyday experiences to the religious community, has been able to meet the criteria of providing, and encouraging, an authentic religious experience for its members.

Prime Time has been able to adapt its form in such a way that it has, in effect, brought the "rough and tumble of the world" (Beaudoin 1998, 177) within the institutional walls of the church. It has accomplished this through adapting various pop-cultural forms to Christian ends, and through providing authentic religious leaders and experience in a vernacular that not only is understandable to this GenX segment but originates from them. That is, a particular religious institution has been created within which Xers can create their own authentic religious expressions and experiences, in the context of traditional Christian beliefs. This simultaneously authenticates both the sponsoring church—Loveland—and the GenX congregation.

Prime Time, then, offers a fascinating example of Christianity contextualized into a very specific social context—that of the young African-American hip-hop scene—that enables these Xers to be both authentically Christian and authentically black, without compromising either identity.

Notes

Although this chapter was coauthored, we have chosen, for ease of writing, and of reading, to use the first person singular throughout.

1. Kim Algallar also attempted to set up other formal interviews with church staff, but all of these proved unsuccessful.

2. In June 1999 a memo issued by Pastor Shawn indicated that LL Prime Time had changed its name to Real Life. However, as of December 1999 it remained listed in the weekly church bulletin, *Lovenotes*, as LL Prime Time. For ease of reference, and because it is still listed as Prime Time, that is the name we use throughout this chapter.

3. See Aldon Morris (1986) on the organization and structure of the African-American church. Morris suggests that although behavior within the black church is organized, it is not highly formalized, so can give the appearance of emotionality, or disorganization.

References

Beaudoin, Tom. 1998. *Virtual Faith: The Irreverent Spiritual Quest of Generation X*. San Francisco: Jossey-Bass.

Morris, Aldon D. 1986. *Origins of the Civil Rights Movement: Black Communities Organizing for Change*. New York: Free Press.

Wesson, Vann. 1997. *Generation X: Field Guide and Lexicon*. San Diego, Calif.: Orion Media.

10

Friday Night Live

It's Not Your Parents' Shabbat

J. Liora Gubkin

Widowed princess, having had sufficient experience with princes, seeks frog.

—*Personal ad*, Jewish Journal of Greater Los Angeles

Across the page from the personal ads in the *Jewish Journal of Greater Los Angeles* appears an advertisement for Friday Night Live, a creative and innovative Shabbat service targeted toward young professionals. And on the second Friday of every month, more than fifteen hundred young Jews throughout Los Angeles and beyond gather to sing, dance, pray, and socialize—known in Jewish parlance as *schmoozing*. The word is out, for Generation X Jews from Santa Barbara to Orange County, that Sinai Temple is the place to celebrate Shabbat and meet young, single Jews.

Rabbi David Wolpe, the brains behind and spiritual leader of Friday Night Live, begins the service each month by telling the makeshift congregation that Shabbat "is an opportunity to connect with God and with each other. Here at Friday Night Live," Wolpe continues, "we do that through music." The unique blend of contemporary and traditional music, led by music director Craig Taubman, serves as a bridge through which to cultivate community. Many who attend FNL are searchers: whether for a spiritual experience, friendship, or their *bashert* (soulmate). They come to feel connected to a community in a religious tradition where community is a central value; in fact it's a commandment, an important aspect of Jewish law.

Granted, the Jews who attend FNL are not observant in a traditional sense of the word. While a small minority of those who attend FNL also pray (*daven*) in an Orthodox community, particularly the Orthodox outreach group Aish Ha-Torah, Sinai Temple is not in walking distance from the Pico-Robertson area, where a large percentage of L.A.'s Orthodox Jews live, and most Orthodox Jews would protest both the mixed seating and the instrumental music that are the hallmarks of this Shabbat celebration. Most attendees are unaffiliated Jews, dissatisfied with the liberal or secular Jewish tradition of their parents. As Heyden, a twenty-year-old computer science student, describes the Reform Judaism of his youth, "I grew up with the stand up, sit down, turn the page service and hated it."

Like Heyden, participants at FNL are primarily nonaffiliated, but many attend multiple venues for Jewish spiritual searchers in the L.A. area such as Aish Ha-Torah and the Travelling Shabbat Singles. Nonaffiliated does not necessarily mean inactive. Generation X Jews participate in a general dual trend within American Judaism, in which a growing "religious minimalism" by the majority is coupled with intense engagement by a minority. "American Judaism," notes one writer on the topic, "is suffering a staggeringly high rate of defection and indifference, even as it simultaneously experiences a creative renaissance and return to tradition by Jews across the spectrum of Jewish life" (Wertheimer 1993, 66). At Friday Night Live one finds young Jews for whom this monthly service is their sole religious experience praying next to Jews who have just come from a Shabbat dinner and will return to synagogue Saturday morning.

Not content with the Judaism, or lack of Judaism, they were raised with, many of these Generation X Jews deliberately refuse to peg themselves into a denominational hole. Again, they are part of a larger Jewish trend. According to the 1990 National Jewish Population Survey, 41 percent of Jewish households were affiliated with a synagogue. The numbers are even lower in Los Angeles, and lower still among Generation X Jews. The absence of family is clearly one reason for their nonaffiliation. In addition, they are perhaps disturbed by the acrimonious relationship between various Judaisms that mars communal leaders' calls for unity among the Jewish people. Although, as Jack Wertheimer (1993) notes, "All four major movements in American Judaism [Conservative, Orthodox, Reconstructionist, and Reform] have repositioned themselves in ways that have heightened religious polarization" (95), at Friday Night Live, issues of who is a Jew, patrilineal descent, and the legitimacy of marriages performed by Reform rabbis in the land of Israel recede into the background. Young Jews come to Friday Night Live in search of a feeling, a religious experience, not correct theology or ideology. They are open to whatever group fills that longing for community and gives these GenX Jews a place to belong.

Beth, a twenty-three-year-old systems engineer, is fairly typical in this respect. She describes her religious upbringing as being on "the conservative side of Reform." These days she prays with multiple communities, a "denominational mutt" searching to find where she fits best. Beth poignantly speaks of belonging to "a lost generation" of young adults plagued with high rates of intermarriage and divorce who are "trying to find who we are and where we belong." As high rates of divorce of their parents has been a benchmark experience of Generation X, concern with intermarriage in the Jewish community has emerged as a central crisis issue at approximately the same time. With these spiritual and social needs looming, Wolpe enrolled Taubman and began Friday Night Live in June 1998. Postcollege, prefamily, "this is the population we lose," Wolpe says.

The homogeneity of the group, at least on a superficial level, fosters a sense of community. There is a separate family-oriented service prior to Friday Night Live, and although a few younger and older people infiltrate the service, the vast majority are Generation X Jews. The "young feel of the congregation" infuses it with energy, says Scott, a forty-year-old computer consultant. Without the presence of families, the service leaders can focus their attention on the population at risk. "When you look around the room and there are no families," says Heyden, "you feel more free to be yourself."

But does Friday Night Live truly provide a place to belong? Given its phenomenal growth and sustained success, it is clear that FNL fulfills some need for community. But what kind of community is this—a congregation of fifteen hundred to two thousand young professionals who gather once a month for an hour-long service and two hours of informal social activities? This chapter will present this quasicommunity, the religious experiences of those who attend, the vision of its charismatic leaders, and the challenges FNL faces as it attempts to reach Generation X Jews into the next millennium.

Music: Unifying Language, Universal Medium

Traffic bottlenecks in both directions at the mammoth complex of Sinai Temple, located at the intersection of Wilshire and Beverly Glen in West Los Angeles. Several attendants hired for the evening direct traffic into the underground parking structure as others collect keys of those who park behind the early arrivals. The underground structure is full. The time is 7:15 P.M. Inside, people schmooze before they enter the sanctuary. As Jesse, a thirty-year-old teacher, notes, you never know who you will see. People scan the crowd for familiar faces, and throughout the building one hears the form of chitchat known as "Jewish geography":

"Wow, I haven't seen you since we attended camp Ramah [a Jewish summer camp] in 1984."

"Didn't you volunteer at the last Jewish Federation Super Sunday?"

"Can you believe it's been five years since we taught together for the Bureau of Jewish Education?"

People who have arrived alone, especially women, seek out other loners to find safety in numbers. Several hover over the long table at the sanctuary entrance. Here one finds flyers for a workshop to learn to read Hebrew in one day; a listing of upcoming singles events at Sinai Temple; a twelve-page booklet containing transliterations of the songs and prayers of the Shabbat service; and a plate to place your business card on if you want to be contacted to join the FNL Planning Committee.

The table is physically located at the entrance of the sanctuary, and its contents offer entry points into Jewish community. The prayer booklet is particularly interesting in this regard. Transliteration is provided, so everyone—even those without a Jewish knowledge base—has access to the prayers that will be sung in Hebrew, the sacred language of the Jewish people. In addition, the slim, gray booklet assures newcomers that the service will not be too long. Here you can judge a book by its cover; the service lasts less than an hour. The translations provided in the booklet are also geared toward the Generation X crowd. In lieu of a complete translation, each prayer is followed by a phrase that expresses the sentiment of the Hebrew. A comparison with the full prayerbook (siddur) is instructive. For the *Aleinu* prayer, to give one illustration, the booklet reads, "It is up to us to praise the Holy One of Blessing." In keeping with both the emphasis on the voluntary nature of religion for this generation and the general discomfort with the language of commandment in liberal Judaisms, to praise God is construed as an individual choice in this translation. It is, perhaps, a more user-friendly interpretation of the prayer's opening line, which is translated in the siddur, "We rise to our duty to praise the Lord of all, to acclaim the Creator."

One enters the sanctuary and is transported to an earlier era. The fixed, theater-style seats are plush and deep green with a rich wood backing that holds siddurs and bibles. Ensconced in these seats, reminiscent of pews, facing the raised area of religious worship (*bimah*) with its soaring, free-standing ark, stained-glass windows, and elaborate, gold eternal light, one cannot help but be filled with awe. The setting presents a disconcerting contrast to the intimate and participatory aesthetic Wolpe and Taubman attempt to establish. In full awareness of the clash between the architecture of the sanctuary and the content of the Friday Night Live service, Wolpe comments that "religion moves in patterns and waves. An earlier generation wanted grandeur; now intimacy is in fashion. . . . Neither are wrong; Judaism has a place for both *ahava*, love, and *yirah*, awe."

The band begins to play up on the *bimah*. For this particular Friday Night Live the instruments include cello, bass, percussion, accordion, clarinet, and two guitars. (When the band is introduced toward the end of the service, we learn that the second guitarist played with Paul McCartney's group Wings.)

Wolpe and Taubman, with open collars and rolled-up sleeves, descend from the *bimah* and work the crowd. Taubman starts quietly, "Romemu Adonai Eloheinu." The repetitive beat and soulful tune captivate the congregation. He translates the words, "Praise Adonai our God." He sings the tune again and again; each time more voices join his in song. The intensity builds as Taubman encourages everyone to raise their hands above their head and follow his lead, putting one's whole self into the music. A grand crescendo as a thousand voices join in song, and the magic of Friday Night Live begins.

If Friday Night Live does constitute a community, truly it is formed through the music. Luke, a thirty-year-old writer, describes the service as "Rockin' Shabbas." "Normally *davening* is such a pathetic experience in Jewish life," Luke laments. "The liberals are dead and the Orthodox go on forever, but this is a nice combination of passion with some traditional liturgy and musical instruments." Beth puts it simply: "The singing together is so beautiful, I get chills." Lisa Schiffman's description of her experience of music during a prayer service in her memoir *Generation J* (1999) aptly captures the FNL experience: "During the songs, a change happens. These individuals become something more. They become part of a whole, a community. They become part of a heritage, a civilization. They're connected by voice, by sound, by melody. Sometimes they become part of each other, part of whatever they call God" (94–95). For some the music is simply enjoyable; for others it elevates and transforms. The contrast between Heyden's earlier religious experiences and his enthusiasm for Friday Night Live is stunning. "I am looking for Shechinah [God's immanent presence]. When I'm here, I find it. That's the transformative point for me."

The song is soulful, spiritual prayer. As Wolpe (1993) has described the power of song, "The Hebrew word for song, *shir*, denotes more than musical song; it means poetry, lyric, the use of words that seek to overbound the everyday, to ratchet language up to a different level, to celebrate and explore. To sing is to elevate the ordinary. A song is a statement made sublime" (170). For many FNL participants, worship becomes possible in this setting. Scott believes the music provides the opportunity to connect with God and each other that Wolpe hopes FNL cultivates. For Scott, singing as part of this congregation is "being in awe of God." At its best, the experience of singing these ancient prayers in a sacred language with tunes that lift the spirit of the current generation allows these individuals—members of "the lonely generation"—to merge beyond the boundaries of self. Beth's passion for the music is palpable as she explains, "I want to be here and pray; it's a celebration of praying—loudly like you want the whole world to hear you."

One can read this aspect of Friday Night Live through a postmodern lens. These GenXers are not searching for rational knowledge as much as pursuing truth at a collective level. What one comes to understand from observing and participating in Friday Night Live is that experience is key. Taubman, self-described as "on the cusp of Generation X," carefully chooses music to create space for this experience. On the Friday Night Live CD (yes, you can play this music in the comfort of your own home), Taubman describes his own process when making this music: "Every once in a while I find that more than a writer I am a discoverer. The music found on this album is such a discovery. As I prepared for the Shabbat service, I would read and study the liturgy and music would pour from the pages of the siddur." As he explores musical possibilities, Taubman's first questions are keyed to the experience. He asks himself, "Does the music move me? Am I engaged in the moment?"

For many at Friday Night Live, magic blossoms in that moment. "Music is the touchstone," says Heyden. "It's part of an atmosphere that makes you comfortable being Jewish in your own way. That's the magic." The music succeeds, in large part, because it enables participants to maintain their own spirituality and simultaneously participate in the larger group. With no theology, doctrine, or creed made explicit, everyone can be Jewish "in [their] own way." Taubman appreciates the generosity of the music. "Music is a universal language," he says. "Whether or not you understand the context or content of a particular song, music is a powerful medium that conquers that adversity." Tina, at twenty-two a newcomer to her heritage—she began the process of claiming her Jewish identity while in college—concurs; "I don't know if I necessarily believe the prayers," she says, "but in a room full of people who are part of something larger, you don't have to understand or agree. Being with this community, you can feel good about yourself and know you're part of something special."

When we get to the Amida (the standing prayer), one of the central components of the Shabbat service, everyone rises, and the room echoes with a thunderous sound as the chairs spring upright. The back wall that connects the sanctuary to the social hall has been opened; there are more than fourteen hundred people standing. Wolpe prepares the congregation for the silent prayer with a message particularly appropriate in the face of the rampant consumerism of the holiday season and the general materialism of so many young professionals in Los Angeles: "Use this time to think about what you really want—not just what others want you to want." A hush descends over the crowd as Taubman steps forward, strums the opening notes on his guitar, and sings softly, "Adonai s'fatai tiftach / Ufi yagid t'hilatecha" (Open my lips so that my mouth may sing your praise.) Taubman alternates between singing the words and humming a *niggun*, a spiritual, wordless tune, which gently fades as the intensity of silent prayer emerges. The Amida concludes with what is perhaps the most unusual part of the Friday Night Live service to occur in a main-line, liberal congregation. As the congregation sings Oseh Shalom, the blessing for peace, the band plays along and several hundred people join in a somewhat contrived spontaneous dancing through the aisles of the congregation. Panned by some as forced and faked, praised by others as the highlight of their Shabbat experience, dancing is one more way FNL pursues a religious experience.

Making Meaning Particular

As the rabbi of Friday Night Live, Wolpe has a mission. Each month he uses his sermon as a platform to teach GenX Jews that they can pursue meaning-ful religious experience within Judaism, that Jewish tradition has what they are looking for. If the music at FNL functions as a unifying and universal medium, Wolpe's sermon is the medium that makes meaning particular.

Wolpe is particularly well suited to bring this message to the audience. The son of a rabbi and a teacher who studied at both the University of Judaism in Los Angeles and Jewish Theological Seminary in New York, the leading insti-tutions of Conservative Judaism, he traversed his own path away from and back to Judaism. At the age of forty-one, moreover, he can relate to the con-cerns and struggles of Generation X Jews and often integrates personal stories into his sermon.

In the midst of a very full schedule—a husband and father, he is the full-time rabbi at Sinai Temple, teaches at their day school, writes prolifically, and is in constant demand as a speaker—Wolpe works diligently toward his goal to "provide a message that is thought provoking each month." The power of Wolpe's speech is no coincidence; he sees Judaism itself as a religion of word and speech. In his book *In Speech and in Silence,* Wolpe writes, "The Jewish tra-dition is a tradition of words. What we say, how we speak, what it means to connect to another human being—these are central concerns of the Jewish tradition" (35). Wolpe understands the power of words and is committed to using them well. Words are a primary vehicle through which we connect to each other and connect to God: "The central religious objects in Judaism are scrolls, book, commentaries; the central quest in Judaism is the attempt to bring the sacred into language, to make the ineffable expressible" (114).

In fact, Wolpe is renowned for his speaking ability. One Jewish profes-sional who had the "burden" of following Wolpe's keynote speech at a con-ference for Jewish educators compared him to the lyrical biblical psalmist, King David: "From David to David there is no one like David." One may be tempted to dismiss this as hyperbolic flattery, but from the rapt attention he holds of those present at FNL to the remarks made by everyone interviewed for this chapter—many of whom described him as "charismatic"—it is clear that Wolpe and his sermons are a key component of FNL's success.

In his sermons Wolpe does not assume any knowledge of Judaica, but he also does not talk down to the congregation. Instead, he tackles the issues of faith, love, spirituality, soul, and the search for meaning, which is craved by so many of the GenXers. The December 1999 Friday Night Live coincided with the final night of Hanukkah, a holiday familiar to even nonobservant Jews. Wolpe began his sermon with a question from the great sixteenth-century rabbi Joseph Caro, a mystic who was also responsible for one of the most important documents of Jewish law. Caro asked, "Why do we celebrate Hanukkah for eight days?" According to rabbinic tradition, we celebrate Hanukkah for eight days because when the Jews reclaimed the Temple in Jerusalem after the Maccabees defeated the army of King Antiochus, there was only enough oil found hidden away in the Temple to last one day. Miraculously, however, it lasted through eight days until more oil was found to keep the eternal light aflame. Caro asks, "Shouldn't we celebrate Hanukkah for seven days, since the oil was supposed to last one day? Aren't the following seven days the true miracle of Hanukkah?"

"It's a good question!" Wolpe exclaims as he notes the last flame flickering on the menorah to his right, lit hours earlier. There is a Hanukkah miracle, suggests Wolpe, and it is neither seven nor eight days. The true miracle is that someone hid a container of oil in the Temple in the first place. Wolpe evokes the scene. Imagine the fierce battle. Imagine the pigs' blood in the holy of holies. Despite overwhelming odds, someone decided to hide oil for the eternal light. It must have seemed a meaningless gesture. Friends and family probably thought the anonymous hero of this story was absolutely crazy. Wolpe then makes this historical event meaningful for our own lives. Here a small, unknown act made a huge difference. Here is positive evidence of the reality of miracles, and the possibility for miracles in our own lives. Wolpe states emphatically that he does not use the word *miracle* metaphorically. He argues for an openness of the soul, a recognition that to perform a small act of faith can change the world.

In his focus on the reality of miracles, Wolpe is emblematic of the shift from modern to postmodern spirituality. Rabbis of both eras preach the significance of the good deed, but the language of the prophet has given way to the language of the mystic. A sermon in the Judaism of my youth was likely to conclude with the words of the prophet Amos, "Let justice roll down like waters, and righteousness like an ever-flowing stream," followed by a call for social justice. Today the catchphrase is *tikkun olam*, the repair of the world, adapted from the complex cosmology of the sixteenth-century Jewish mystics, in which God *needs* human partners to repair a broken world. Most Jews at

Friday Night Live are not aware of the implicit theology, but what is clear is that it is mystical, rather than rational, imagery that speaks to this generation.

The following month Wolpe directs the congregation's attention to the other central prayer of the Shabbat service, the Shema, which is called by many "the watchword of our faith" and is traditionally recited three times a day. He notes that anyone not already familiar with its contents will find it on page 29 and 30 of the prayerbook: "Shema Yisrael Adonai Eloheinu Adonai Echad" (Hear, O Israel: The Lord our God, the Lord is One). Wolpe draws attention to the texts preceding and following this famous declaration: Ahavat Olam speaks of God's love for all humankind and for the people of Israel; Ve'ahavta says we should love God with all our heart, soul, and might. The Shema, Wolpe notes, is both preceded and followed by a declaration of love. Then he returns to the opening line of the Shema and notes its peculiarity as a prayer. "To whom is the Shema directed? Not to God. It is directed to Israel—to us." The word *echad*, he continues, usually translated as "one," can also mean "alone." Wolpe asks what it would mean to think of the Shema as a plea to us that God is alone. God loves us and needs us to love God in return. Jewish worship, Wolpe concludes, is essentially about reciprocal love.

It is not just music and community, Wolpe asserts. Rather, the deep mystery that is God's love is at the center of Judaism. Wolpe addresses a potential criticism from the skeptics among FNL participants. (Although there may be more of an openness to belief in God among Generation X, a recent survey [Cohen 1991] found that nearly 20 percent of the Jews questioned expressed skepticism about the existence of God.) You cannot simply say you do not believe in God, Wolpe declares, because then you have to say who exactly is the God you don't believe in. "If you are referring to the old man in the sky, well, I don't believe in him either and haven't for a long time." Wolpe speaks of the mystery that is God, the root of soulfulness, and the proof, which often must be taken on faith, of ultimate meaning.

Part of the appeal of Wolpe's words resides in his ability to seamlessly shift between ultimate meaning and popular culture. One sees this encapsulated in his ongoing commentary on the ubiquitous cell phone. When a phone rang in the sanctuary after the opening song, which compares Shabbat to a bride and welcomes her into our midst, Wolpe used the opportunity to explore the metaphor that Jews, ideally, are married to time rather than enslaved by it. When a lost cell phone was brought to him by security, Wolpe announced that he was going to use this opportunity to perform the mitzvah (good deed) of returning lost things, although it pained him greatly. In both cases, Wolpe used his wit and charm to mediate between Jewish values and contemporary life. The words of two FNL participants sum it up: "The rabbi is funny, and he talks to us! . . . He says exactly the right thing at exactly the right moment."

J. Liora Gubkin

Searching for Connection—Frogs and Princes Present

Following the sermon, announcements, and closing prayers the hard-core schmoozing begins. For some, this is the reason to attend FNL. In fact the crowd is substantially augmented by those who arrive at the end of the service. There are several postservice activities to choose from. One can participate in Israeli folk dancing, partake in discussion with Wolpe, listen to a concert in the chapel, or nosh on the pasta salad and brownies that quickly disappear. People wander between the activities, sampling what is available and checking out where the action is. It is clearly a singles scene. It is, as Luke, a devoted attendee of FNL, describes it, "a 'meet' market for Moses."

In my observer capacity I was able to overhear a variety of interactions. One of my favorite snippets of conversation occurred in the social hall, where two men were debriefing after being rebuffed by a woman. "She wasn't ignoring you," the one consoled, "she just wasn't paying attention." In another instance, I was chatting about FNL with a female acquaintance when a socially awkward man came up to her and said, "Hi. Do you want a boyfriend?" Her response was a polite but firm no.

Yet as a Generation X Jew myself, I was a participant as well. Thus, I too was privileged to partake in the fine art of flirting. Immediately following the service one guy made a beeline toward me—I had ignored the rule about safety in numbers—told two terrible jokes, which, thankfully, I have forgotten, and then asked, "So, are you going to give me your phone number?" This was particularly amusing because I was liberally (almost desperately) handing out my number in hopes of securing follow-up interviews for this chapter. Let's just say, this man does not make an appearance in this story. These social interactions take place primarily, but not exclusively, after the service, when one can clearly see men and women checking each other out. "There is also a 'see and be seen' type atmosphere," notes Jesse. "I wouldn't go as far as to say 'meat market,' but an element of that is there." At the January FNL, for example, an attractive man sitting in the row ahead of me turned around and complemented me on my beautiful voice. This was quite flattering, except, as my family will attest, I cannot carry a tune to save my life. To conclude this tale of princes and frogs, however, I am happy to report that I even secured a date. We met while watching Israeli dancing. My mother is ecstatic.

While most would agree that the service succeeds at fostering a sense of connection, many would also agree with Scott, who wishes the people behind Friday Night Live "would make more of a clear effort to bring the rest of the event in line with that ideal. Most people don't make eye contact. It's very much like a bar scene but without the alcohol." Others, however, are far less cynical. Beth enjoys the social component of FNL, especially because it is a place to find young men who are deliberately choosing to be Jewish. Finding a Jewish partner is a key concern for many of the singles at FNL. They do not want to become one of the statistics on intermarriage reported in the National Jewish Population Survey of 1990, which stated that more than half of the weddings that involved American Jews were interfaith. The results also showed that nearly 75 percent of the children raised in interfaith households are not being raised as Jews.

Intermarriage quickly becomes connected to children, which quickly becomes connected to the perpetuation of Judaism. Suddenly, it is not just about a date; the survival of an entire people is at stake. Concern, anxiety, and fear lurk just beneath catchy phrases like "bar without alcohol" and "'meet' market for Moses." The specter of intermarriage, especially for this generation raised with a hyperconsciousness of the Holocaust, haunts Jewish single life. In a December 1999 issue of the *Los Angles Jewish Journal*, the singles column was devoted to interfaith dating. In addition to the statistics from the 1990 National Jewish Population Survey, the column included a sidebar entitled "Five Steps to Better Ensure a Jewish Marriage" excerpted from a publication with the ominous title *It All Begins with a Date*. Steps 4 and 5 encourage parents to create a positive Jewish environment in the home and to enroll children in outside Jewish activities such as youth groups and summer camps. Steps 1 to 3 directly confront issues of dating and marriage: "One: Tell your children you expect them to marry someone Jewish. Explain why. Two: Let them know that this standard applies even to dating. Three: Start talking to them about this when they are very young. Don't wait until their first date." Whether or not Jews at FNL find their *bashert* in the midst of this mammoth singles scene, they have heard the message against intermarriage and for "Jewish continuity" loud and clear.

Socializing may be the original draw to FNL for many attendees, but the event is often criticized as being overwhelming and too crowded to actually meet new people. Wolpe dismisses the complaint. "In some ways it's a false concern," he says. "Usually what they mean is that they see people that they want to meet and don't succeed." Taubman replies that the breakdown into various activities such as dancing and discussion is an attempt to make the event more intimate and accessible.

Community without Commitment? A Challenge for Friday Night Live

For the moment, Friday Night Live succeeds because it provides what these GenX Jews are searching for: spiritual experience, a sense of belonging, a date. The majority of participants leave feeling good about themselves, and about their Judaism: they experience joy in singing and dancing to an eclectic synthesis of ancient prayers and contemporary music; they receive assurance from a charismatic leader that Jewish tradition has something to offer; and through their sheer numbers, they are reminded they are not alone. "I knew; I was so certain it would succeed," says Wolpe. "I did not have a moment of doubt." Success, however, comes with a price. If anything threatens to curtail FNL, it is a lack of funding. Although generous benefactors support FNL, it is currently running a deficit of $30,000, a burden that is assumed by Sinai Temple. Nevertheless, Wolpe maintains a commitment to freely give this event to the Generation X population and not to ask for their financial support.

One may question the wisdom of not asking for anything in return. Does community require mutual obligation in order to be sustained? In all its denominational forms, Judaism would answer the question with a resounding yes. As Wolpe's eloquent analysis of the Shema makes clear, God needs us; we also need each other. Taubman wants to extend FNL beyond the once-a-month experience, to "feel good that evening but also take it further." In an interview on the one-year anniversary of FNL, he suggested outreach programs such as making links between FNL and Habitat for Humanity or Jewish Big Brothers. At this point, however, Wolpe maintains that "people want more of the same."

Can there be community without commitment? Perhaps FNL is simply one stop along the way in the GenX search for meaning. Perhaps, over time, FNL will integrate Taubman's vision. The future is unknown. What is clear, however, is that as the numbers continue to increase, Friday Night Live remains the place for young Jews to celebrate Shabbat on the second Friday night of every month.

References

Cohen, Steven M. 1989. *Content or Continuity? Alternative Bases for Commitment: The 1989 National Survey of American Jews.* New York: American Jewish Committee.

Harlow, Jules, ed. 1989. *Siddur Sim Shalom: A Prayerbook for Shabbat, Festivals, and Weekdays.* New York: Rabbinical Assembly.

Schiffman, Lisa. 1999. *Generation J.* New York: HarperSanFrancisco.

Wertheimer, Jack. 1993. *A People Divided: Judaism in Contemporary America.* New York: HarperCollins.

Wolpe, David. 1992. *In Speech and in Silence: The Jewish Quest for God.* New York: Henry Holt and Company.

11

Losing Life to Save It

An "Insider" Account of the Church of the Redeemer Community in South Central Los Angeles

Timothy Sato

For those who want to save their life will lose it, and those who lose their life for my sake, and for the sake of the gospel, will save it. For what will it profit them to gain the world and forfeit their life?

—*Mark 8:35*

The first gunshot interrupted a calm Monday morning. Across the street a young man was holding a gun with two hands, white smoke erupting from the barrel. Immediately, I hit the pavement as he fired another round in our direction. *Clack! Clack!* I put my head down and prayed that no one would be killed. *Clack! Clack! Clack! Clack!* The last shot echoed for a moment before fading into an unusual silence on the busy street.

Several feet away, a Latina grandmother was on the ground, grimacing in pain. Fortunately, she was hit in the lower leg, and the injury did not seem life threatening. I called 911 from a nearby pay phone, and the operator instructed me to put a clean cloth on the wound and elevate her leg. I took off my dress shirt, placed it over the bullet wound, and talked to her for a few short minutes until the paramedics arrived. Somehow, her son was already standing by her side as the ambulance pulled up to the curb.

An hour later, after changing my shirt and making a few phone calls, I walked back to the same bus stop, caught the bus, and went downtown. On the way, I thanked God for preserving my life once again and prayed that the woman would recover fully—able to live in our neighborhood without pain and without fear. I did not find, as had Winston Churchill, that the experience of being shot at "without result" was exhilarating. Rather, I felt sad and angered that our neighborhood was still a place where grandmothers were shot while waiting for the bus.

211

Much has changed since that time. The oppressive violence that once reigned in our neighborhood has become a distant memory. In fact, I was only reminded of the bus stop incident—an event that took place five years ago—by a recent flyer posted by a movie company. The flier notified neighbors that in the course of filming, some streets would be blocked and warned of "full-load automatic gunfire" from 3:00 P.M. until midnight. In Hollywood's wisdom, the street was going to be renamed "Resurrection Avenue," and the filming would take place during the Church of the Redeemer's Friday-night meeting. My wife and I, along with other neighbors, opposed the exploitation of our neighborhood to provide images of death and destruction, but rejoiced as we realized that the sound of gunfire would not simply blend in with the other sounds of the neighborhood as it had in the past.

Generation X in the 'Hood

The media portrayal of Generation X is a confusing mélange of images. One extreme highlights the entrepreneurial spirit and pioneering work of the cyber-elite "digerati" as they ascend untold heights of wealth and cultural influence. The other extreme continues to hold fast to the idea that this generation is comprised of slackers, indifferent voters, and martini-swilling swing dance aficionados—children of privilege untested by war, recession, or national crisis. Yet another view champions Generation X as a highly idealistic group, actively volunteering, creating new political networks, and forming cross-ethnic relationships at an unprecedented rate.

Where do the members of the Church of the Redeemer fit into these clashing views of GenX? On one level, members are eclectic and entrepreneurial, creating leadership structures as the need arises, participating in a nondenominational church that meets in a house, and living lives that are outside the normative experience of their peers. Yet members are also very traditional—heeding advice, for example, from people who are older than their parents and viewing the Bible as the living word of God.

Nearly all of the members of the Church of the Redeemer are part of Generation X. They are primarily middle- and upper-middle-class white, Asian, black, and Latino evangelical Christians who have intentionally moved to the inner city for the long term. Among the members are engineers, teachers, managers, health professionals, a preacher/basketball coach, an accountant, an artist, a management consultant, and other people who, by education and earning power, could easily live in other neighborhoods. Influenced by InterVarsity Christian Fellowship and by a movement called Christian community development, these young adults are investing their talents and resources to develop their lives of faith and bless their neighbors in the inner city.

Some might view this intentional move to the city as a political statement, but members of the Church of the Redeemer have a very pragmatic, almost apolitical approach to their efforts. An *Atlantic Monthly* article declared that our generation appears "to have enshrined political apathy as a way of life" (Halstead 1999). While some members of the church might fit this description, others are actively networking with politicians and with a local community organizing group. Nonetheless, many of the members would agree that "the exercise of worldly politics rests upon a quite unfounded confidence in the moral competency of human beings" (Eller 1987, xii). Political structures, in the view of many in the church, can do some good, but they are not going to be the agents of the neighborhood's salvation. Thus, when member Richard Parks was encouraged by neighbors and the councilman's office to run for a seat on a neighborhood council, he declined. "I want people to see that the church, not politics, is the reason for change taking place in the neighborhood," he said in a recent conversation. Members vote, develop relationships with the council office, and apply for city grants to paint murals, but they do not put their hope in politics to bring about transformation.

Moving to the Neighborhood. In the fall of 1992 four of us moved to the western border of University Park in Los Angeles, less than a mile from the University of Southern California, and three miles north of the flash points of the riots.[1] Our vision was to live in a multiethnic community in South Central Los Angeles for at least one year. There, in the inner city, we would seek to live out the most basic of our convictions: to love God with all of our strength and our neighbor as ourselves. During the course of our experience with InterVarsity Christian Fellowship, a parachurch ministry to college students, each of us became convinced of God's passion for justice and love for the poor and oppressed. While we knew that to move into areas of the inner city could be dangerous, and would certainly elicit concern from our families and ridicule from some friends, we had learned in the Bible that this kind of "losing life" actually amounted to gaining what we called "Life with a capital L."

What began as a one-year commitment has become a shared experience with seven years of history. Over the course of time, this initial group of four has become the Church of the Redeemer, a house church of twenty-four members with grassroots ministries such as a tutoring program, Bible studies, a gym night for children, and other activities.

Although it is physically close to USC, moving to the neighborhood was like moving a world away. In our first few years in the neighborhood, we became accustomed to gunfire and were experts at hitting the floor, crawling to the phone, and dialing 911. (Remarkably, the number of gun battles far outnumbered the casualties.) During the first twelve months that we lived in two adjacent houses, the liquor store across the street was the site of six shootings, multiple assaults, and one murder. As we met more of our neighbors, we discovered that the elderly were afraid and stayed in their homes as much as possible. At one of the first block club meetings we attended, an eighty-year-old African-American lady told us about drawing a gun from her purse to ward off some would-be muggers. Children played in their yards or parking lots, but were not allowed to play anywhere else.

The sound of helicopters overhead became commonplace to us, as did the loudly voiced incredulity of some of our friends, coworkers, and a few neighbors. Quite simply, some people could not comprehend the fact that college-educated middle- and upper-middle-class people would willingly move to a neighborhood that many people considered dangerous and others were trying desperately to leave. The footage of fires and looting from the Los Angeles riots was fresh in the civic consciousness, and rubble-strewn lots from burned-out businesses languished on many streets, and yet here we were, moving of our own volition into the very neighborhood that had seemed consumed by flames months earlier. While some people doubted us, others dismissed us as "nice people" doing something idealistic for a few years before we began our careers and moved to the upper-middle-class Westside neighborhoods of Los Angeles.

Perhaps those of a generation earlier saw a phase similar to their "hippie phase." The members of our church, averaging about twenty-six years of age, cannot possibly know yet whether they are right or not. However, we have not considered our actions to be idealistic or rebellious; nor are we looking to save people or transform the neighborhood overnight. Our plans did not include vision of utopian community or forming the groundswell of a new political movement. The revolution we have learned about and sought is two thousand years old, and had been lived by many Christians before us. Although we pray and work for change, we are not certain what will result from our efforts.

During a process of learning and growth, each of us has changed considerably. We have learned a great deal from our friends and neighbors, and have befriended amazing people of faith, courage, and perseverance. After seven years in the neighborhood, we are just beginning to learn to love God and our neighbors as ourselves. Having experienced challenge, transformation, and deep Christian community, we now consider the neighborhood to be our home and are committed to remain there, yet knowing that the success or failure of our experiment may not be determined for years or decades.

The Neighborhood. Like other parts of South Central, University Park has gone through many transitional periods. During the 1920s, the Anti-African Housing Association, later called the University District Homeowners Association, battled to keep blacks, Japanese, and other ethnic minorities from crossing Budlong Avenue, two blocks to the east of the house where the Church of the Redeemer now meets (Davis 1990, 164). The association signed an agreement that read, "It is hereby agreed by the undersigned property owners not to sell or agree to sell any property owned by us in the streets between Vermont Avenue and Budlong Avenue to people other than the Caucasian Race" (McClenahan 1929, 91).

Needless to say, the racist homeowners were not successful in their attempts to keep nonwhite property owners out of the neighborhood. The 1990 census found that the neighborhood was nearly 50 percent black and 47 percent Latino, the remainder divided between Asians and a small minority of whites. In 1992, when we moved here, white flight to the suburbs had taken place decades before, and black flight was in progress, as many people with resources fled the neighborhood's violence and struggling schools. Still, the neighborhood is ethnically diverse, with an increasing number of Latino residents. The neighborhood has economic diversity as well, with working-class neighbors, professionals, and retired people living in very close proximity.

The housing stock is a mix of single-family homes, apartments, "fourplexes," and bungalows. Some of the neighborhood's Craftsman houses have been lovingly restored, while others are in disrepair, and other houses are hybrids of various styles. A few streets are lined with trees, while others are barren.

There are many charming aspects to the neighborhood. On summer evenings, kids play in the streets, riding bikes and playing football. Men from Mexico and Central America push carts selling *paletas* (frozen fruit bars), or *elote*, a delicious corn on the cob smothered in mayonnaise, Parmesan cheese, and chili pepper. One man rides a bike with a cart in front, yelling, "Tamale, tamale, tamales!" and stops to sell them to African-American ladies, kids, and anyone who calls for him to stop. Produce trucks cruise the neighborhood in the late afternoon and early evening. After Thanksgiving, strings of lights cover many windows, doors, and balconies along the dark streets.

In our neighborhood, music is a constant presence. Ice cream trucks drive by in the late afternoon and into the night, playing a cacophony of songs from their speakers: "Raindrops Keep Falling on My Head," "Pop Goes the Weasel," "God Rest Ye Merry Gentlemen," "The Entertainer," "It's a Small World," and other year-round hits. A man with impeccable taste in jazz drives a tiny car with powerful speakers through the neighborhood, blasting Miles Davis.

Thanks to a local community development corporation, there is a small pocket park with a playground, picnic tables, and a basketball court relatively close by. Children play on jungle gyms, and teenagers play basketball on a blacktop court. Kids play street football, ride bikes in driveways, and use any available space to play.

Other aspects of the neighborhood are less appealing. For instance, a pink-walled monstrosity barely hiding oil derricks sits in the middle of the neighborhood, and a sign at the entrance reads, "WARNING. Detectable amounts of chemicals known to the State of California to cause cancer, birth defects, or other reproductive harm may be found in and around this facility."

Clear transformation has begun in the grimmer aspects of the neighborhood environment. Seven years ago, Kenwood Avenue was a war zone. Teenage gang members dominated the street and sold drugs at the corner liquor store. Violence was so prevalent that a young woman was shot in the leg as she sat on her front steps. Gunfire, fully automatic and otherwise, was a common phenomenon. Fortunately, despite the ongoing presence of the drug trade, violence has dramatically declined. Reid Proctor, our unofficial church historian and a math teacher with a profound mind for facts, figures, and trivia, recently gave a definitive answer: "I can't remember the last time [we hit the floor], it's been at least two or three years!" Members of the Church of the Redeemer see this as a direct answer to prayer and attribute the peace to God's work in the neighborhood.

Putting Down Roots. When we arrived, we did not have a wealth of urban experience, and so spent our time simply getting to know our neighbors and the scene. We lived in adjacent houses and cooked meals together, shared expenses, had Bible studies, prayed, and invited people over for dinner. As we invited new acquaintances over, a "ministry of hospitality" emerged as the primary focus rather than programs that might be short-lived because of our lack of experience and knowledge.

We did not have illusions that we would be able to build friendships and gain trust immediately. One neighbor would only speak to us through the thick metal mesh of his security door for an entire year. When he finally opened his door, he apologized, saying, "I guess I haven't been too hospitable." We also befriended the owners of Lucy's Tires, Lucy Rivera and her two sons, Vidal and José. Lucy, a woman of incredible courage and faith, has been an inspiration. The Riveras moved away for a time, but to the delight of many in the church, recently returned because of the strength of their relationships in the neighborhood.

During the course of time, we have had experiences that we will never forget. One night as Richard Parks and I walked to our weekly Bible study, we glanced across the street to see a man who was half on the sidewalk and half in the gutter and in danger of rolling out into the street. Richard suggested that we should go across the street and see what was happening. The man, who was just steps away from the liquor store, had no shoes and was so intoxicated that he could not walk. We helped him across the street and onto our couch for the night.

The next morning, he reported that "friends" had seen his predicament and passed him by. Others took advantage of him, stealing his hat and shoes as he wallowed in the gutter. He was deeply moved that strangers had cared for him when his own friends ignored him. Situations like this honed faith and sharpened a felt need for a God who was present, immediate, and responsive. Richard described experiences like these as living "in the reality of the kingdom of God." Feeding the hungry, clothing the naked, and sheltering the homeless were not abstract principles, they were actual situations requiring more than just a theoretical understanding of the Bible.

As we learned more about the neighborhood, we soon realized that the corner liquor store was a source of many problems. Gang members sold drugs as they milled around in front of video games. The store's operator sold drug paraphernalia, like tiny plastic bags used to hold rock cocaine, and had the audacity to sell alcohol to minors and cups of ice with purchases of hard liquor; not surprisingly, public drinking was rampant and prostitution was commonplace at the corner. On separate occasions, gunfire hit our house and an adjacent fence and building, and when we looked through the bullet holes later, we could see the neon sign of the liquor store.

Richard and I, along with neighbors, block club leaders, the lead police officer for the area, and the city councilman's office, identified the store as one of the rogue businesses in the neighborhood. We and others went door to door with petitions and succeeded in getting the neighborhood its day at City Hall. We had often felt like "lambs before wolves," and on the day of the zoning hearing, we walked into what looked like a slaughter.

A very prominent attorney who promised to make the liquor store a "test case" for discrimination against business owners in the city represented the owner. She had regularly appeared in the media after the 1992 riots as a spokeswoman for the Korean-American community, and we recognized her immediately. The owner of the liquor store property was himself a prominent attorney who later gave a major donation to USC's law school. (He owned the property, and had sold the business to a Korean-American family.) We were overwhelmed—just a handful of retired people and residents taking a day off from work—even though we had the support of the councilman's office and assistance from the Community Coalition. Amazingly, both attorneys for the store seemed confused and offered eloquent and unintentional condemnations of the store they sought to defend. The Korean-American attorney, for reasons best known to herself, called the store "a homicide waiting to happen." Subsequently, neighbors, the zoning administrator, and later the city council's zoning committee adopted the phrase to describe the liquor store. They forced the business to close its doors and revoked the property's liquor license. Today, on the site of the liquor store, a new market selling fresh produce, milk, meat, and other necessities attracts a parking lot full of shoppers, but no loiterers, no drug traders, and no prostitutes. The story of the liquor store serves as a symbol and sign of "God's redemption" in the neighborhood.

In the Book of Jeremiah, God directs the Israelites, "Build houses and settle down; plant gardens and eat what they produce" (Jeremiah 29:5). In essence, God instructs the people to become invested in the city of their exile, Babylon, and to settle down for the duration. Rather than constantly praying to leave, or maintaining a permanent state of readiness to depart, the people are called to become invested citizens in a "foreign" land. Closing the liquor store, starting a church, buying homes in the neighborhood, and developing deep friendships are all examples of the Church of the Redeemer's members "settling down."

Early on in our time in the city, several of us distinctly remember Derek Perkins (the youngest son of Dr. John Perkins and codirector of the Harambee Christian Family Center, in Pasadena, California) challenging us to make a multiyear commitment. He said that it might take five years of living in a neighborhood before people finally stopped thinking that we were students, and maybe ten years before we would earn any trust from the people there. Fortunately, we have been able to build trust with people at a faster rate, but Derek's words inspired us to take a long view of the time and energy we have invested in the neighborhood. Instead of expecting certain outcomes immediately, we prepared ourselves to learn and progress at a more deliberate speed.

Part of the process has been developing deep relationships with friends who live here. Quite literally, we have a web of friendships that seemed unimaginable at points in our past. We've met people whom we would have never met living in affluent areas. Instead of stereotyping homeless people, welfare moms, and other urban types, we know people personally. We are invested in how someone finds a place to live. We know kids who are struggling with simple reading and basic math, so we started a tutoring program. The struggles and pains of our neighbors are becoming our needs and concerns, especially as we start families and become deeper friends with our neighbors.

Sources of Inspiration

InterVarsity Christian Fellowship (IVCF). Of the twenty-two people who have relocated to this neighborhood to join the Church of the Redeemer, all have come from the college-based Christian fellowship called InterVarsity. About sixty years old in the United States, with a fifty-year-old international spin-off called the International Fellowship of Evangelical Students (IFES), this non-denominational organization of evangelical Christian students seeks to reach mainly undergraduate students, although there is a sizable outreach to graduate students as well. Outreach on the majority of campuses centers on small group Bible study, weekly worship services, and other large and small group activities. The organization is nationally run, from the main office in Madison, Wisconsin, but local chapters have quite a bit of autonomy; the character of chapters from campus to campus can vary widely.

The southern California chapters of InterVarsity were, for a few years, sharply distinct from the rest of the country, following a revival of sorts that actually began in northern California, at Stanford University. The renewal movement was self-consciously eclectic, drawing on the best Christian traditions of social justice, spiritual disciplines, charismatic experience, and evangelical belief. Tom Pratt, a student at Stanford during the renewal, former InterVarsity staff worker, and current president of a nonprofit organization called Servant Partners, described the movement as follows:

> The renewal was about many things, but one of the most important was the obedience of faith—that faith is active in works, right out of [the Book of] James. We emphasized this strongly and I think we did that specifically as a prophetic reaction against the kind of easy "believism" cheap grace emphasis that so many evangelicals were into. We were trying to take the commandments of God really seriously—at face value. If he says we're supposed to do this for the poor, than it means we're supposed to go do that for the poor. We can't edit parts out, even if we don't see people around us who are like-minded doing these things.

A key component of the renewal movement was the chapter's intense study of the Bible, using the "inductive method." In this method of study, introduced by an InterVarsity staff worker and missionary, Paul Byer, groups of students use Bible texts typed out double-spaced and engage in observation of repeated words and phrases, contextual and historical study, and finding meanings of important words in the original Greek or Hebrew. Individual observation is followed by group interpretation, which may or may not be led by someone who has studied the text before. The group tries to come to a consensus about the author's intent in writing the text, and if the members succeed, they discuss what application they can make of the text to their lives.

Although the method can be a purely academic exercise, many students who believe what they study have a high degree of ownership of biblical texts. Many IVCF chapters study the Gospel of Mark as an introduction to inductive study; one, because it is the shortest gospel—a group of ten or fifteen students actually has a fighting chance of studying the whole thing in a year—and two, because it is centered on the life and actions of Jesus. Mark is not merely an introduction, however, but a touchstone for members' basic values. Mark 8:36 and the text surrounding it has changed hundreds of students' lives: "For what does it profit one to gain the whole world and lose one's life?" For many people, including probably all members of the Church of the Redeemer, this has meant vastly reorienting the priorities they had entering college, for instance, from getting a high-paying, self-fulfilling job and buying a big house to working alongside the poor and living in the inner city.

Another text that sums up the value of justice and social action is Isaiah 58:6, where God asks Israel how they can expect mercy when their own poor are starving: "Behold, in the day of your fast you seek your own pleasure and oppress all your workers ... is not this the fast that I choose; to loose the bonds of wickedness, to undo the thongs of the yoke, to let the oppressed go free, and to break every yoke?"

Such study led many students in northern and later southern California to choose new commitments to their Christian faith, and thus, fifteen years later, hundreds of graduates are living Christian lives in their workplaces, local churches, and ministries with a high degree of commitment. In California, this commitment does not mean joining the Christian Coalition, Operation Rescue, or other "fundamentalist" groups; California InterVarsity grads, perhaps like many in their generation, are apolitical, and tend not to identify with the political "Christian agenda."

Many graduates, in fact, see primary importance in identifying not with power groups but with the powerless. During their college years, hundreds of graduates have had experience with short-term projects of practical service in the United States, and in Africa, Asia, and Latin America. Rejecting the paternalistic view of Christian missions that sought to Americanize foreign peoples, these short-term projects often have as a major goal learning languages and cultures in order to understand, appreciate, and even adopt aspects of others' worldviews. Pragmatically, members of the Church of the Redeemer understand that until oppressed peoples' needs become their own needs, they cannot truly work alongside them for justice with long-term integrity.

The number of InterVarsity graduates seeking to employ themselves in long-term ministry and relocation to inner-city areas in the United States and abroad has grown so much that several former InterVarsity staff have formed a new nonprofit organization called Servant Partners. The mission of Servant Partners is "To unite people from diverse class and ethnic groups in Christian discipleship and community transformation within urban poor communities."[2] Thus, the organization helps graduates to organize themselves into ministry teams and to provide training for "relocators," those who intentionally move into "poor" communities. According to Tom Pratt, around 150 of these relocators (along with 20 Servant Partners staff) are involved in the southern California area, in Pomona, northwest Pasadena, Lincoln Heights, and South Central. "Sister movements" involving approximately 70 people are taking place in Seattle, Boston, and Northern California.

Servant Partners considers itself to be an outgrowth of the renewal movement within InterVarsity. Thus, much of its philosophy of ministry, language, and methods is a translation of campus concepts into the urban context. In large part due to this connection with InterVarsity, the Church of the Redeemer has a close relationship with Servant Partners. To date, six interns have become members of the church, and Servant Partners is the fiscal agent for the tutoring program. Moreover, Kevin Blue, a member of the church's leadership team, recently became a part-time staff member of Servant Partners.

John Perkins and the Christian Community Development Association. The Christian community development movement has greatly influenced the urban ministry ideas within InterVarsity and Servant Partners. Coincidentally, one of InterVarsity's first urban projects was in Pasadena, home of the Harambee Christian Family Center and Dr. John Perkins. (Perkins is the founder of three Christian ministries in Mississippi and Pasadena, and is the chairman of the Christian Community Development Association.) Through the Harambee connection, InterVarsity staff and students were exposed to his prophetic vision of neighborhood transformation.

Dr. Perkins has written extensively about Christian community development and is its chief spokesperson. In his view, the gospel is holistic: "Christian community development begins with people transformed by the love of God, who then respond to God's call to share the gospel with others through evangelism, social action, economic development, and justice" (1995, 21). His "three Rs"—relocation, reconciliation, and redistribution—summarize his vision for developing at-risk communities. Relocation, the first R, means moving into neighborhoods and letting needs become your own rather than merely doing something for (or to) the poor. Bob Lupton, a CCDA board member with a ministry in Atlanta (1995), writes that "being a vested member of the community one is called to serve is an important key to effectiveness" (75).

The second R, reconciliation, is the process of admitting racism, developing trust, and building mutual friendships. The process includes, but goes far beyond, admiring mutable, superficial cultural traditions and foods. Rather, deep bonds of trust and friendship are developed as people of different races learn and appreciate the bones, sinews, and heart of each others' culture. Spencer Perkins, another son of John Perkins, and Chris Rice described their experience with racial reconciliation at the Voice of Calvary Church in Mississippi (Perkins and Rice 1993). Through years of ministry in a multiethnic church, they distilled three guiding principles for racial reconciliation: admit (that racism exists), submit (forgive and reconcile), and commit (build relationships across ethnic lines). John Perkins himself was brutally beaten and left for dead, the victim of an unjust arrest and targeting of white police officers in Mendenhall, Mississippi. Remarkably, because of his faith, he was able to forgive the officers and continues to preach a gospel that is rooted in reconciliation between people and God and people to each other.

The final R, redistribution, is not a radical overturning of the existing economic system. Rather, "redistribution must involve us—our time, energy, our gifts, and our skills" (Perkins 1982, 154). CCDA also advocates for economic development, job creation strategies, starting neighborhood businesses, and other strategies to provide economic opportunity for low-income people.

Today, CCDA has more than three thousand individual members and hundreds of affiliated churches, and there are hundreds of other ministries working in urban areas that do not consider themselves to be part of CCDA. Many of the Los Angeles CCDA members are churches or well-established ministries—such as World Impact and World Vision—and the vast majority are not members of Generation X. Still, according to Richard Parks, GenXers are actively engaged in "the movement of God's spirit" in urban areas.

The "three Rs" of the Christian Community Development Association and the many influences from InterVarsity are more than principles. They are essential elements to understanding the motivation for the members of the Church of the Redeemer. The members of the Church of the Redeemer are normal people. They have jobs, buy houses, raise kids, and go to church. Nonetheless, they have chosen to pursue lives vastly different from the ones they envisioned as they entered college. They have perceived a call from God and are seeking to live out obedient lives in the urban context. The following stories are of four members of the church: Jeff and Amy Blain, Richard Parks, and Kevin Blue.

The Blains. Jeff and Amy Blain have a young daughter, Michaela, and are expecting another child in a few months. Last year, the Blains purchased a home two blocks away from the house where the Church of the Redeemer meets. Amy, a nurse, is from Redmond, Washington, the home of Microsoft Corporation. Jeff, a production manager with Sonoco, is from Simi Valley, California, also known as the home of the jury that failed to convict the police officers who beat Rodney King. Both Jeff and Amy grew up in the church but "had no categories for loving the poor."

During their years at USC, Jeff and Amy became active participants in

InterVarsity, most formatively in Bible studies on campus. Many students, attempting to apply the scripture studies to their daily lives, went regularly to meet homeless people around the campus. As Amy and Jeff encountered these people and studied the Bible, they became convinced that "it was not God's intent" that classes or races should live separately. They were also convinced that they were called to "love the least"—those who were economically oppressed, outcast, or marginalized. The riots of 1992, two weeks before USC's graduation, solidified their realization that anger against racial and class injustices was felt across a broad spectrum of the city.

After marrying and moving to northern California, Jeff and Amy became involved in a multiethnic church in the town of Benicia, California. There, they formed deep relationships. After Jeff's company transferred him back to southern California, the couple moved to South Central Los Angeles to become part of the church. The Blains recently purchased a house in the neighborhood, putting down roots a little bit deeper. They share the house with two single men, also members of the Church of the Redeemer, dividing chores and common expenses.

Amy and Jeff's commitment to the inner city is focused on "obedience to God" and the pursuit of faith that will result in their own growth. The Blains are also very active in the life of the church. Jeff leads a gym night for youth and emcees the church service, while Amy is part of the tutoring planning committee and has started an informal group with neighborhood mothers with young children.

Richard Parks. Richard Parks was born in Thousand Oaks and moved to Los Angeles to attend USC. At college, he began to question some of his underlying values as he studied scripture during his involvement with InterVarsity Christian Fellowship. Richard says that his study of the Bible "pruned from my heart sin and selfishness." He realized that materialism was a stumbling block for him, and his plans to pursue wealth and comfort changed. As graduation approached, Richard began to discern God's call for his life in the inner city. A summer volunteering with Voice of Calvary ministries in Jackson, Mississippi, greatly influenced him, especially as he saw the depth of racial reconciliation at the church. A desire grew in him to be part of an urban ministry in Los Angeles.

Now, in addition to living out that desire, Richard is the assistant director of a research center, the Southern California Studies Center at USC. He also recently completed his M.B.A. from USC's Marshall School of Business. Instead of pursuing a fast-track corporate job like many of his peers at the business school, Richard plans to work in the nonprofit sector, developing housing and beginning economic development projects.

Richard has invested his time in building relationships with neighbors, local businessmen, and block club leaders. He has also been instrumental in local projects like closing the liquor store, planting trees in the neighborhood, and organizing a mural project funded by the city. He describes the value of being present in the neighborhood instead of merely volunteering or sending a monetary gift:

> By our presence, I think we have experienced the joy of being neighbors and . . . our impact has been significantly greater. The other issue is that my neighbor's needs are my needs, so the liquor store at the end of the street where there are drive-by shootings, gang members hanging out, and all kinds of public fighting and prostitution taking place, that's just not a problem that people are telling me about, but it's a problem that I experience with my neighbors. As a result, we better understand how we can work with our neighbors to change the situation and we have a clear stake in the outcome.

Richard and roommate Kevin Blue are also known for their Christmas parties and barbecues. According to Richard, the experience in University Park has caused us to "throw ourselves at Jesus's feet" and depend on him. He describes his life as full of meaning, "significant," and "joyful." Though some people may consider Richard's decision to be unwise, he regards his decisions collectively as the "road that has led to life."

Kevin Blue. Kevin Blue, like many inner-city pastors, wears many hats to support his ministry. The leader of the Church of the Redeemer's elders team, Blue is also a teaching specialist with InterVarsity, a highly successful coach for the girls' basketball program at a nearby private school, and a staff member with Servant Partners. Before moving to the neighborhood more than five years ago, Blue led the staff team of USC's InterVarsity chapter.

After his junior year in college, Kevin spent the summer tutoring in a mixed Latino and black neighborhood in Pasadena, where he began to realize that "a large part of the church's mission in the world is to provide good news to the poor." He also realized that the things that he had valued, such as his concern for racial reconciliation and justice issues, were "of the kingdom." These values in part arose from his experience as a black man and as a student at a multiethnic high school. As the team leader at USC, Kevin helped to inspire dozens of people through preaching and demonstrating practically God's love for the poor.

While Blue is a Los Angeles native, his family lived in a middle-class neighborhood and had prepared him to leave the city altogether. Rather than choosing this path, however, he has chosen to invest his life and talents in the inner city. "It was strictly the call of God and the direction the gospel of Jesus points me in that got me to consider environments like this." When asked about the appeal of serving in the urban context, Kevin said,

> I don't think it is very appealing to most people. . . . That kind of life, where it's obvious that you trust God, for a lot of people looks stupid. It's an affront to prideful thinking that we should be doing other things, controlling our own lives and making decisions on our own as opposed to asking God for wisdom. The thing that is attractive to people—that is, for people who are really drawn to God—is it actually requires you to make decisions of faith, and you actually have to trust God. You get to know God, and see God come through for you. There's no greater delight for anyone who is seeking God than to find that God is real, and that he actually comes through for you when you need him to, not only for you personally but for others around you.

The Church of the Redeemer

The Church of the Redeemer has twenty-four members and meets in the living room of Ellen Bauer's house on Raymond Avenue. In addition to members, there are people from the neighborhood, friends, parents, and other visitors. Every week, couches are moved against the wall and a hodgepodge of folding, rocking, and dining room chairs are arranged into uneven "pews." At times, when all of the chairs are filled, more folding chairs—even lawn chairs—are brought out to accommodate the congregation. In front of the rows of chairs, a full-size Yamaha keyboard—purchased at a yard sale in the neighborhood—sits on an aging elementary school desk covered with a green cloth. To the right of the keyboard player, there is a wooden chest. For six days of the week, the chest functions as a table, but on Sundays it is an altar complete with a vase full of fresh flowers and a fragrant candle.

At 10:30 on Sunday morning, only a few people are in the living room sanctuary, but by 10:45 the room echoes with the piano, tambourine, and voices singing in unison. The mixture of songs ranges from contemporary Vineyard worship music, Spanish songs, traditional hymns at an upbeat tempo, and gospel. Some people raise their hands, while others keep them at their sides. During a cappella songs like "Sign Me Up" ("for the Christian Jubilee") the congregation claps and stomps to the rhythm of the tambourine. When the upbeat songs end, there is usually an "amen" from Mrs. Evelyn Washington, the senior member and only retired person in the church. An announcement period follows that includes a time to share reports of thanksgiving or prayer requests.

After worship, the emcee, one of several people depending on the schedule, invites the speaker to come forward, and a glass of water is quickly placed on the floor in case the speaker needs a drink. A black metal music stand serves as the lectern. Behind the speaker, there is a framed print by John August Swanson depicting workers in a field, trees, and a quote from Psalm 85: "Justice and peace shall kiss."

The "talks" or sermons generally focus on a specific passage (or passages) from the Bible using examples from everyday life, current movies, and stories from the neighborhood. Most of the speakers have been connected to InterVarsity Christian Fellowship in some form, either as staff or as volunteers. They analyze the passage, discuss its relevance to our situation, and then lead us in thinking about ways to apply the scripture to our lives. Sermons cover a broad range of topics, the parables of Jesus, Nehemiah, the Book of Revelation, and many others.

When the sermon concludes, the last remarks and benediction made, there are snacks and drinks on the dining room table. The Sunday meetings represent the only time all of the members of the church are present. Thus, the conversations are lively and people hang around long after the service is complete, eating bagels and *pan dulce*.

The community life hinges on three categories that several of us learned in our senior years of college. In 1990 Tom Pratt, former InterVarsity staff worker and current president of Servant Partners, said that successful Christian communities maintain three important concepts: mission, fellowship, and accountability. From the time we began the ministry in University Park, we have attempted to keep the three concepts intact.

The church's formal ministries focus on youth. One of the church elders, Rebecca Sato (my younger and wiser sister), leads the tutoring program, planning curricula, designing the program, and working with a planning committee that assists with fund-raising. This year, the Adventures Ahead tutoring program received a $15,000 grant from USC's Good Neighbors program. Since the tutoring program is not yet incorporated, Servant Partners serves as the fiscal agent. The grant enabled the tutoring program to purchase curriculum materials and money for field trips and other activities.

During Halloween, the Church of the Redeemer held its third annual carnival. The carnival involves blocking the street at both ends and filling the street with games, food, a large "jumper" for the young kids, and other attractions. Near the end of the evening, someone offers a brief testimony about God's love for the neighborhood. The annual event is one of the only street fairs in the neighborhood and draws hundreds of people.

The ministry of hospitality remains a central component of the mission of the church. A dizzying array of dinners, desserts, and movie nights occurs regularly. Neighborhood kids constantly knock on doors to play video games, use the Internet, or ask for help with homework after tutoring.

The social connections between members are also strong. For example, some church members have experienced periods of financial difficulty, during which a member of the church may make some phone calls asking for anonymous contributions, quickly generating funds. At other times, members make a pledge to help with a person's expenses until they find a new job, or the crisis is over. Various members also frequently have dinner, meet informally, or watch *The X-Files* together.

Accountability groups, regular meetings for prayer and confession, occur regularly. Currently, the groups are single-sex and contain three to four people. Each week, or when the groups arrange to meet, the members talk about "struggles" from the previous week, give each other advice, and pray about upcoming challenges. The topics are highly personal: all areas of sin, including thought life, unedifying things watched on TV, financial struggles and anxieties, laziness, lack of love for people, covetousness for material things, anger, bitterness, despondency—whatever the sins of that week are revealed, and the person receives prayer.

Many members of the church also pray each Sunday morning before the worship meeting, as they have nearly every week for seven years. This time is usually devoted to prayer for specific issues or people in the neighborhood (as opposed to prayers for church members' families or other more personal concerns). Over time, the church has seen many direct answers to its petitions and requests, which have deepened the members' commitment and hopefulness.

Leadership. The Church of the Redeemer is led by three people called the "elders," though the senior member is only in his early thirties. This team discusses the vision for the church, plans the teaching schedule for the sermons, and serves as a catalyst for other leadership activities. Kevin Blue leads the team, with Ellen Bauer and Rebecca Sato completing it.

Rather than perceiving itself as the sole directive body, the elders team functions as a catalyst for other people to take initiative in various tasks. The elders team was envisioned as a group of leaders providing direction to other leaders, and it grew out of the frustrations of growth. Originally, decisions were made collectively. When differences in opinions existed among the original four people, consensus was much easier to reach, but it could still take a month or more to make some decisions. The sheer logistics of coordinating a meeting for twelve people necessitated the formation of a leadership body. Larger decisions such as starting the church, choosing a name, adopting a covenant statement, and other activities are still completed with input from every person in the group. The elders team regularly solicits input on points of decision and maintains formal and informal lines of communication with the members of the church.

Challenges to the Church. In a setting like University Park, difficulties abound. The specter of violence has passed for the moment, but there are many other painful realities. Henri Nouwen (1983) writes that compassion, from its Latin roots, means "to suffer with." Thus, compassion is not a simple emotion or token gesture. Instead, compassion in its true form entails taking on a measure of suffering. Kevin Blue calls this process "absorbing pain." Absorbing pain means seeing the pain of others and minimizing it by joining with them to endure the pain. It also means working with people to mitigate painful situations.

At times, suffering with people can be extremely difficult, generating frustration, even anger. In one situation, several people in the church were extremely concerned about a mother who attended the church but regularly neglected her teenage son and young daughter. From time to time, the woman would ask for help with job hunts, child care, and finances, and people from the church would assist, until the situation seemed to be generating an unhealthy dependence. Other members of the church provided help with budgeting and job hunting. The woman, however, seemed to take responsibility for herself and her children for very short periods before returning to old patterns. Eventually the family was evicted from their apartment and chose to move to a homeless shelter outside of the neighborhood. People from the church remain in contact with the family, but their situation has not changed during the last year. In this situation, suffering with the family and absorbing the pain were difficult and challenging prospects without a happy ending.

One tremendous challenge for the single men and women, the majority of the church, is the issue of singleness and marriage. In crude terms, the eligible pool of single Christian men and women who are interested in inner-city ministry is limited. Although there are single men and women in the church, none of the members is currently dating another member. This, especially in the postcollege years, is often disturbing and anxiety producing.

Although racial reconciliation with all its difficulties is a major goal for the church, we have not yet experienced the kind of reconciliation over deep issues that other churches, like Voice of Calvary in Mississippi, have had. In one sense, the fact that church has not experienced racial conflict is extremely positive. Part of this is that members of the church run the tutoring programs and other events that minister to children in the neighborhood, resulting in tremendous goodwill from parents and guardians. Another reason is that the church, although using some Spanish songs and reading passages in Spanish, has not dealt with the need for a sustained bilingual service. Some members speak Spanish, but more must learn to create a church that is more truly representative of the neighborhood. A "diverse fellowship of neighbors" is a primary goal of the church, with racial reconciliation as the motivating factor. While relationships are developing across ethnic lines, incorporating this diverse group into the church body seems a difficult task.

The members of the Church of the Redeemer are pursuing a dream that is far from the normative experience of their generation. While they seek the happiness, meaningful lives, job satisfaction, and deep friendships that many GenXers idealize, each of the members believes that the choice to live in the inner city is central to their pursuit of meaning and joy. C. S. Lewis (1927), a favorite author of many in the church, offers a fitting description: "Indeed, if we consider the unblushing promises of reward and the staggering nature of the rewards promised in the Gospels, it would seem that Our Lord finds our desires not too strong, but too weak. We are half-hearted creatures, fooling about with drink and sex and ambition when infinite joy is offered us. . . . We are far too easily pleased" (27). For the Church of the Redeemer, this means that the temptations of worldliness are nothing in comparison to living a life of full pursuit of God. Money, sex, and ambition are nothing if one takes the passage from Mark 8:36 literally. What would it profit to gain the whole world (financial success, prestige, a fancy car) and lose one's life?

Like many groups of evangelical Christians, the Church of the Redeemer hopes that the transformation of individuals in the neighborhood will eventually change society. Thus, they hope to send missionaries abroad (one has already left Los Angeles to work for a Christian agency in Guatemala) or to start similar churches in the inner city. Considering themselves to be part of a long history of Christian concern and compassion for the poor, the oppressed, the orphan, and the widow, they view themselves as people seeking to live a faithful Christian life of compassion and love for justice in a world obsessed with self-fulfillment.

Notes

I would like to thank Caroline Sato and Richard Parks for their feedback, insight, and encouragement.

1. USC has demonstrated a commendable commitment to education in the neighborhood's Family of Five Schools, offering enrichment programs and scholarships to students who meet vigorous academic standards. In 1998 USC's Good Neighbors

program also channeled $517,549 in donations to schools and charitable organizations around the University Park and Health Sciences campuses.

2. Mission statement from the Servant Partners website, www. servantpartners.org.

References

Blain, Amy. 1999. Interview by Caroline Sato. Los Angeles, October.

Blue, Kevin. 1999. Interview by author. Los Angeles, November.

Davis, Mike. 1990. *City of Quartz: Excavating the Future in Los Angeles.* New York: Vintage Books.

Eller, Vernard. 1987. *Christian Anarchy: Jesus' Primacy over the Powers.* Grand Rapids, Mich.: Eerdmans.

Halstead, Ted. 1999. "A Politics for Generation X." *Atlantic Monthly* 284, no. 2 (August): 33–42.

Lewis, Clive Staples. 1996. *The Weight of Glory.* New York: Touchstone.

Lupton, Bob. 1995. "Relocation, Living in the Community." In *Restoring At-Risk Communities,* edited by John M. Perkins. Grand Rapids, Mich.: Baker Books.

McClenahan, Bessie. 1929. *Changing Urban Neighborhood: A Sociological Study.* Los Angeles: University of Southern California.

Nouwen, Henri J. M. 1983. *Compassion: A Reflection on the Christian Life.* New York: Doubleday.

Parks, Richard. 1999. Interview by author. Los Angeles, November.

Perkins, John M. 1982. *With Justice for All.* Ventura, Calif.: Regal Books.

———, ed. 1995. *Restoring At-Risk Communities,* Grand Rapids, Mich.: Baker Books.

Perkins, Spencer, and Chris Rice. 1993. *More Than Equals.* Downers Grove: InterVarsity Press.

Pratt, Tom. 1999. Interview by author. Pasadena, Calif., November.

Conclusion:
Toward a Theory of
Generation X Religion

Richard W. Flory

As we have seen from the preceding chapters, GenXers are active and innovative in developing structures through which they can both express their religious beliefs and find the spiritual experiences they seek. In our ethnographies of these religious communities, we have obviously left out certain segments of Generation X religious expression. As Donald and Arpi Miller pointed out in their introductory chapter, those segments of Generation X religion that were not included here tend toward expressions that exist outside institutional boundaries, such as individual "dabblers" and "spiritual seekers," and those who might develop various hybrids of religious beliefs. We have also left out those GenXers who have remained in more traditional religious settings, attending the churches, temples, and synagogues in which they were raised. Thus, we are well aware that we are not presenting an exhaustive sampling of Generation X religious expressions, but we are certain that these ethnographies represent a significant segment of religiously active GenXers, which in turn allows us to ask questions about how generational differences affect religious organization and expression.

In this concluding chapter, I hope to initiate a conversation about how to understand Generation X religion, ultimately asking whether it has unique features that can be explained by generational factors, or conversely, if it isn't just the same old religion with a different look. With that goal in mind, I will address the following: first, set some theoretical and comparative context for these ethnographies, both in terms of religion in America and generational analysis; second, analyze the major characteristics of Generation X religion that emerge from across the cases; third, develop a typology of Generation X religion that will help us place it in the constellation of religious expressions; and fourth, develop the beginnings of a theory of Generation X religion. The closing section of the chapter will provide a few recommendations for religious leaders who are perhaps concerned about where the next generation of believers will come from, or are interested in otherwise serving the religious and spiritual needs of GenXers.

Theoretical and Comparative Context

Religion in the 1990s. Religion in the 1990s has been largely interpreted through several related approaches that, taken together, provide both a theoretical and a comparative context for understanding Generation X religion. Older models that emphasized the inevitable secularization of religion have been refuted and largely abandoned in favor of models that emphasize why religion continues to be a dynamic force in American society. These models utilize the conception of a religious marketplace, in which churches and other religious organizations adapt to the demands of their "consumers" in order to survive and thrive.[1] Thus, variables such as organizational form, religious leadership, doctrinal beliefs, and the techniques used to attract new members must constantly be adapted to take into account the shifting needs and desires of religious consumers.

Drawing on this line of interpretation, two studies have particular importance for understanding Generation X religion. The first is Donald Miller's analysis (1997) of what he terms "New Paradigm" churches; that is, those that have successfully responded to the changes in American culture that began in the mid-1960s. He argues that these churches are more successfully meeting the needs of their congregations than mainline churches, "successfully mediating the sacred, bringing God to people and conveying the self-transcending and life-changing core of all true religion. They offer worship in a musical idiom that connects with the experience of broad sectors of the middle class; they have jettisoned aspects of organized religion that alienate many teenagers and young adults; they provide programming that emphasizes well-defined moral values and is not otherwise available in the culture. In short, they offer people hope and meaning that is grounded in a transcendent experience of the sacred" (3). In other words, they have successfully adapted their organizations, their message, and their leadership to address the demands of the religious marketplace. It is important to note in this regard that the membership of these churches is dominated by the baby-boom generation and thus has adapted to the needs of that generational segment, as opposed to either their parents' or their children's generations, by appropriating elements from the larger culture, particularly in musical tastes and organizational form. That is, they are contemporary and democratized in their approach to worship and mediating the sacred.

Conclusion: Toward a Theory of Generation X Religion

While Miller deals with the baby-boom generation only as a function of the particular churches he is studying, Wade Clark Roof specifically engages in an analysis of the spiritual quests of baby boomers. In his most recent book, Roof (1999) argues that a (spiritual) quest culture has been created by boomers as they seek spiritual meaning, in which the search for an "authentic inner life and personhood" is the dominant theme in American religion today:

> Americans are asking questions such as, "Does religion relate to my life?" "How can I find spiritual meaning and depth?" and "What might faith mean for me?" This inward search for greater spiritual depth was evident in a poll in 1994 which reported that 65 percent of Americans believed that religion was losing its influence in public life, yet almost equal numbers, 62 percent, claimed that the influence of religion *was increasing in their personal lives.* If as many social scientists argue, religion has to do with two major foci of concerns—*personal meaning* and *social belonging*—then most certainly it is around the first of these that religious energies revolve today. (7; emphasis in original)

Thus for Roof, what he frames as the primary religious "map" orienting religion in America is the quest for private, personal spiritual meaning.

Taken together, we would conclude that boomer religion, owing to that generation's formative experiences in the 1960s and their aftermath—civil rights, the women's movement, free speech, free love, "don't trust anyone over thirty," and various forms of self-expression—has developed a form that has appropriated contemporary culture both in the worship setting and in the programs of their groups, a more democratized and lay-oriented organizational and authority form with, above all else, a primary emphasis on one's personal and private spiritual pilgrimage. These analyses of boomer religion provide a point of comparison for our discussion of Generation X religion; that is, to what extent do Xers exhibit similar characteristics in their religious endeavors, and how can these be understood as a result of their generational experiences?

Generational Analysis and Generation X Religion. Generational analysis in the social sciences has a long history, with its beginnings usually associated with Karl Mannheim's essay "The Problem of Generations" ([1927] 1952).[2] According to Mannheim, individuals in any given generation share a common social and historical location that limits their potential range of experience, "predisposing them for a certain characteristic mode of thought and experience, and a characteristic type of historically relevant action" (291–92).[3] In this, a generation is analogous to a social class in that persons in the same

233

age grouping will experience social reality from the same (age) perspective at crucial formative times of their lives, thus providing them with an outlook particular to their generation. Howard Schuman and Jacqueline Scott (1989) have shown that adolescence and early adulthood is "the primary time period for generational imprinting" and that generational effects seem to be the result of the interaction of personal and national history. Thus, depending on one's generation, the salience of certain social and political events and developments will take on different meaning, particularly as they interact with one's personal experience during those formative years.

Assuming this basic theoretical perspective, we must first identify those crucial experiences encountered by Xers as late adolescents and early adults that formed their generational consciousness, and then determine the relationship between Xers' generational consciousness and the forms that their religious commitments take. Accepting what was outlined in the introductory chapter as "benchmark experiences" for GenXers, only a brief outline of these is necessary here.

First, there exists a *rootlessness* among GenXers, due on the one hand to highly mobile families that relocated often, out of necessity or desire, for economic opportunities, and on the other hand the high rate of divorce among parents, thus necessitating shuttling between families and having multiple homes. Second, there are *diminishing economic and career opportunities* for Xers as changes have taken place in the economy, and increased preparation and training have been required for poorer paying jobs. Third, the *technological literacy* demonstrated by Xers and the *ascendency of images over printed words* among them have resulted in a changed epistemological perspective and more accessible opportunities for visual self-expression, and a reliance on various pop culture media such as movies, television shows, and rock music for moral authority. Fourth, this is the generation of *multiculturalism*; racial integration and affirmative action laws passed by boomers have been lived by Xers.

Primary Characteristics of Generation X Religion

Across the diverse groups described in each of the ethnographies in this volume, five major characteristics of Generation X religion emerge, which I discuss here as separate entities, although all are related to each other in actual practice. First, Generation X religion emphasizes the sensual and experiential, combining the sacred and the profane and incorporating text, image, music, dance, and the body as venues for the expression of religious beliefs. Second, Generation X religion is entrepreneurial in finding cultural and institutional space to create new religious expressions based on their existing lifestyle interests. Third, Generation X religion is on the one hand similar to boomer religion in that it emphasizes personal identity, religious experience, and spiritual seeking, but it differs in that it roots the quest for religious identity in community, rather than a more purely personal spiritual quest. Fourth, race, ethnic, and gender diversity and inclusiveness is an explicit goal of Generation X religion. Fifth, there is an insistence on an "authentic" religious experience in GenX religion, both on the part of the individual and as found in the religious communities that GenXers choose to join, that acknowledges the ambiguities, trials, and successes of life.

Experiential Religion. In contrast to more traditional forms of religion, GenX religion emphasizes the experiential and participatory dimension over the more passive, rationalistic, or propositional form of previous generations. Thus, instead of Xers simply attending church or synagogue and passively taking in the music, religious symbolism, and instruction, GenX religion combines many different elements, all of which work to involve the person both in the religious meetings and ritual and in the community itself.

Music is the element common to all the cases in this volume, and serves several functions: first to create the atmosphere that each group identifies with; next to create particular emotional/spiritual states; and finally, to cause the person to interact with the music, the beat, lyrics, and others in the group. Of course music in religion often serves these same functions regardless of its generational appeal, but among these groups there is a marked difference from non-GenX religious groups, in that the music is not simply differentiated along "traditional" and "contemporary" lines. Instead, although the music is shared across the generation in some sense, it is more specifically tailored to each group's identity, combining its religious and spiritual sensibilities with its ethnic and/or cultural identity.

Thus Goths, whose primary venue for meeting is the club scene, orient themselves around "Gothic rock," which expresses their fears, wishes, desires, and the like. The Gothic community only comes together physically around its music. Similarly, LL Prime Time meetings, ministering primarily to African-American GenXers, are oriented around hip-hop and R&B music, while Victory Outreach utilizes oldies, hip-hop, and R&B to appeal to Latino Xers, all of which speaks to the spiritual and identity needs of each group.

Closely related to music is dance, whether as an integral part of the program when the group meets, or by individuals within the context of the group meeting. LL Prime Time and the Goths actually structure at least part of their community around dance, Goths in dance clubs, and Prime Time with both dance teams (steppers) as part of the meeting and individuals who dance throughout the musical portion of the service. Similarly, Harvest Rock, although it does not include any structured setting for its members to dance, does provide the symbolic space for several people to dance individually during the musical worship time, so long as it is not disruptive of the service and is perceived as being an authentic spiritual expression, within the context of the larger worship service.

A third element of the experiential dimension is the integration of multimedia and mixed media, such as websites, video, artwork, and other presentation media, both in religious services and to aid in extending the reach of the group. The International Church of Christ has an extensive website and produces a high quality newsmagazine video to update church members on developments in the ICC around the world. This also functions both to establish and reinforce the identity of the individual as a "disciple" and to promote a sense of community with fellow believers around the world. Mosaic, on the other hand, utilizes the skills of its members in producing artwork to set the mood for the worship service, and multimedia productions to create a worship experience that fully involves all of the senses during the service, during which one might be alternately watching a video production, clapping hands in time to the music, and singing, all within the space of a few minutes.

Finally, each of these elements of religious experience utilizes the body in some fashion. On one level, there is an enormous amount of body contact between the members of—and visitors to—these groups. For example, during the services at Prime Time, everyone is not only standing, dancing, clapping, and singing but hugging each other as well. Several of the songs require those in attendance to go find someone to hug, whether a member or a visitor—in fact, visitors are well integrated into this part of the service. Even when the time arrives in the service to greet visitors, several of the members walk over and greet visitors with handshakes, hugs, and kisses. Such contact seems a very important part of the community.

Perhaps the most extreme use of the body is through religious tattooing. As was seen among the Goths, and the Christians at Sid's Tattoo Parlor, tattooing (and body piercing, particularly for the Goths) is at once an act of establishing a personal identity and identifying with a particular group. Thus GenX evangelicals simultaneously set themselves apart from other evangelicals by modifying their bodies, contrary to long-standing evangelical teaching, and publicly identify themselves with a particular form of evangelical Christianity by tattooing Bible verses and other Christian symbolism on their bodies. Goths on the other hand, have less overt religious imagery in their tattoos, but do seem to tend toward fantasy or otherworldly body art, such as winged horses or "Giger's alien."[4]

But perhaps as important is what seems to be the understanding of being tattooed and pierced as a religious or spiritual experience in itself. This is more obvious among the Goths; Julia Winden Fey notes that they explain their tattoos and piercings as ways of "finding meaning through controlling, pleasuring, and/or beautifying themselves." A similar rationale can also be seen among evangelical GenXers, whose tattoos in effect sacralize their bodies through the imagery marked upon them, and who also commented on how the pain of getting a tattoo was one of the attractions of tattooing. Thus pain and control over one's body through tattooing and piercing, in the symbolic context of the religious community, is a spiritual experience in itself.

Entrepreneurial Religion. A second characteristic of Generation X religion is that it is entrepreneurial in finding cultural and institutional space in which to create new religious expressions based on existing lifestyle interests. In this, Xer religion flourishes where there are no, or at least far fewer, rigid structures created by others into which Xers have to fit. This of course can take place either within existing religious organizations or as completely independent and autonomous groups, but the point remains, traditional hierarchical institutional structures militate against innovative Generation X religion. Tom Beaudoin (1998, 163) provides an interesting example of this in a brief discussion of Catholic Church sponsored websites. Beaudoin suggests that even the symbolism used in the websites, while perhaps well understood and deemed important by the sponsoring organization, is at best uninteresting and unintelligible to GenXers, and fails to adequately confront what he terms the "lived theology" of GenXers.

As such, Xers have sought out, and in many cases have created, their own institutional space in which to pursue their religious and spiritual pursuits, largely based on their existing lifestyle interests and concerns. Thus there is an elective affinity between GenX religious groups and their members, such that a wide variety of GenX religious groups results, even within the same religious tradition. For example, we have presented nine different Christian GenX groups, each with strong ties to a generally conservative theology in which the authority of Scripture, the person of Jesus, and so on, would all be generally agreed upon. However, the lifestyle affinities of each group, ranging from the alternative (punk, skinhead, rockabilly) to Latino urban morality plays to competing Korean college ministries to the hip-hop orientation of LL Prime Time, result in their being completely separate groups that have no relationship with—and perhaps even no knowledge of—each other. The organizational similarity between these groups is that they have either established themselves within existing organizations that have allowed them the freedom to pursue their religious goals in whatever form they desire, or they have been able to create independent entities through which they can pursue their religious goals. In this, Xers have created a strong link between GenX culture and religion. That is, as each group is organized around the different GenX cultural expressions of its members, such as tattooing, Gothic music, or hip-hop and R&B, Xer culture is fully embraced in Xer religion. This is considerably different from the relationship between baby-boomer culture and religion, in which although the "profane" may be put to the service of the sacred, it is not completely embraced, resulting in a religious culture set apart from, or even oppositional to, the secular. In contrast, Xers have embraced pop-cultural forms, sacralized them, and formed religious groups around them.

Identity in Religious Community. A third characteristic of Generation X religion, and one related to the idea of elective affinity, is the emphasis placed on creating a more or less unique individual identity that is rooted in the confines of the religious community. Although similar, this is significantly different from the more purely personal religious quest of baby boomers (see Roof 1993, 1999), in that one's identity becomes transformed in the religious community; one is first a religious believer, and second a Korean, African-American, Latino, "alternative," or whatever. Further, personal identity and the religious community are linked through a narrative in which individuals relate their experiences, how they have come to be who they are, the journeys they have traveled, and the like. In this process, personal narrative is validated only through incorporating the values of the religious community into that narrative, and in effect, making the community narrative one's own.

This has been seen in various ways in these case studies, but perhaps the examples that stand out the most are the evangelical tattooers at Sid's, and the Latino street dramas produced by Victory Outreach. In each, a story is told, relating the person's life path to where they find themselves at the current time, and how they have found meaning in their respective religious communities. For the evangelical tattooers, the narrative is on the one hand permanent, in that it has been permanently etched on their bodies. But as we found when interviewing them, interpretation of the tattoos can change over time. At the time of these interviews, the narrative was organized around the evangelical tattooing community, in which one's past life, usually depicted in older tattoos, remains, and is used as a map of one's life story. Thus the evangelical tattoo artist Rob Silva keeps the tattoos from his pre-Christian "punk" days as a reminder of what he was then, and as a way to relate his story to interested parties (sociologists included). For the Latino Xers involved in street dramas, the narrative process is similar; one acts out a past from which one was "saved," yet maintains the external symbols of that past, primarily in the presentation of self, partly as a reminder of one's past and partly as a way to reach out to others who find themselves enmeshed in that former life. As

Arlene Sánchez Walsh frames this process, former identities become "sacralized" in the service of the religious narrative.

Race-, Ethnic-, and Gender-Inclusive Religion. Most of the cases presented here state as one of their explicit goals to have a race/ethnic-inclusive group. Those that do not are race/ethnic-specific groups, and even they have found ways to include a broader range of groups than they originally were founded to serve. This inclusivist goal is by all accounts a moral commitment rooted in the core values of each community, thus yielding somewhat different definitions of inclusiveness, depending on the particular religious community. Mosaic, Harvest Rock, and LACC, for example, are all committed to having racially diverse congregations, and each succeeds in varying degrees to fulfill this goal. Their commitment to inclusiveness ends, however, with their understanding of biblical moral teachings. From their perspective it is biblical, and thus required of them, to seek religious unity across race and ethnic boundaries, and to create new identities in which such ascribed characteristics are subsumed under a dominant religious identity. None of these groups would embrace the ideals of the more laissez-faire Goths, who extend their commitment to inclusiveness to include both sexual identity and practice. It is also clear, however, that Mosaic, LACC, and Harvest Rock do embrace those who are "struggling" with various sexual identity and practice issues, so long as this is a part of their authentic religious and spiritual journey.

Changes in traditional gender roles and relationships are neither as intentional nor as obvious as the efforts for race/ethnic inclusiveness. Most of the organizers and leaders of these groups are men, with more or less equal numbers of participants, both men and women. Overall, as is the case with most religious groups in America, gender issues among these groups are generally correlated with the ideology and structural location of the group: the more conservative or traditional the ideology and more tied to an existing organization, the fewer opportunities there are for women in the group; the less conservative or traditional the ideology and the more independent the group, the more opportunities there are for women. Some change, however, is taking place within the GenX context.

For example, Arlene Sánchez Walsh reports that Teresa Arce, the GenX pastor at the Lord's Vineyard, embodies an egalitarian ideal based on a "shared faith and equality before God." Similarly, the Church of the Redeemer has a leadership board that consists of three persons—two females, and one male—this even though the theological roots of this group would suggest a more traditional male leadership. And finally, the evangelical tattooers and the Goths provide space for both men and women to express their religious experience in the same manner—that is, within the context of each group. Among these groups at least, stereotypes relating religion, culture, and gender are being challenged.

Authentic Religion. The final characteristic of Generation X religion can be framed as an insistence on authenticity in how one approaches one's religious beliefs, as measured by how those beliefs are lived in everyday life. This is admittedly a more implicit dimension that emerges across each of the cases, an emphasis found in the different ways that the members of the groups talk about their involvement, what attracted them, and why they remain involved in a particular group. The emphasis on authenticity is seen in three related areas: the importance of authentic leaders, the importance of authentic experience, and the importance of authentic belief.

The authenticity of leaders tends to be measured by the degree to which the leaders of any particular group act in nonjudgmental and nonhypocritical ways. For example, Lance, the pastor of Committed Fellowship, is considered to have an authentic religious identity, not because he claims some sort of external authority but rather because of the way he talks about and lives out his faith, and how he interacts with the members of the church. Thus Abe, who on his first visit to Committed was, by his own description, "in full Nazi uniform," complete with swastikas and Doc Martens boots, and smoking a cigarette outside the warehouse meeting hall, was attracted to the nonjudgmental atmosphere of Committed because in a brief interaction with Lance—who did not identify himself as the pastor of the church—he was simply accepted as he was, swastikas, cigarette, and all. Similarly, Pastor Che Ahn of Harvest Rock Church consistently presents himself as simply a fellow religious traveler, often relating his own religious experience to the members of the church, pointing up his conviction that there is hope and healing for those who believe. For Che Ahn, his is not a message of religious instruction in the traditional sense, but rather a message of religious experience that the members of Harvest Rock can also experience.

Religious experience is considered authentic by GenXers when it is honestly lived, and acknowledges both the ups and downs of life. For Goths, authenticity is found in embracing the value of all aspects of life, the "dark side" as well as the good things that life has to offer. As Carlos, a member of the Gothic subculture, says, "The way I see it . . . in order to get a better experience in life, it's kind of best to see both the light and the dark. You know, the happiness and the sadness. Life and death. Just to try to experience both of them in order to maybe appreciate the other one." For members of the LACC, authenticity in religious beliefs is developed as they are paired with a "discipler," one with whom they can work through various struggles they may have, thus feeling that they are really living out what they say they believe and developing a "unified sense of identity and purpose." A similar perspective is found among members of the Church of the Redeemer community, who are under no illusions that their efforts in the inner city will simply solve the many problems they encounter. They are resolved instead, as Tim Sato has framed it, "to suffer with" those in their neighborhood as a part of their religious commitment to live in solidarity with the poor and the oppressed. They know that they will not be successful in all of their efforts, but the authenticity of their beliefs requires that they continue to be a presence in their community, sharing the good as well as the bad.

Finally, authentic religious belief is identified by experience, narrative, creativity, and example, not by rational argumentation for the truth claims of a particular religious belief system. For Xers, rationalistic apologetics are largely irrelevant to their religious commitments, having been replaced by an experience-based epistemology. Thus, religion is not true because someone can construct some detailed argument for it; rather it is what it does, how it makes one feel, and perhaps the commitments that it requires of its adherents that make it so. We must note, however, that to this end, written text remains important, but functions as background that provides the parameters for one's religious commitments, and as religious narrative itself, not something that should be subject to objective verification. Thus we see Goths identifying with Anne Rice's vampire novels, and the existential dilemmas faced by Lestat and Louis, in the midst of their own spiritual crisis. Sacred text functions in a different manner in the Church of the Redeemer community in Los Angeles. Members of this community clearly believe the truth claims of the Bible, but they interpret it more as a model for how they should live their lives than as proof of what they believe. Thus the stories they find in the text become lived out as a part of their own (individual) narrative, as well as the narrative of the community.

A Typology of Generation X Religion

Taking into account the above characteristics of GenX religion, as well as the institutional characteristics of each case, we can develop a typology that gives us a better feel for where these religious communities exist in the larger constellation of religious organizations. Creating a typology along the two basic dimensions of *organizational form* and *authority type* would theoretically allow us to map all religious organizations, GenX or not. This of course is beyond the scope of this chapter, although I will use these two basic dimensions to map our GenX cases, and with that in mind, we can create a mental mapping of where they are in contrast to other GenX groups not included here, or to more traditionally oriented religious groups.

Conceptualizing organizational form and authority type as each having three categories—denominational, nondenominational, and independent for organizational form; hierarchical, democratic, and consensus for authority type[5]—results in mapping the vast majority of our cases within the nondenominational and independent forms of organization, and as having either democratic or consensus types of authority. Only LACC is both denominational and hierarchical, and Victory Outreach is hierarchical but independent, with the remaining cases in the categories noted above. Owing to the types of cases presented in this book, this typology may not seem too surprising; after all, how many heavily tattooed "gang-banger looking" parishioners are there in the average Episcopal or Presbyterian church? As well, boomer-oriented religion might also be found along the same general dimensions of organization and authority.

Yet the grouping of these cases does correlate with much of the "common wisdom" about Generation X in general, and in their approach to religion in particular. Beaudoin (1998) has argued that GenXers approach religion with "a lived theology that is very suspicious of institutions. Indeed, Xers have a heavily ingrained . . . suspicion or skepticism (even cynicism) in general. This skepticism surfaces most acutely in regard to those who purport to be looking out for the generation's good" (52). As regards these groups, and where they are located on the organizational and authority dimensions, Xers tend toward the democratic and consensus authority types, generally eschewing hierarchical authority and maintaining weak ties, if any at all, to controlling organizations such as a denominational structure. Further, the majority of the groups were founded and organized by Xers, and all of them are run by Xers, even those that are on the hierarchical authority dimension.

This typology then shows that at least on these two dimensions, Generation X religion, owing to Xers' suspicion of institutions and authority, is located where we would expect it to be—generally independent of larger organizational ties, and thus control, and run on democratic or consensus authority principles. But based on what we know from the analyses by Miller and by Roof, this is not significantly different from where baby-boomer religion would be located. What then, if anything, is unique about Generation X religion?

Making Sense of Generation X Religion

GenX and Boomer Religion Compared. Taking the above discussion into account, we can now address the following questions: first, Is Generation X religion qualitatively different from the religion of their parents' generation (baby boomers)? and second, In what ways are any differences attributable to the unique experiences of GenXers?

Similarities between GenX and boomer religion fall into three basic categories. First, each has developed religious organizations that are similar to each other in terms of their structure, governance, nondescript buildings and utilitarian worship space, and approaches to the sacred. Thus, most are either independent or nondenominational, and tend toward a lay-oriented leadership style. Their emphasis is decidedly not on their buildings and worship place—most are in rented storefronts or warehouse space that remain relatively unadorned with religious symbols—yet they have appropriated a variety of "profane" cultural forms as mediators of the sacred. Second, GenXers and boomers both demonstrate the power of a religious consumption ethic; that is, individuals can "shop" for whatever group seems to fit their desires and needs. This is related to the kind of lifestyle they have already fashioned for themselves, or to which they aspire, finding a group with which they have an elective affinity and thus aligning themselves. For boomers, this may be a "New Paradigm" or "mega" church, complete with a veritable smorgasbord of small groups, each intended to meet one or another spiritual and/or psychological need (see Wuthnow 1994a, 1994b; Miller 1997). For Xers, as we have seen, the choice is based more on finding a group with a perspective compatible with one's lifestyle and how one understands one's personal identity. Finally, both Xers and boomers are "seekers," looking for spiritual experience and fulfillment through their various religious involvements.

There are, however, several differences between GenX religion and boomer religion. First, although GenX and boomer religious groups may have a similar structure, they are different in substance. Boomers continue to rely on a rationalistic belief that truth is "out there" and can be discovered (indeed has been discovered, if one simply believes the correct thing). That is, a key component of boomer religion—regardless how independent or nonhierarchical they may be—is authoritative instruction from religious text on religious truth; what truth is, and how to apply it to life. GenXers, on the other hand, while they may have the same or similar organizational form, are oriented around a quite different reality; religious truth, while important to Xers, is not necessarily a fixed target, and is found through their religious experience, not in the properly exegeted text. Truth, for Xers, owing perhaps to their cynicism and skepticism, is best conveyed through stories and myth, and is authenticated through the lived experience of themselves and others, rather than through the pronouncements—and propositional arguments—of external authorities.

A second difference between Xers and boomers is the way they relate to the religious marketplace. For boomers this is much like the way people relate to department stores: there are many to choose from, each with similar products, and as such they are largely interchangeable, depending on how easy or difficult they may be to get to, what services they have to offer, or whether they can meet personal needs. Thus, the difference between shopping at Bloomingdale's rather than Saks, or worship at Calvary Chapel rather than the Vineyard, is one of degree rather than type. In contrast, GenXers, even though, as noted above, they are as much consumers as boomers, are more producers than consumers; they are not simply religious consumers, although they are that, but also producers, actively creating new groups in the marketplace for themselves, regardless of whatever might have been provided for them by existing religious groups.

Thus the groups that we have included here, all of which embrace GenX cultural expressions and celebrate them as unique and authentic religious expressions, show religious entrepreneurship in the service of meeting their religious needs. As noted in the typology above, these groups are founded by Xers to meet their own needs, and are, in the main, run on a democratic or consensus basis—authority is found in the group itself, not in some externally established leader.

Finally, although boomers and GenXers are religious seekers, Xer seeking is more than just a quest for an individualistic spiritual experience—Xers are instead looking for and creating community, belonging, and authenticity, which can only be measured within the religious community. The desire seems to be first for community and belonging, and second for personal fulfillment; or, perhaps more accurately, personal fulfillment comes through commitment to the community, and through the experience of belonging to such a religious/spiritual community. Thus, authentic religion and spiritual experience comes through doing, through the experience of living out the religious narrative of the community. The importance of community for Xers cannot be emphasized enough. This is not community in the abstract, as with many churches that seek to develop community through various small group programs, but is a lived reality for Xers. As I was told by one Xer, "'We' are all we have." Building community in this context seems completely natural and essential for Xers.

Relating Generational and Religious Experience. As I noted at the beginning of this chapter, to make any real claims about generational effects on religion we would need to link the particular experiences of Generation X to its members' religious activities. I'm *not* arguing here for a direct cause-effect relationship between what were presented earlier as the benchmark experiences of GenXers and their religion; rather, I posit that the constellation of these experiences shapes the religious forms we have seen. Thus experiences outlined above such as rootlessness, declining economic opportunities, technological literacy and immersion in pop culture, and a lived multiculturalism lead to new religious forms. For example:

- Rootlessness and declining economic opportunities result in a search for community and belonging in which one's *compadres* can be relied upon for more than just moral support.

- Technological and pop-cultural literacy, as learned through computers, movies, and MTV, and the epistemological understanding that this embodies give GenXers the ability to use various technology and art forms to shape their own religious expressions and experience. These are neither text based, nor do they have a traditional linear structure; rather they are malleable, multidimensional narratives, and allow for the legitimate expression of religious experiences through music, dance, and even the body, precisely because this religion is no longer conceived of as a linear, text-based reality.

- A lived multiculturalism naturally results in a desire to have new religious institutions mirror the world as it has been experienced. This, after all, can be understood as a twist on the old line that churches are segregated by the choice of the members, by worship style, and by the populations surrounding particular churches. For GenXers, their religious communities are inclusive for precisely the same reasons.

The GenX Difference. As GenXers seek spiritual experience and religious belonging, they have created (and are creating) new religious forms based on their generational experiences, characterized by what I see as significant changes from previous generations, in three related areas. First, GenXers evidence a move from written text to narrative and image as a basis for religious belief.[6] This is not to say that text has been abandoned completely; in fact, the images and stories are in some way rooted in text, whether that text is the Bible or Anne Rice's vampire novels, but for Xers image and story have become dominant, and text background. Second, there is a move for Xers away from rationalistic, propositional truth claims reliant on the proper exegesis of written text to truth validated by experience in the religious community. And finally, there is a move from the essentially individualistic spiritual quest that characterizes baby boomers to a religious/spiritual identity rooted in the larger community.

These new forms represent in their own context traditional, although minimal theologies that subvert other more ideological elements traditionally associated with religion—in particular, ascribed statuses associated with race, ethnicity, and gender, as well as how the sacred is mediated through stories and images rather than in propositional form. Thus GenXers create new religious communities that explicitly embrace diversity and inclusiveness, and so encourage a religious identity expressly incorporating race, ethnicity, and gender into a unifying narrative that joins the person and the community. These changes signal a major shift in how religious truth is appropriated, expressed, and understood. How these changes will play out over time, and whether they will be institutionalized in some form or taken in entirely new directions, remains to be seen. Regardless, Generation X religion demonstrates the vitality of religion, given the freedom to express itself.

Postscript: Some Recommendations for Religious Leaders

When we first started organizing this volume, one of my initial tasks was to determine just what sorts of published resources existed concerning Generation X religion by performing various searches in library catalogs and online bookstores. These results showed that the vast majority of the books published on Generation X and religion concern how one or another religious group might figure out how to "reach" Xers with a particular religious message and attract GenXers to their group. If published volumes can be used as a measure of concern, it seems that most religious leaders are troubled by what they perceive to be a generation relatively uninterested in religion, and how they might make, for example, evangelical Christianity, or Catholicism, or Judaism, more interesting or attractive to GenXers.

As we have demonstrated in this book, however, Xers are quite interested in religion and spirituality, although in somewhat unconventional ways. Thus, without stepping too far beyond the limits of what is generally considered acceptable practice for social science, I would like to offer a few recommendations, based on the findings here, to religious leaders who are interested in serving the religious and spiritual needs of Generation X. This is not an exhaustive list, nor are there any easy formulas for categorizing GenXers; nonetheless, these do provide a place to start.

First, religious leaders need to understand the shift from (written) text to narrative, image, and experience in religious belief, and how that works itself out in how GenXers perceive religion. More bluntly, since appeals based on rationalistic apologetics are largely irrelevant to GenXers, religious groups/leaders must tell stories, learn to understand the stories of contemporary pop culture, appreciate the resonance of these stories in Xers' lives, and equip GenXers to tell their own stories in religiously relevant terms.

Second, leaders need to trust Xers to do the right thing. Given the institutional space and freedom to innovate and create new forms of religious tradition, Xers will create vibrant groups that serve their own religious and spiritual needs within the context of the "parent" religious tradition. Xer-originated (and run) groups are more likely to be interpreted as "authentic" and thus have a higher likelihood of success among GenXers—it is no accident that virtually all of the cases included here are groups organized and led by GenXers themselves.

Third, downplay hierarchies of authority and their implications. This may be particularly problematic for traditionally hierarchical organizations such as the Catholic Church, or some mainline denominations, but as we have seen, distrust of authority is a reality for Generation X, resulting in a generally democratic or consensus form of authority in the majority of the cases included here. There is probably a reason why most of the groups included in this volume tend toward traditions that are structurally more free to innovate and create new forms of religious expression, but I think that this is still possible within the context of more traditional religious organizations. Although this might be accomplished in many different ways, some perhaps unique to the particular institutional setting, the most obvious way is to follow the suggestion above—to trust GenXers to create their own groups within the tradition, and to provide the institutional space and freedom for them to develop as fits their needs.

Finally, it seems natural for Xers to follow the social implications of different religious teachings, particularly in the local setting, where results, however minimal, can be seen. This generation wants to live out its religious commitments, although it does not want to align itself with old ideologies such as established political agendas from political parties, which ring hollow and inauthentic. Instead, working on local issues, such as improving neighborhoods, whether through taking up residence or volunteering in established programs, allows Xers to emphasize doing, to create their narrative through experience.

These are simply a few general recommendations, based on what we were able to uncover about Generation X religion. The list is not so much exhaustive as suggestive, intended to provide some context for religious leaders to think through how to provide the institutional space to meet the religious needs of Generation X.

Notes

I would like to thank Don Miller, Tim Caron, Scott Young, and Malia Cheshire for reading previous drafts of this chapter and for providing helpful suggestions. In addition, I am grateful to Kelly Moore and the Center for the Study of Women at Barnard

College, and to Randall Balmer and the Columbia University Seminar on American Religion, for the opportunity to present this research, and for their wise questions and comments about GenX religion.

1. See, for example, Finke and Stark 1992; Finke 1997; and Warner 1993.

2. Analyses using generations as an independent variable have usually followed developments in social history—there were several volumes published on youth movements, generations, and so on, during the 1960s and early 1970s, and several more have been published during the 1990s in response to Generation X. See, for example, Cottle 1972; Eisenstadt 1956; and Howe and Strauss 1991, 1993.

3. Mannheim further specified what he termed "generation units," which were essentially oppositional groups within the same generation, reacting to the same social and political events in different ways, but still based on their particular generational experiences. This further distinction and how it might work out in either baby-boomer religion or Generation X religion is beyond the scope of this chapter, as we are concerned here with the more generally innovative ways in which Generation X has developed its own religious forms. These distinctions might be teased out from among the cases included in this book, but my inclination would be to think of the groups that we have intentionally left out of this volume, such as the more individualistic, noninstitutional "dabblers" and those who have simply remained within the churches, temples, and synagogues of their heritage, as belonging to different "generation units" than those included here. Future research in this area might then work toward identifying and comparing different generation units within the broader Generation X.

4. Giger's alien is the model that was used for the creatures in the *Alien* movies starring Sigourney Weaver.

5. Democratic authority is conceptualized as there being a leader(s), but decisions and participation are lay-oriented; in a consensus, the group decides various paths of action, and all participate equally.

6. For a provocative analysis of these and related developments in electronic media and their effects, see Stephens 1998.

References

Austin, Joe, and Michael Nevin Willard, eds. 1998. *Generations of Youth: Youth Cultures and History in Twentieth-Century America*. New York: New York University Press.

Beaudoin, Tom. 1998. *Virtual Faith: The Irreverent Spiritual Quest of Generation X*. San Francisco: Jossey-Bass.

Cottle, Thomas J., ed. 1972. *The Prospect of Youth: Contexts for Sociological Inquiry*. Boston: Little, Brown and Company.

Eisenstadt, S. N. 1956. *From Generation to Generation: Age Groups and Social Structure.* New York: Free Press.

Finke, Roger. 1997. "The Illusion of Shifting Demand: Supply-Side Interpretations of American Religious History." Chapter 4 in *Retelling U.S. Religious History,* edited by Thomas A. Tweed. Berkeley and Los Angeles: University of California Press.

Finke, Roger, and Rodney Stark. 1992. *The Churching of America, 1776–1990: Winners and Losers in Our Religious Economy.* New Brunswick, N.J.: Rutgers University Press.

Howe, William, and Neil Strauss. 1991. *Generations: The History of America's Future, 1584–2069.* New York: Quill/William Morrow.

———. 1993. *Thirteenth Gen: Abort, Retry, Ignore, Fail?* New York: Vintage.

Mannheim, Karl. [1927] 1952. "The Problem of Generations." Chapter 7 in *Essays on the Sociology of Knowledge.* London: Routledge and Kegan Paul.

Miller, Donald E. 1997. *Reinventing American Protestantism: Christianity in the New Millennium.* Berkeley and Los Angeles: University of California Press.

Roof, Wade Clark. 1993. *A Generation of Seekers: The Spiritual Journeys of the Baby Boom Generation.* New York: HarperCollins.

———. 1999. *Spiritual Marketplace: Baby Boomers and the Remaking of American Religion.* Princeton, N.J.: Princeton University Press.

Schuman, Howard, and Jacqueline Scott. 1989. "Generations and Collective Memories." *American Sociological Review* 54: 359–81.

Stephens, Mitchell. 1998. *the rise of the image and the fall of the word.* New York: Oxford University Press.

Warner, R. Stephen. 1993. "Work in Progress toward a New Paradigm for the Sociological Study of Religion in the United States." *American Journal of Sociology* 98: 1044–93.

Wuthnow, Robert. 1994a. *Sharing the Journey: Support Groups and America's Quest for Community.* New York: Free Press.

———. 1994b. *I Come Away Stronger: How Small Groups Are Shaping American Religion.* Grand Rapids, Mich.: Eerdmans.

Contributors

Richard W. Flory is assistant professor of sociology at Biola University, La Mirada, California. He has recently completed a manuscript analyzing the development and change in protestant fundamentalist higher educational institutions, from the 1920s to the 1990s. His current research examines the role of journalism in the creation of a secular public sphere in the United States, between 1870 and 1930.

J. Liora Gubkin is a Ph.D. candidate in the School of Religion at the University of Southern California.

Douglas Hayward is associate professor of anthropology and intercultural studies and chair of the Department of Anthropology, Intercultural Education, and Missiology at Biola University, La Mirada, California.

Lori Jensen is a Ph.D. candidate in the Department of Sociology at the University of Southern California.

Sharon Kim is a Ph.D. candidate in the Department of Sociology at the University of Southern California.

Kimberly Leaman Algallar is currently involved in the development of Points of Light, a community-reaching Christian ministry based in Pomona, California.

Arpi Misha Miller graduated Phi Beta Kappa from the University of Southern California in 1998 and is traveling the world and studying Spanish before applying to a doctoral program in sociology.

Donald E. Miller is Executive Director of the Center for Religion and Civic Culture, and Firestone Professor of Religion at the University of Southern

California. He is the author or co-author of five books, including *Reinventing American Protestantism: Christianity in the Next Millennium* (University of California Press, 1997), *Survivors: An Oral History of the Armenian Genocide* (University of California Press, 1993), *Homeless Families: The Struggle for Dignity* (University of Illinois Press, 1993), *Writing and Research in Religious Studies* (Prentice Hall, 1992), and *The Case for Liberal Christianity* (Harper and Row, 1981).

LaDawn Prieto received her M.S.W. from the University of Southern California, and is currently working in a private, nonprofit social work agency in Los Angeles County.

Timothy Sato is the program coordinator for institutional studies at the Center for Religion and Civic Culture at the University of Southern California.

Arlene Sánchez Walsh is a Ph.D. candidate in history at the Claremont Graduate University, and program coordinator for community studies at the Center for Religion and Civic Culture at the University of Southern California.

Gregory C. Stanczak is a Ph.D. candidate in the Department of Sociology at the University of Southern California, where he is writing a dissertation on the Los Angeles Church of Christ.

Julia Winden Fey is an instructor in the Department of Philosophy and Religion and the resident master of the State Residential College at the University of Central Arkansas. She is completing work on a dissertation in feminist sexual ethics and the Gothic subculture in her free time.

Index